This Belongs to:

_____

Copyright © 2024

All rights reserved
Published in association with the literary agency of
Fill in Publishing.

Fillinpublishing.com

Fill in Publishing presents the 4E journey
For
Intimate Connections
Strengthening the bond of love and understanding between couples

Unlike most publishing companies we take you on a journey that will transform your life. You will assume the role of the main character in every book, shaping both the narrative and your own future in collaboration with the guiding force of Wisdom.

The 4Es of destination are an essential component for any Authentic Journey to unfold.

EDUCATION

The 1st E of destination that all Fill in publications have are the E's of Education. That is knowing *what, why* and *how* things work.

EQUIPPING

Fill in publishing recognizes that a successful journey doesn't only come from knowing what, why and how things work, so all of our publications provide the second E of Equipping. That is Equipping you to navigate with and navigate through the what, whys and how's of Education.

EXPERIENCE

It's is great to understand the E of Education. It is even better to know the E of Equipping so we can successfully navigate through life's challenges and opportunities. But there is a saying that says, Experience is the best teacher.
This is why all Fill in Publishing books will have the 3rd E of Experience. An opportunity to take your E of Education and E of Equipping to a higher level and impower you to put the rubber to the road and merge your Education and Equipping to a hands-on Experience. Experience empowers us to refine and better Educate and Equip ourselves.

EVALUATION

This leads to the 4th and last E Fill in publishing has in all its publications. This is the E of Evaluation so you will become better and even better.

Every book with Fill in publishing is a **4E journey**. A journey where you will;
- *Be Educated,*
- *Get Equipped,*
- *Gain Experience*
- *Refine with Evaluation*

This making you the main character, author, architect and benefactor of every book empowered by the guiding force of Wisdom.

Introduction

Discover the key to harmonious and satisfying communication by embracing these 4 practical steps.

Watch as your experiences evolve from frustrating to fulfilling.

Imagine a world where you and your partner share an intimate, close relationship like no other. A bond so strong that it withstands the test of time and brings you both immeasurable joy and fulfillment. This is not just a dream, but a reality that can be achieved by taking these 4 simple steps.

By embracing the idea of creating an intimate close relationship, you open the doors to a world of endless possibilities. Picture the moments of pure connection, where you truly understand each other's thoughts and emotions.

Building an intimate close relationship requires effort and dedication, but the rewards are beyond measure. It means investing time and energy into understanding your partner's needs, desires, and feelings. It means being present in their lives, actively listening, and offering unwavering support. It means being vulnerable and allowing your partner to see the real you, flaws and all.

Not only will this intimate close relationship bring you immense happiness, but it will also enhance other aspects of your life. Studies have shown that individuals in strong, intimate relationships tend to have better physical and mental health. They experience lower levels of stress, increased longevity, and a greater sense of overall well-being.

So, why wait any longer? Take the leap and embark on this 4E journey towards creating an intimate close relationship with your partner. The rewards are immeasurable, and the love and connection you will experience will be unlike anything you have ever known. Don't settle for anything less than the extraordinary. Start building your intimate close relationship today and unlock a world of love, intimacy , and fulfillment.

For someone I want to see succeed

Reward Series

on
Intimate Connections

A Reward is not a Bribe

Reward

- Reward is to give a gift to (someone) in recognition for their completed services, efforts, or achievements.
- This motivates one to accomplish goals for rewards

Rewards create Perks

- An Advantage or benefit following from a job or situation
- This keeps the benefits going after the reward.

~~Bribe~~

- Bribe is to give a gift to (someone) before they accomplish their services, efforts, or achievements with the intent to get paid back with their services, efforts, or achievements. This is not a Bribe.

Your Reward Opportunity

I_____
Promiser

Will agree to present:_____
Recipient

With_____
Reward

If you fill out and share _____ journey experiences with your partner
Quantity

by:_____
Deadline date

NOTE: This can be for yourself

Table of Contents

What this book will do for your relationship..........................1
    Why read it and why use it

Why feelings are the root to successful intimate relationships..1
    Seven profound quotes to explain why

Defining the word "Facts" "Defining the word "Feelings"...2
    Defining the two words Facts and Feelings. Giving us a grasp of what we are working with and what we are working for

"Your not listening to me!" or "Thanks for listening to me." 3-4
    Giving value to your partners self-worth, heart, emotions, and their opinion.

"It is crucial to bear in mind"..4
    Facts play a crucial role in any relationship

The Land mine experience or the Peace of mind experience...5-7
    Which one do you identify with?

For those seeking a path to wellness in their relationship, this message is intended for you.....................8
    Providing the nourishment you need to thrive, revitalize and rejuvenated.

This message is for individuals who are not in need of a solution but can still reap the benefits. 8
    By doing so, you not only prevent potential issues from arising but also enhance your relationship to make it even more fulfilling and rewarding.

Table of Contents

The step-by-step process...8
   The upcoming pages will guide you on how to establish an emotional connection

The journey of intimacy using 2 simple pages................9-10
   Introduction to the pages that will create intimacy

Step #1. The 4 categories to become a great listener...11-12
   Preparing to listen, How to listen, How to respond, and The pitfalls to avoid

Step #2. Identifying your own feelings 13-14
   Knowing your pleasant and unpleasant feelings

Step #3. Giving value 15
   How Partner A shares and Partner B listens

Step #4. Exchanging value 16
   How Partner B shares and Partner A listens

Evaluate your intimacy before and after
   12 questions to ponder before you start............................19-20

40 Opportunities to create intimacy..........................21-100
   Practicing opportunities

Definitions and Explanations
Extremely In-depth insights and explanations reference guide to each item under the 4 categories to becoming a great listener.....**101-109**

Meet Wisdom...**110**

Seeing is Seeing - Feeling is Believing (For a workshop class)
   Proving this is true...**111-116**

☞ **This requires each partner to have their own book** ☜

What this book will do for your relationship.

Discover the secret to true intimacy with this book. Learn why feelings and emotions are the key to a deep connection with your partner. Say goodbye to the divisive 'Facts First Approach' and embrace the 'Feelings First Approach' that fosters closeness and understanding in personal relationships. With this book, you'll gain the tools to emotionally connect with your partner and create a truly intimate bond. Don't settle for a surface-level relationship - take the first step towards a deeper connection today. Let this book guide you towards a fulfilling and loving partnership.

Discover the undeniable truth:

Feelings are the very foundation of thriving intimate connections. Delve into these seven profound quotes that unravel the essence of emotional depth and pave the way to lasting love.

People don't care how much you know until they know how much you care.
Theodore Roosevelt

In order to move on, you must understand why you felt what you did and why you no longer need to feel it.
Mitch Albom

Feelings or emotions are the universal language and are to be honored. They are the authentic expression of who you are at your deepest place.
Judith Wright

Thoughts are the shadows of our feelings - always darker, emptier and simpler.
Friedrich Nietzsche

I continue to be fascinated by the fact that feelings are not just the shady side of reason but that they help us to reach decisions as well.
Antonio Damasio

Empathy is seeing with the eyes of another, listening with the ears of another, and feeling with the heart of another.
Alfred Adler

The best and most beautiful things in the world cannot be seen or even touched. They must be felt with the heart.
Helen Keller

Defining the word "Facts"

The meaning of facts can be rephrased in various ways, depending on the context. Essentially, facts are pieces of information that are true and can be verified through evidence or observation. They are objective and independent of personal opinions or beliefs. Facts play a crucial role in bolstering arguments and drawing conclusions, particularly in disciplines like science, history, and law. Undoubtedly, they provide a solid foundation for logical reasoning and objective analysis. However, it is important to acknowledge that facts alone cannot fully address the profound emotional and psychological needs of individuals. The innermost desires and yearnings of a person's soul cannot be solely satisfied by factual information; they require a deeper level of empathy, understanding, and connection. While facts are indispensable in certain domains, it is equally vital to recognize the significance of emotional intelligence and subjective experiences in comprehending the complexities of human existence.

Defining the word "Feelings"

Feelings can be defined as the complex and intricate emotions that arise within an individual in response to various stimuli and experiences. They encompass a wide range of emotions, including happiness, sadness, anger, fear, love, and many more. Feelings are not only subjective experiences but also have a profound impact on our thoughts, behaviors, and overall well-being. **Feelings can be intense and overwhelming, influencing our decision-making processes and shaping our relationships with others.** Understanding and acknowledging our feelings is crucial for self-awareness and emotional intelligence, as it allows us to navigate through life's challenges and connect with others on a deeper level.

It is very important to acknowledge that Feelings, Personal beliefs, and Subjective experiences influence how individuals interpret and respond to facts.

Are you familiar with expressions such as;
"Your not listening to me" or "Thanks for Listening to me"

By truly listening and empathetically responding to your partner's feelings, you will not only validate their self-worth, heart, emotions, and opinions, but also provide them with the value they crave and deserve. This is what most individuals yearn for, and what every single person truly needs. These illustrations vividly depict why the Facts First approach *(Illustration 1)* often falls short, while the Feelings First approach *(Illustration 2)* triumphs.

"Your not listening to me"

Are you familiar with the spine-chilling words that are staring right at you from the illustration 1 below? Do they send shivers down your spine and make you break out in a cold sweat? We know the feeling all too well. But fear not, for we have the solution to your woes. Let us help you conquer those dreaded words and emerge victorious!

Illustration 1

"You're not Listening to me"
Each (Asterisk *) represents the "Facts First" Approach

The neighbor yelled at me and made me feel discouraged and very angry.

*Why did you talk to her?
*What did she yell about?

Your not listening to me.

*I can repeat every word you said.
*"The neighbor yelled at you and made you feel discouraged and very angry."

"Thanks for Listening to me"

Imagine hearing those magical words, "Thank you for listening to me," just like illustration 2 below. Wouldn't that be amazing? Well, guess what? You can make it happen with just four simple steps outlined in this book. So, are you ready to become a master listener and earn the gratitude of those words "Thanks for listening to me"

"It is crucial to bear in mind"

This system does not aim to disregard or overlook all facts within our relationships. Facts play a crucial role in any relationship. However, it is equally important to recognize that emotions, feelings, and opinions serve as **the first connecting links** that enable us to comprehend and acknowledge these facts.

Do you live with,
The Land Mine experiences
Or do you live with
The Peace of Mind experience

Imagine a scenario where the mere presentation of facts can ignite a firestorm of explosive consequences. It's akin to stepping on a land mine, triggering a chain reaction of accusations, blame, ridicule, and even personal attacks. However, there is a better way to navigate this treacherous terrain.

By acknowledging and understanding a person's feelings and emotions **first**, we can pave the way for a more fruitful exchange of information. Let me share a personal experience to illustrate this point. Picture me driving through the bustling streets of Los Angeles, only to find myself dangerously heading down a one-way street in the wrong direction. The panic, drama, and fear that engulfed me in that moment were as unexpected and jarring as the detonation of a land mine.

Now, let's draw a parallel between this horrible experience and the approach of presenting facts first. Just like my ill-fated detour, it may seem like the most direct route to my desired destination was the shortest path to take. However, be warned, it will undoubtedly lead to unexpected collisions and disastrous outcomes. I had to travel an additional 2 blocks south of my intended destination to reach it using the correct route. Despite the longer distance, it provided a much safer and successful journey.

To truly comprehend the gravity of this situation, I urge you to turn your attention to illustration 3 on the next page. These visual representations vividly depict the potential consequences of the facts first approach. It is only by recognizing and addressing emotions and feelings upfront that we can pave the way for a more harmonious and productive exchange of facts.

To summarize, we should strive for a more empathetic and compassionate approach. By prioritizing emotions and feelings, we can unlock a deeper understanding of the facts and foster an environment where fruitful discussions can flourish. Together, you can navigate the minefield of communication and forge a path towards mutual understanding and intimacy.

In response to a spouse coming home late from work, the scenario for illustrations 3 on page 6 and illustration 4 on page 7 depicts the various emotions and reactions that may arise in such a situation.

Illustration 3
The Land Mine experience

Each (Asterisk *) represents the "Facts First" Approach
(The Scenario: The spouse comes home late from work.)

You're finally home.
*Where have you been?
*Why are you so late?

*I don't want to talk about it!

*What did I do wrong?

*Nothing just leave me alone.

Well that's a great greeting. Maybe you shouldn't have come home at all, if home is so bad for you.

Do you really want to go there?

*You started this!

Illustration 4
The Peace of Mind experience

Each (Asterisk *) represents the "Feelings First" Approach

(Scenario: The spouse comes home late from work.)

 Long day? I was *worried. Are you alright?

I am extremely *frustrated and *angry

 It sounds *bad? What happened?

I *suffered 3 hours in traffic because of a high speed car chase. They closed the freeway and I *hate sitting in traffic. It made me late, *frustrated and *angry.

 I am *glad you made it home safe. You sound very *disappointed also.

Yes I am *Disappointed and *discouraged. I was *hoping to spend some *good quality time with you before you go to work.

 I feel *bad and understand.

I *appreciate that and I *love you.

7.

For those seeking a path to wellness in their relationship, this message is intended for you.

If you've ever found yourself in the frustrating situation of feeling like your words are falling on deaf ears or stepping on emotional landmines, then this journey is exactly what you need. Just as certain foods can provide comfort and relief when you're exhausted or unwell, this book will serve as a refreshing journey that will quench the thirst in your relationship, providing it with the nourishment it needs to thrive and making it feel revitalized and rejuvenated.

This message is for individuals who are not in need of a solution but can still reap the benefits.

You don't need to be going through the frustrating experience of feeling unheard or the explosive experience of stepping on a metaphorical landmine in order to make progress in the book.

Just as certain foods can provide hydration and nourishment when you're sick, these ingredients can also benefit your body when you are not sick. Even if you already have a healthy relationship, it's still beneficial to consume these elements to maintain good nourishment, hydration, and overall well-being in your relationship.

Instead of waiting until something goes wrong, take the opportunity to nourish your relationship through this journey. By doing so, you not only prevent potential issues from arising but also enhance your relationship to make it even more fulfilling and rewarding.

The step-by-step process that will demonstrate how to effectively implement this strategy for both these relationships.

The upcoming pages will guide you on how to establish an emotional connection and build a deep level of intimacy with your partner in 4 simple steps.

The remaining pages of the book will provide you with numerous opportunities to practice and cultivate a beautifully intimate relationship with your partner in the months ahead. It's like a continuous process of growth and improvement, allowing you to strengthen your bond and create a lasting connection.

A Journey of Intimacy

PLEASANT FEELINGS

OPEN	INTERESTED	ALIVE	STRONG
☐ ~~Understanding~~	☐ Absorbed	☐ Animated	☐ Certain
☐ ~~...~~	☐ Affected	☐ ~~Courageous~~	☐ ~~...~~
☐ Inter~~ested~~	☐ ~~Fascinated~~	☐ Impulsive	☐ Rebellious
☐ Kind	☐ Inquisitive	☐ Liberated	☐ Secure
☐ Receptive	☐ ~~...~~	☐ ~~...~~	☐ Sure
☐ Reliable			☐ Tenacious
☐ Satisfi~~ed~~			☐ Unique
☐ Symp~~athetic~~			
☐ Under~~standing~~			

LOVE			HAPPY
☐ Admi~~ring~~			☐ Cheerful
☐ Affect~~ionate~~			☐ Delighted
☐ Attrac~~ted~~			☐ Ecstatic
☐ Close			☐ Elated
☐ Comf~~ortable~~			☐ Festive
☐ Consi~~derate~~			☐ Fortunate
☐ Devot~~ed~~			☐ Glad
☐ Draw~~n~~			☐ Gleeful
☐ Loved			☐ Great
☐ Lovin~~g~~			☐ Important
☐ Passi~~onate~~			☐ Joyous
☐ Sensi~~tive~~			☐ Jubilant
☐ Symp~~athetic~~			☐ Lucky
☐ Tender			☐ Merry
☐ Touched			☐ Overjoyed
☐ Warm			☐ Satisfied
	☐ Optimistic	☐ Serene	☐ Sunny
	☐ Re-enforced	☐ Surprised	☐ Thankful

> With these two pages, you will embark on an extraordinary journey of intimacy in the 4E realm. These concise yet powerful 2 pages hold the key to unlocking a world of connection, passion, understanding and vulnerability.
>
> Within their carefully crafted words, you will find the roadmap to deepening your bond with your partner.

Read and check off
✓

Preparing to listen
- ☐ Remember to put your mind and feelings in neutral gear.
- ☐ Your body posture must say, *"I' am open, very interested, affirmative, attentive."*
- ☐ Maintain good eye contact.
- ☐ Give the speaker a verbal door opening, showing your readiness to listen.

While Listening
- ☐ Track what the speaker is saying in both content and feeling levels
- ☐ Stay with the content of communication
- ☐ Listen for and identify the basic general feeling; anger, fear, joy, resentment, etc.
- ☐ Suspend judgment; open yourself to the presence of their heart.

Responding
- ☐ Use oral responses, which are affirming, which say, *"I am with you"*, *"I understand."*
- ☐ Feed general feelings back to the speaker. *"You seem to feel this has been a good experience for you"*
- ☐ Stay an inch ahead of the speaker, not a mile.

using two simple pages

> You will explore new levels of emotional closeness, and discover the true essence of intimacy.
>
> Over the next few pages, we will guide you through a 4 step unforgettable experience, showing you how to navigate each page and transform it into the journey of intimacy.

UNPLEASANT FEELINGS

HELPLESS
- ☐ Alone
- ☐ ~~Despairing~~
- ☐ Fatigued
- ☐ Forced
- ☐ Frustrated
- ☐ Hesitant
- ☐ In A Stew
- ☐ Incapable
- ☐ Inferior
- ☐ Paralyzed
- ☐ Pathetic
- ☐ Tragic
- ☐ Useless
- ☐ Vulnerable
- ☐ Woeful

SAD
- ☐ Anguished
- ☐ Desolate
- ☐ Desperate
- ☐ Dismayed
- ☐ Grief
- ☐ Grieved
- ☐ Lonely
- ☐ Mournful
- ☐ Pained
- ☐ Pessimistic
- ☐ Sorrowful
- ☐ Tearful
- ☐ Unhappy

CONFUSED
- ☐ Disillusioned
- ☐ Distrustful
- ☐ Lost
- ☐ Misgiving

DEPRESSED
- ☐ A Sense
- ☐ Abondoned
- ☐ Ashamed
- ☐ Diminished
- ☐ Disappointed
- ☐ Scared
- ☐ Shaky
- ☐ Suspicious
- ☐ Terrified
- ☐ Threatened
- ☐ Timid
- ☐ Wary
- ☐ Worried

ANGRY
- ☐ Aggressive
- ☐ Annoyed
- ☐ Bitter
- ☐ Boiling
- ☐ Cross
- ☐ Enraged
- ☐ Fuming
- ☐ Hateful
- ☐ Hostile
- ☐ Incensed
- ☐ Inflamed
- ☐ Infuriated
- ☐ Insulting
- ☐ Irritated
- ☐ Offensive
- ☐ Provoked
- ☐ Resentful
- ☐ Sore
- ☐ Unpleasant
- ☐ Upset
- ☐ Worked Up

HURT
- ☐ Aching
- ☐ Afflicted
- ☐ Agonized
- ☐ Alienated
- ☐ Appalled
- ☐ Crushed
- ☐ Dejected
- ☐ Deprived
- ☐ Heartbroken
- ☐ Humiliated
- ☐ Injured
- ☐ Offended
- ☐ Pained
- ☐ Rejected
- ☐ Tormented
- ☐ Tortured
- ☐ Victimized
- ☐ Wronged

Notes:
_____
_____
_____

8 Pitfalls to avoid
- ☐ Me-too-ism. Don't start telling your story, or comparing your story to theirs.
- ☐ Moralizing, preaching, being judgmental
- ☐ Asking a direct question to satisfy your own curiosity
- ☐ Being an interviewer rather then a listener
- ☐ Giving advice (try fixing it)
- ☐ Cheap consolation. *"Oh, that's not to bad"*
- ☐ Arguing or disagreeing with the speaker
- ☐ Analyzing or interpreting
- ☐ Ignoring obvious heavy emotions

Date: _____

PLEASANT FEELINGS

☺ OPEN	☺ INTERESTED	☺ ALIVE	☺ STRONG
☐ Accepting	☐ Absorbed	☐ Animated	☐ Certain
☐ Ama...			...amic

STEP #1

In each two-page journey, you will uncover a treasure trove of four essential categories that will equip you with the necessary skills to truly listen and connect with your partner. These categories include:

♡ 1. "Preparing to Listen,"

👂 2. "While You Are Listening,"

👄 3. "Responding,"

⛰ 4. "8 Pitfalls to Avoid While Listening."

With each of the 4 categories below, you will read and check off the suggestions provided. Then show your partner. This will serve as a clear indication to your partner that you have dedicated the necessary time to acquaint yourself with the listening skills.

☐ ...			...ed
☐ Touc...			...shed
☐ Warm	☐ Optimistic	☐ Serene	☐ Sunny
	☐ Re-enforced	☐ Surprised	☐ Thankful

Read and check off ✓ **The 4 categories to become a great listener**

1. ♡

Preparing to listen
- ☑ Remember to put your mind and feelings in neutral gear.
- ☑ Your body posture must say, *"I am open, very interested, affirmative, attentive."*
- ☑ Maintain good eye contact.
- ☑ Give the speaker a verbal door opening, showing your readiness to listen.

2. 👂

While Listening
- ☑ Track what the speaker is saying in both content and feeling levels
- ☑ Stay with the content of communication
- ☑ Listen for and identify the basic general feeling; anger, fear, joy, resentment, etc.
- ☑ Suspend judgment; open yourself to the presence of their heart.

3. 👄

Responding
- ☑ Use oral responses, which are affirming, which say, *"I am with you"*, *"I understand."*
- ☑ Feed general feelings back to the speaker. *"You seem to feel this has been a good experience for you"*
- ☑ Stay an inch ahead of the speaker, not a mile.

UNPLEASANT FEELINGS

😞 **HELPLESS**	😕 **CONFUSED**	😟 **DEPRESSED**	😠 **ANGRY**
☐ Alone	☐ Disillusioned	☐ A Sense of Loss	☐ Aggressive
☐ Desp...			☐ Annoyed

For more depth and understanding

For a comprehensive understanding of each of these items, you can find detailed information on pages 107 to 114. These pages provide in-depth insights and explanations about each individual item mentioned in the 4 categories to become a great listener, ensuring that you have all the necessary information at your fingertips. By referring to these specific pages, you will gain a thorough understanding of the intricacies and nuances associated with each item.

For a more comprehensive understanding of the four categories of excellent listening mentioned at the end of every page, you can refer to pages 101 to 109. These pages provide detailed definitions and explanations for each item mentioned.

☐ Sorro...		Heartbroken
☐ Tearful	☐ Scared	☐ Humiliated
☐ Unhappy	☐ Shaky	☐ Injured
	☐ Suspicious	☐ Offended
	☐ Terrified	☐ Pained
	☐ Threatened	☐ Rejected
	☐ Timid	☐ Tormented
	☐ Wary	☐ Tortured
	☐ Worried	☐ Victimized
		☐ Wronged

Notes:
_____
_____
_____

4.

8 Pitfalls to avoid

- ☑ Me-too-ism. Don't start telling your story, or comparing your story to theirs.
- ☑ Moralizing, preaching, being judgmental
- ☑ Asking a direct question to satisfy your own curiosity
- ☑ Being an interviewer rather then a listener
- ☑ Giving advice (try fixing it)
- ☑ C... ...on. "Oh, that's not to bad"
- ☑ ...disagreeing with the speaker
- ☑ ...interpreting
- ☑ Ig... ...vious heavy emotions

Date: 7-11-2022

12.

PLEASANT FEELINGS

☺ OPEN	☺ INTERESTED	☺ ALIVE	☺ STRONG
☐ Accepting	☐ Absorbed	☐ Animated	☐ Certain
☐ Amazed	☐ Affected	☐ Courageous	☐ Dynamic

STEP #2

In the next step, each of you will individually explore your own emotions by marking any pleasant or unpleasant feelings. This exercise will allow you to become more conscious of your emotional reactions during conversations, helping you to better understand yourself.

☺ LOVE	☺ POSITIVE	☺ GOOD	☺ HAPPY
☐ Admiration	☐ Anxious	☐ At ease	☐ Cheerful
☐ Affectionate	☐ Bold	☐ Blessed	☐ Delighted
☐ Attracted	☐ Brave	☐ Bright	☐ Ecstatic
☐ Close	☐ Challenged	☑ Calm	☐ Elated
☑ Comforted	☐ Confident	☑ Certain	☐ Festive
☐ Considerate	☐ Daring	☐ Clever	☐ Fortunate
☐ Devoted	☐ Determined	☐ Comfortable	☐ Glad
☐ Drawn toward	☑ Eager	☐ Content	☐ Gleeful
☐ Loved	☐ Earnest	☐ Encouraged	☐ Great
☐ Loving	☐ Enthusiastic	☐ Free and easy	☐ Important
☐ Passionate	☐ Excited	☐ Peaceful	☐ Joyous
☐ Sensitive	☐ Hopeful	☐ Pleased	☐ Jubilant
☐ Sympathy	☐ Inspired	☐ Quiet	☑ Lucky
☐ Tender	☐ Intent	☐ Reassured	☐ Merry
☐ Touched	☐ Keen	☐ Relaxed	☐ Overjoyed
☐ Warm	☐ Optimistic	☐ Serene	☐ Satisfied
	☐ Re-enforced	☐ Surprised	☐ Sunny
			☐ Thankful

Read and check off

✓

Preparing to listen
- ☑ Remember to put your mind and feelings in neutral gear.
- ☑ Your body posture must say, *"I' am open, very interested, affirmative, attentive."*
- ☑ Maintain good eye contact.
- ☑ Give the speaker a verbal door opening, showing your readiness to listen.

While Listening
- ☑ Track what the speaker is saying in both content and feeling levels
- ☑ Stay with the content of communication
- ☑ Listen for and identify the basic general feeling; anger, fear, joy, resentment, etc.
- ☑ Suspend judgment; open yourself to the presence of their heart.

Responding
- ☑ Use oral responses, which are affirming, which say, *"I am with you", "I understand."*
- ☑ Feed general feelings back to the speaker. *"You seem to feel this has been a good experience for you"*
- ☑ Stay an inch ahead of the speaker, not a mile.

UNPLEASANT FEELINGS

😟 HELPLESS
- ☐ Alone
- ☐ Despair
- ☐ Distressed
- ☐ Dominated
- ☐ Empty
- ☐ Fatigued
- ☐ Forced
- ☐ Frustrated
- ☐ Hesitant
- ☐ In A Stew
- ☐ Incapable
- ☐ Inferior
- ☐ Paralyzed
- ☐ Pathetic
- ☐ Tragic
- ☑ Useless
- ☐ Vulnerable
- ☐ Woeful

😕 CONFUSED
- ☐ Disillusioned
- ☐ Distrustful
- ☐ Doubtful
- ☐ Embarrassed
- ☐ Hesitant
- ☐ Indecisive
- ☐ Lost
- ☐ Misgiving
- ☑ Perplexed
- ☐ Pessimistic
- ☐ Shy
- ☐ Skeptical
- ☐ Stupefied
- ☐ Tense
- ☐ Unbelieving
- ☐ Uncertain
- ☐ Uneasy
- ☐ Unsure
- ☐ Upset

😞 DEPRESSED
- ☐ A Sense of Loss
- ☐ Abominable
- ☐ Ashamed
- ☐ Bad
- ☐ Despicable
- ☐ Detestable
- ☐ Diminished
- ☐ Disappointed
- ☐ Discouraged
- ☐ Disgusting
- ☐ Dissatisfied
- ☑ Guilty
- ☐ In Despair
- ☐ Lousy
- ☐ Miserable
- ☐ Powerless
- ☐ Repugnant
- ☐ Sulky
- ☐ Terrible

😠 ANGRY
- ☐ Aggressive
- ☐ Annoyed
- ☐ Bitter
- ☐ Boiling
- ☐ Cross
- ☐ Enraged
- ☐ Fuming
- ☐ Hateful
- ☐ Hostile
- ☐ Incensed
- ☐ Inflamed
- ☐ Infuriated
- ☐ Insulting
- ☐ Irritated
- ☐ Offensive
- ☐ Provoked
- ☐ Resentful
- ☐ Sore
- ☐ Unpleasant
- ☐ Upset
- ☐ Worked Up

😢 SAD
- ☐ Anguish
- ☐ Desolate
- ☐ Desperate
- ☐ Dismayed
- ☐ Grief
- ☐ Grieved
- ☐ Lonely
- ☐ Mournful
- ☐ Pained
- ☐ Pessimistic
- ☐ Sorrowful
- ☐ Tearful
- ☐ Unhappy

😐 INDIFFERENT
- ☐ Bored
- ☐ Cold
- ☐ Disinterested
- ☐ Dull
- ☐ Insensitive
- ☐ Lifeless
- ☑ Neutral
- ☐ Nonchalant
- ☐ Preoccupied
- ☐ Reserved
- ☐ Weary

😨 AFRAID
- ☐ Alarmed
- ☐ Anxious
- ☐ Frightened
- ☐ Menaced
- ☐ Nervous
- ☐ Panic
- ☐ Quaking
- ☑ Restless
- ☐ Scared

😔 HURT
- ☐ Aching
- ☐ Afflicted
- ☐ Agonized
- ☐ Alienated
- ☐ Appalled
- ☐ Crushed
- ☐ Dejected
- ☐ Deprived
- ☐ Heartbroken
- ☐ Humiliated
- ☐ Wronged

Notes:
_____
_____
_____
_____

> Don't forget to place the date below

8 Pitfalls to avoid
- ☑ Me-too-ism. Don't start telling your story, or comparing your story to theirs.
- ☑ Moralizing, preaching, being judgmental
- ☑ Asking a direct question to satisfy your own curiosity
- ☑ Being an interviewer rather then a listener
- ☑ Giving advice (try fixing it)
- ☑ Cheap consolation. *"Oh, that's not to bad"*
- ☑ Arguing or disagreeing with the speaker
- ☑ Analyzing or interpreting
- ☑ Ignoring obvious heavy emotions

Date: _____7-11-2018_____

PLEASANT FEELINGS

☺ OPEN	☺ INTERESTED	☺ ALIVE	☺ STRONG

STEP #3

Partner A **Partner B**
Shares **Listens**

One partner will have 5 to 10 minutes to share their pleasant and unpleasant feelings. *A timer can be very beneficial.* While the other partner practices the four categories of effective listening. ♡ 👂 👄 ■

This exercise will not only allow you to express yourself, but also provide your partner with the opportunity to practice their active listening skills, ensuring that they truly comprehend and empathize with your feelings.

☐ Passionate	☐ Excited	☐ Peaceful	☑ Jubilant
☐ Sensitive	☐ Hopeful	☐ Pleased	☑ Lucky
☐ Sympathy	☐ Inspired	☐ Quiet	☐ Merry
☐ Tender	☐ Intent	☐ Reassured	☐ Overjoyed
☐ Touched	☐ Keen	☐ Relaxed	☐ Satisfied
☐ Warm	☐ Optimistic	☐ Serene	☐ Sunny
	☐ Re-enforced	☐ Surprised	☐ Thankful

Read and check off

Preparing to listen
- ☑ Remember to put your mind and feelings in neutral gear.
- ☑ Your body posture must say, *"I am open, very interested, affirmative, attentive."*
- ☑ Maintain good eye contact.
- ☑ Give the speaker a verbal door opening, showing your readiness to listen.

While Listening
- ☑ Track what the speaker is saying in both content and feeling levels
- ☑ Stay with the content of communication
- ☑ Listen for and identify the basic general feeling; anger, fear, joy, resentment, etc.
- ☑ Suspend judgment; open yourself to the presence of their heart.

Responding
- ☑ Use oral responses, which are affirming, which say, *"I am with you", "I understand."*
- ☑ Feed general feelings back to the speaker. *"You seem to feel this has been a good experience for you"*
- ☑ Stay an inch ahead of the speaker, not a mile.

UNPLEASANT FEELINGS

😳 HELPLESS	😵 CONFUSED	😐 DEPRESSED	😠 ANGRY
☐ Alo...			...gressive

STEP #4

Partner B Shares   Partner A Listens

In order to enhance communication and understanding between you and your partner, you both switch roles. The Listener becomes the partner that shares their pleasant and unpleasant feelings for 5 to 10 minutes. By switching roles, you will have the opportunity to experience both perspectives and gain a deeper understanding of each other's thoughts and feelings. This exercise can help foster empathy, active listening, and effective communication skills within your relationship.

☐ Grieved   ☐ Lifeless   ☐ Frightened   ☐ Alienated
☐ Lonely
☐ Mournful
☐ Pained   *While listening, writing down key points here can improve your retention and understanding.*
☐ Pessimistic
☐ Sorrowful
☐ Tearful
☐ Unhappy

☐ Shaky   ☐ Injured
☐ Suspicious   ☐ Offended
☐ Terrified   ☐ Pained
☐ Threatened   ☐ Rejected
☐ Timid   ☐ Tormented
☐ Wary   ☐ Tortured
☐ Worried   ☐ Victimized
   ☐ Wronged

Notes:
_____
_____
_____

8 Pitfalls to avoid

- ☑ Me-too-ism. Don't start telling your story, or comparing your story to theirs.
- ☑ Moralizing, preaching, being judgmental
- ☑ Asking a direct question to satisfy your own curiosity
- ☑ Being an interviewer rather then a listener
- ☑ Giving advice (try fixing it)
- ☑ Cheap consolation. *"Oh, that's not to bad"*
- ☑ Arguing or disagreeing with the speaker
- ☑ Analyzing or interpreting
- ☑ Ignoring obvious heavy emotions

Date: _____7-11-2018_____

UNPLEASANT FEELINGS

😟 HELPLESS
- ☐ Alone
- ☐ Despair
- ☐ Dist...
- ☐ D...
- ☐ ...
- ☐ ...
- ☐ In...
- ☐ Inca...
- ☐ Inferi...
- ☐ Paralyze...
- ☐ Pathetic
- ☐ Tragic
- ☐ Useless
- ☐ Vulnerable
- ☐ Woeful

😕 CONFUSED
- ☐ ...illusioned
- ☐ ...
- ☐ ...
- ☐ ...
- ☐ ...
- ☐ ...
- ☐ ...
- ☐ ...
- ☐ ...

😣 DEPRESSED
- ☐ A S... ...
- ☐ ...
- ☐ ...
- ☐ ...

😠 ANGRY
- ☐ Aggressive
- ☐ Annoyed
- ☐ ...ter
- ☐ ...ng
- ☐ ...
- ☐ ...
- ☐ ...sed
- ☐ ...amed
- ☐ ...nfuriated
- ☐ Insulting
- ☐ Irritated
- ☐ Offensive
- ☐ Provoked
- ☐ Resentful
- ☐ Sore
- ☐ Unpleasant
- ☐ Upset
- ☐ Worked Up

😢 SAD
- ☐ Anguish
- ☐ Desolate
- ☐ Desperate
- ☐ Dismayed
- ☐ Grief
- ☐ Grieved
- ☐ Lonely
- ☐ Mournful
- ☐ Pained
- ☐ Pessimistic
- ☐ Sorrowful
- ☐ Tearful
- ☐ Unhappy

😑 IND...
- ☐ Bored
- ☐ Cold
- ☐ Disinterested
- ☐ Dull
- ☐ Insensitive
- ☐ Lifel...
- ☐ Neut...
- ☐ Non...
- ☐ Preoccupie...
- ☐ Reserved
- ☐ Wea...

😨 ...FRAID
- ☐ Alarmed
- ☐ Anxious
- ☐ Cowardly
- ☐ Doubtful
- ☐ Fearful
- ☐ ...tened
- ☐ ...aced
- ☐ ...ous
- ☐ ...
- ☐ ...king
- ☐ ...ess
- ☐ ...
- ☐ ...
- ☐ ...icious
- ☐ Terrified
- ☐ Threatened
- ☐ Timid
- ☐ Wary
- ☐ Worried

😞 HURT
- ☐ Aching
- ☐ Afflicted
- ☐ Agonized
- ☐ Alienated
- ☐ Appalled
- ☐ Crushed
- ☐ Dejected
- ☐ Deprived
- ☐ Heartbroken
- ☐ Humiliated
- ☐ Injured
- ☐ Offended
- ☐ Pained
- ☐ Rejected
- ☐ Tormented
- ☐ Tortured
- ☐ Victimized
- ☐ Wronged

> Unleash your imagination as you embark on a journey through pages 21 to 100, where you'll find an abundance of 40 opportunities to cultivate deep, intimate bonds that will foster a profound understanding between you and your partner.

One Shares one Listen

The other Shares The other Listens

Notes: _____
_____
_____

- ☐ Me-too-ism. Don't start telling ... ...tory to theirs.
- ☐ Moralizing, preaching, being ju...
- ☐ Asking a direct question to satis... ou...
- ☐ Being an interviewer rather then a liste...
- ☐ Giving advice (try fixing it)
- ☐ Cheap consolation. *"Oh, that's ...*
- ☐ Arguing or disagreeing with the...
- ☐ Analyzing or interpreting
- ☐ Ignoring obvious heavy emotio...

Date:

Evaluate your intimacy before you go forward

1. **How often do you find yourself using or hearing the words**
"You don't understand me"
☐ Always ☐ Often ☐ Sometimes ☐ Rarely ☐ Never

2. **How often do you find yourself using or hearing the words**
"Thank you for understanding me"
☐ Always ☐ Often ☐ Sometimes ☐ Rarely ☐ Never

3. **How often do you find yourself expressing or being exposed to the statement**
"You just don't get it"
☐ Always ☐ Often ☐ Sometimes ☐ Rarely ☐ Never

4. **How often do you find yourself expressing or being exposed to the statement**
"I'm glad you got it"
☐ Always ☐ Often ☐ Sometimes ☐ Rarely ☐ Never

5. **How often do you find yourself in a situation where you've spoken or been privy to the words**
"I don't feel connected"
☐ Always ☐ Often ☐ Sometimes ☐ Rarely ☐ Never

6. **How often do you find yourself in a situation where you've spoken or been privy to the words**
"I love our connection"
☐ Always ☐ Often ☐ Sometimes ☐ Rarely ☐ Never

7. **How often have you uttered or listened to the phrase**
"I don't know how I feel"
☐ Always ☐ Often ☐ Sometimes ☐ Rarely ☐ Never

8. **How often have you uttered or listened to the phrase**
"Thanks for helping me to understand how I feel"
☐ Always ☐ Often ☐ Sometimes ☐ Rarely ☐ Never

9. **How often have you expressed or been told**
"I want quality time"
☐ Always ☐ Often ☐ Sometimes ☐ Rarely ☐ Never

10. **How often have you expressed or been told**
"I appreciate this quality time"
☐ Always ☐ Often ☐ Sometimes ☐ Rarely ☐ Never

11. **How often have you vocalized or been a recipient of the remark**
"You don't hear what I am saying"
☐ Always ☐ Often ☐ Sometimes ☐ Rarely ☐ Never

12. **How often have you vocalized or been a recipient of the remark**
"It's nice to be heard"
☐ Always ☐ Often ☐ Sometimes ☐ Rarely ☐ Never

19.

Re-evaluate your intimacy after you reach page 62

1. **How often do you find yourself using or hearing the words**
"You don't understand me"
☐ Always ☐ Often ☐ Sometimes ☐ Rarely ☐ Never

2. **How often do you find yourself using or hearing the words**
"Thank you for understanding me"
☐ Always ☐ Often ☐ Sometimes ☐ Rarely ☐ Never

3. **How often do you find yourself expressing or being exposed to the statement**
"You just don't get it"
☐ Always ☐ Often ☐ Sometimes ☐ Rarely ☐ Never

4. **How often do you find yourself expressing or being exposed to the statement**
"I'm glad you got it"
☐ Always ☐ Often ☐ Sometimes ☐ Rarely ☐ Never

5. **How often do you find yourself in a situation where you've spoken or been privy to the words**
"I don't feel connected"
☐ Always ☐ Often ☐ Sometimes ☐ Rarely ☐ Never

6. **How often do you find yourself in a situation where you've spoken or been privy to the words**
"I love our connection"
☐ Always ☐ Often ☐ Sometimes ☐ Rarely ☐ Never

7. **How often have you uttered or listened to the phrase**
"I don't know how I feel"
☐ Always ☐ Often ☐ Sometimes ☐ Rarely ☐ Never

8. **How often have you uttered or listened to the phrase**
"Thanks for helping me to understand how I feel"
☐ Always ☐ Often ☐ Sometimes ☐ Rarely ☐ Never

9. **How often have you expressed or been told**
"I want quality time"
☐ Always ☐ Often ☐ Sometimes ☐ Rarely ☐ Never

10. **How often have you expressed or been told**
"I appreciate this quality time"
☐ Always ☐ Often ☐ Sometimes ☐ Rarely ☐ Never

11. **How often have you vocalized or been a recipient of the remark**
"You don't hear what I am saying"
☐ Always ☐ Often ☐ Sometimes ☐ Rarely ☐ Never

12. **How often have you vocalized or been a recipient of the remark**
"It's nice to be heard"
☐ Always ☐ Often ☐ Sometimes ☐ Rarely ☐ Never

Before starting, evaluate your intimacy on page 9

PLEASANT FEELINGS

OPEN
- ☐ Accepting
- ☐ Amazed
- ☐ Confident
- ☐ Easy
- ☐ Free
- ☐ Interested
- ☐ Kind
- ☐ Receptive
- ☐ Reliable
- ☐ Satisfied
- ☐ Sympathetic
- ☐ Understanding

INTERESTED
- ☐ Absorbed
- ☐ Affected
- ☐ Concerned
- ☐ Curious
- ☐ Engrossed
- ☐ Fascinated
- ☐ Inquisitive
- ☐ Intrigued
- ☐ Nosy
- ☐ Snoopy

ALIVE
- ☐ Animated
- ☐ Courageous
- ☐ Energetic
- ☐ Free
- ☐ Frisky
- ☐ Impulsive
- ☐ Liberated
- ☐ Optimistic
- ☐ Playful
- ☐ Provocative
- ☐ Spirited
- ☐ Thrilled
- ☐ Wonderful

STRONG
- ☐ Certain
- ☐ Dynamic
- ☐ Free
- ☐ Hardy
- ☐ Impulsive
- ☐ Rebellious
- ☐ Secure
- ☐ Sure
- ☐ Tenacious
- ☐ Unique

LOVE
- ☐ Admiration
- ☐ Affectionate
- ☐ Attracted
- ☐ Close
- ☐ Comforted
- ☐ Considerate
- ☐ Devoted
- ☐ Drawn toward
- ☐ Loved
- ☐ Loving
- ☐ Passionate
- ☐ Sensitive
- ☐ Sympathy
- ☐ Tender
- ☐ Touched
- ☐ Warm

POSITIVE
- ☐ Anxious
- ☐ Bold
- ☐ Brave
- ☐ Challenged
- ☐ Confident
- ☐ Daring
- ☐ Determined
- ☐ Eager
- ☐ Earnest
- ☐ Enthusiastic
- ☐ Excited
- ☐ Hopeful
- ☐ Inspired
- ☐ Intent
- ☐ Keen
- ☐ Optimistic
- ☐ Re-enforced

GOOD
- ☐ At ease
- ☐ Blessed
- ☐ Bright
- ☐ Calm
- ☐ Certain
- ☐ Clever
- ☐ Comfortable
- ☐ Content
- ☐ Encouraged
- ☐ Free and easy
- ☐ Peaceful
- ☐ Pleased
- ☐ Quiet
- ☐ Reassured
- ☐ Relaxed
- ☐ Serene
- ☐ Surprised

HAPPY
- ☐ Cheerful
- ☐ Delighted
- ☐ Ecstatic
- ☐ Elated
- ☐ Festive
- ☐ Fortunate
- ☐ Glad
- ☐ Gleeful
- ☐ Great
- ☐ Important
- ☐ Joyous
- ☐ Jubilant
- ☐ Lucky
- ☐ Merry
- ☐ Overjoyed
- ☐ Satisfied
- ☐ Sunny
- ☐ Thankful

Read and check off ✓

Preparing to listen
- ☐ Remember to put your mind and feelings in neutral gear.
- ☐ Your body posture must say, *"I am open, very interested, affirmative, attentive."*
- ☐ Maintain good eye contact.
- ☐ Give the speaker a verbal door opening, showing your readiness to listen.

While Listening
- ☐ Track what the speaker is saying in both content and feeling levels
- ☐ Stay with the content of communication
- ☐ Listen for and identify the basic general feeling; anger, fear, joy, resentment, etc.
- ☐ Suspend judgment; open yourself to the presence of their heart.

Responding
- ☐ Use oral responses, which are affirming, which say, *"I am with you", "I understand."*
- ☐ Feed general feelings back to the speaker. *"You seem to feel this has been a good experience for you"*
- ☐ Stay an inch ahead of the speaker, not a mile.

UNPLEASANT FEELINGS

😧 HELPLESS
- ☐ Alone
- ☐ Despair
- ☐ Distressed
- ☐ Dominated
- ☐ Empty
- ☐ Fatigued
- ☐ Forced
- ☐ Frustrated
- ☐ Hesitant
- ☐ In A Stew
- ☐ Incapable
- ☐ Inferior
- ☐ Paralyzed
- ☐ Pathetic
- ☐ Tragic
- ☐ Useless
- ☐ Vulnerable
- ☐ Woeful

😐 CONFUSED
- ☐ Disillusioned
- ☐ Distrustful
- ☐ Doubtful
- ☐ Embarrassed
- ☐ Hesitant
- ☐ Indecisive
- ☐ Lost
- ☐ Misgiving
- ☐ Perplexed
- ☐ Pessimistic
- ☐ Shy
- ☐ Skeptical
- ☐ Stupefied
- ☐ Tense
- ☐ Unbelieving
- ☐ Uncertain
- ☐ Uneasy
- ☐ Unsure
- ☐ Upset

😔 DEPRESSED
- ☐ A Sense of Loss
- ☐ Abominable
- ☐ Ashamed
- ☐ Bad
- ☐ Despicable
- ☐ Detestable
- ☐ Diminished
- ☐ Disappointed
- ☐ Discouraged
- ☐ Disgusting
- ☐ Dissatisfied
- ☐ Guilty
- ☐ In Despair
- ☐ Lousy
- ☐ Miserable
- ☐ Powerless
- ☐ Repugnant
- ☐ Sulky
- ☐ Terrible

😠 ANGRY
- ☐ Aggressive
- ☐ Annoyed
- ☐ Bitter
- ☐ Boiling
- ☐ Cross
- ☐ Enraged
- ☐ Fuming
- ☐ Hateful
- ☐ Hostile
- ☐ Incensed
- ☐ Inflamed
- ☐ Infuriated
- ☐ Insulting
- ☐ Irritated
- ☐ Offensive
- ☐ Provoked
- ☐ Resentful
- ☐ Sore
- ☐ Unpleasant
- ☐ Upset
- ☐ Worked Up

😢 SAD
- ☐ Anguish
- ☐ Desolate
- ☐ Desperate
- ☐ Dismayed
- ☐ Grief
- ☐ Grieved
- ☐ Lonely
- ☐ Mournful
- ☐ Pained
- ☐ Pessimistic
- ☐ Sorrowful
- ☐ Tearful
- ☐ Unhappy

😑 INDIFFERENT
- ☐ Bored
- ☐ Cold
- ☐ Disinterested
- ☐ Dull
- ☐ Insensitive
- ☐ Lifeless
- ☐ Neutral
- ☐ Nonchalant
- ☐ Preoccupied
- ☐ Reserved
- ☐ Weary

😨 AFRAID
- ☐ Alarmed
- ☐ Anxious
- ☐ Cowardly
- ☐ Doubtful
- ☐ Fearful
- ☐ Frightened
- ☐ Menaced
- ☐ Nervous
- ☐ Panic
- ☐ Quaking
- ☐ Restless
- ☐ Scared
- ☐ Shaky
- ☐ Suspicious
- ☐ Terrified
- ☐ Threatened
- ☐ Timid
- ☐ Wary
- ☐ Worried

😞 HURT
- ☐ Aching
- ☐ Afflicted
- ☐ Agonized
- ☐ Alienated
- ☐ Appalled
- ☐ Crushed
- ☐ Dejected
- ☐ Deprived
- ☐ Heartbroken
- ☐ Humiliated
- ☐ Injured
- ☐ Offended
- ☐ Pained
- ☐ Rejected
- ☐ Tormented
- ☐ Tortured
- ☐ Victimized
- ☐ Wronged

Notes: _____
_____
_____
_____

8 Pitfalls to avoid
- ☐ Me-too-ism. Don't start telling your story, or comparing your story to theirs.
- ☐ Moralizing, preaching, being judgmental
- ☐ Asking a direct question to satisfy your own curiosity
- ☐ Being an interviewer rather then a listener
- ☐ Giving advice (try fixing it)
- ☐ Cheap consolation. *"Oh, that's not to bad"*
- ☐ Arguing or disagreeing with the speaker
- ☐ Analyzing or interpreting
- ☐ Ignoring obvious heavy emotions

Date: _____

22.

PLEASANT FEELINGS

OPEN
- ☐ Accepting
- ☐ Amazed
- ☐ Confident
- ☐ Easy
- ☐ Free
- ☐ Interested
- ☐ Kind
- ☐ Receptive
- ☐ Reliable
- ☐ Satisfied
- ☐ Sympathetic
- ☐ Understanding

INTERESTED
- ☐ Absorbed
- ☐ Affected
- ☐ Concerned
- ☐ Curious
- ☐ Engrossed
- ☐ Fascinated
- ☐ Inquisitive
- ☐ Intrigued
- ☐ Nosy
- ☐ Snoopy

ALIVE
- ☐ Animated
- ☐ Courageous
- ☐ Energetic
- ☐ Free
- ☐ Frisky
- ☐ Impulsive
- ☐ Liberated
- ☐ Optimistic
- ☐ Playful
- ☐ Provocative
- ☐ Spirited
- ☐ Thrilled
- ☐ Wonderful

STRONG
- ☐ Certain
- ☐ Dynamic
- ☐ Free
- ☐ Hardy
- ☐ Impulsive
- ☐ Rebellious
- ☐ Secure
- ☐ Sure
- ☐ Tenacious
- ☐ Unique

LOVE
- ☐ Admiration
- ☐ Affectionate
- ☐ Attracted
- ☐ Close
- ☐ Comforted
- ☐ Considerate
- ☐ Devoted
- ☐ Drawn toward
- ☐ Loved
- ☐ Loving
- ☐ Passionate
- ☐ Sensitive
- ☐ Sympathy
- ☐ Tender
- ☐ Touched
- ☐ Warm

POSITIVE
- ☐ Anxious
- ☐ Bold
- ☐ Brave
- ☐ Challenged
- ☐ Confident
- ☐ Daring
- ☐ Determined
- ☐ Eager
- ☐ Earnest
- ☐ Enthusiastic
- ☐ Excited
- ☐ Hopeful
- ☐ Inspired
- ☐ Intent
- ☐ Keen
- ☐ Optimistic
- ☐ Re-enforced

GOOD
- ☐ At ease
- ☐ Blessed
- ☐ Bright
- ☐ Calm
- ☐ Certain
- ☐ Clever
- ☐ Comfortable
- ☐ Content
- ☐ Encouraged
- ☐ Free and easy
- ☐ Peaceful
- ☐ Pleased
- ☐ Quiet
- ☐ Reassured
- ☐ Relaxed
- ☐ Serene
- ☐ Surprised

HAPPY
- ☐ Cheerful
- ☐ Delighted
- ☐ Ecstatic
- ☐ Elated
- ☐ Festive
- ☐ Fortunate
- ☐ Glad
- ☐ Gleeful
- ☐ Great
- ☐ Important
- ☐ Joyous
- ☐ Jubilant
- ☐ Lucky
- ☐ Merry
- ☐ Overjoyed
- ☐ Satisfied
- ☐ Sunny
- ☐ Thankful

Read and check off
✓

Preparing to listen
- ☐ Remember to put your mind and feelings in neutral gear.
- ☐ Your body posture must say, *"I am open, very interested, affirmative, attentive."*
- ☐ Maintain good eye contact.
- ☐ Give the speaker a verbal door opening, showing your readiness to listen.

While Listening
- ☐ Track what the speaker is saying in both content and feeling levels
- ☐ Stay with the content of communication
- ☐ Listen for and identify the basic general feeling; anger, fear, joy, resentment, etc.
- ☐ Suspend judgment; open yourself to the presence of their heart.

Responding
- ☐ Use oral responses, which are affirming, which say, *"I am with you"*, *"I understand."*
- ☐ Feed general feelings back to the speaker. *"You seem to feel this has been a good experience for you"*
- ☐ Stay an inch ahead of the speaker, not a mile.

UNPLEASANT FEELINGS

😳 HELPLESS
- ☐ Alone
- ☐ Despair
- ☐ Distressed
- ☐ Dominated
- ☐ Empty
- ☐ Fatigued
- ☐ Forced
- ☐ Frustrated
- ☐ Hesitant
- ☐ In A Stew
- ☐ Incapable
- ☐ Inferior
- ☐ Paralyzed
- ☐ Pathetic
- ☐ Tragic
- ☐ Useless
- ☐ Vulnerable
- ☐ Woeful

😕 CONFUSED
- ☐ Disillusioned
- ☐ Distrustful
- ☐ Doubtful
- ☐ Embarrassed
- ☐ Hesitant
- ☐ Indecisive
- ☐ Lost
- ☐ Misgiving
- ☐ Perplexed
- ☐ Pessimistic
- ☐ Shy
- ☐ Skeptical
- ☐ Stupefied
- ☐ Tense
- ☐ Unbelieving
- ☐ Uncertain
- ☐ Uneasy
- ☐ Unsure
- ☐ Upset

😔 DEPRESSED
- ☐ A Sense of Loss
- ☐ Abominable
- ☐ Ashamed
- ☐ Bad
- ☐ Despicable
- ☐ Detestable
- ☐ Diminished
- ☐ Disappointed
- ☐ Discouraged
- ☐ Disgusting
- ☐ Dissatisfied
- ☐ Guilty
- ☐ In Despair
- ☐ Lousy
- ☐ Miserable
- ☐ Powerless
- ☐ Repugnant
- ☐ Sulky
- ☐ Terrible

😠 ANGRY
- ☐ Aggressive
- ☐ Annoyed
- ☐ Bitter
- ☐ Boiling
- ☐ Cross
- ☐ Enraged
- ☐ Fuming
- ☐ Hateful
- ☐ Hostile
- ☐ Incensed
- ☐ Inflamed
- ☐ Infuriated
- ☐ Insulting
- ☐ Irritated
- ☐ Offensive
- ☐ Provoked
- ☐ Resentful
- ☐ Sore
- ☐ Unpleasant
- ☐ Upset
- ☐ Worked Up

😢 SAD
- ☐ Anguish
- ☐ Desolate
- ☐ Desperate
- ☐ Dismayed
- ☐ Grief
- ☐ Grieved
- ☐ Lonely
- ☐ Mournful
- ☐ Pained
- ☐ Pessimistic
- ☐ Sorrowful
- ☐ Tearful
- ☐ Unhappy

😐 INDIFFERENT
- ☐ Bored
- ☐ Cold
- ☐ Disinterested
- ☐ Dull
- ☐ Insensitive
- ☐ Lifeless
- ☐ Neutral
- ☐ Nonchalant
- ☐ Preoccupied
- ☐ Reserved
- ☐ Weary

😨 AFRAID
- ☐ Alarmed
- ☐ Anxious
- ☐ Cowardly
- ☐ Doubtful
- ☐ Fearful
- ☐ Frightened
- ☐ Menaced
- ☐ Nervous
- ☐ Panic
- ☐ Quaking
- ☐ Restless
- ☐ Scared
- ☐ Shaky
- ☐ Suspicious
- ☐ Terrified
- ☐ Threatened
- ☐ Timid
- ☐ Wary
- ☐ Worried

😟 HURT
- ☐ Aching
- ☐ Afflicted
- ☐ Agonized
- ☐ Alienated
- ☐ Appalled
- ☐ Crushed
- ☐ Dejected
- ☐ Deprived
- ☐ Heartbroken
- ☐ Humiliated
- ☐ Injured
- ☐ Offended
- ☐ Pained
- ☐ Rejected
- ☐ Tormented
- ☐ Tortured
- ☐ Victimized
- ☐ Wronged

Notes: _____
_____
_____
_____

8 Pitfalls to avoid
- ☐ Me-too-ism. Don't start telling your story, or comparing your story to theirs.
- ☐ Moralizing, preaching, being judgmental
- ☐ Asking a direct question to satisfy your own curiosity
- ☐ Being an interviewer rather then a listener
- ☐ Giving advice (try fixing it)
- ☐ Cheap consolation. *"Oh, that's not to bad"*
- ☐ Arguing or disagreeing with the speaker
- ☐ Analyzing or interpreting
- ☐ Ignoring obvious heavy emotions

Date: _____

PLEASANT FEELINGS

OPEN
- ☐ Accepting
- ☐ Amazed
- ☐ Confident
- ☐ Easy
- ☐ Free
- ☐ Interested
- ☐ Kind
- ☐ Receptive
- ☐ Reliable
- ☐ Satisfied
- ☐ Sympathetic
- ☐ Understanding

INTERESTED
- ☐ Absorbed
- ☐ Affected
- ☐ Concerned
- ☐ Curious
- ☐ Engrossed
- ☐ Fascinated
- ☐ Inquisitive
- ☐ Intrigued
- ☐ Nosy
- ☐ Snoopy

ALIVE
- ☐ Animated
- ☐ Courageous
- ☐ Energetic
- ☐ Free
- ☐ Frisky
- ☐ Impulsive
- ☐ Liberated
- ☐ Optimistic
- ☐ Playful
- ☐ Provocative
- ☐ Spirited
- ☐ Thrilled
- ☐ Wonderful

STRONG
- ☐ Certain
- ☐ Dynamic
- ☐ Free
- ☐ Hardy
- ☐ Impulsive
- ☐ Rebellious
- ☐ Secure
- ☐ Sure
- ☐ Tenacious
- ☐ Unique

LOVE
- ☐ Admiration
- ☐ Affectionate
- ☐ Attracted
- ☐ Close
- ☐ Comforted
- ☐ Considerate
- ☐ Devoted
- ☐ Drawn toward
- ☐ Loved
- ☐ Loving
- ☐ Passionate
- ☐ Sensitive
- ☐ Sympathy
- ☐ Tender
- ☐ Touched
- ☐ Warm

POSITIVE
- ☐ Anxious
- ☐ Bold
- ☐ Brave
- ☐ Challenged
- ☐ Confident
- ☐ Daring
- ☐ Determined
- ☐ Eager
- ☐ Earnest
- ☐ Enthusiastic
- ☐ Excited
- ☐ Hopeful
- ☐ Inspired
- ☐ Intent
- ☐ Keen
- ☐ Optimistic
- ☐ Re-enforced

GOOD
- ☐ At ease
- ☐ Blessed
- ☐ Bright
- ☐ Calm
- ☐ Certain
- ☐ Clever
- ☐ Comfortable
- ☐ Content
- ☐ Encouraged
- ☐ Free and easy
- ☐ Peaceful
- ☐ Pleased
- ☐ Quiet
- ☐ Reassured
- ☐ Relaxed
- ☐ Serene
- ☐ Surprised

HAPPY
- ☐ Cheerful
- ☐ Delighted
- ☐ Ecstatic
- ☐ Elated
- ☐ Festive
- ☐ Fortunate
- ☐ Glad
- ☐ Gleeful
- ☐ Great
- ☐ Important
- ☐ Joyous
- ☐ Jubilant
- ☐ Lucky
- ☐ Merry
- ☐ Overjoyed
- ☐ Satisfied
- ☐ Sunny
- ☐ Thankful

Read and check off
✓

Preparing to listen
- ☐ Remember to put your mind and feelings in neutral gear.
- ☐ Your body posture must say, *"I' am open, very interested, affirmative, attentive."*
- ☐ Maintain good eye contact.
- ☐ Give the speaker a verbal door opening, showing your readiness to listen.

While Listening
- ☐ Track what the speaker is saying in both content and feeling levels
- ☐ Stay with the content of communication
- ☐ Listen for and identify the basic general feeling; anger, fear, joy, resentment, etc.
- ☐ Suspend judgment; open yourself to the presence of their heart.

Responding
- ☐ Use oral responses, which are affirming, which say, *"I am with you", "I understand."*
- ☐ Feed general feelings back to the speaker. *"You seem to feel this has been a good experience for you"*
- ☐ Stay an inch ahead of the speaker, not a mile.

UNPLEASANT FEELINGS

😔 HELPLESS
- ☐ Alone
- ☐ Despair
- ☐ Distressed
- ☐ Dominated
- ☐ Empty
- ☐ Fatigued
- ☐ Forced
- ☐ Frustrated
- ☐ Hesitant
- ☐ In A Stew
- ☐ Incapable
- ☐ Inferior
- ☐ Paralyzed
- ☐ Pathetic
- ☐ Tragic
- ☐ Useless
- ☐ Vulnerable
- ☐ Woeful

😕 CONFUSED
- ☐ Disillusioned
- ☐ Distrustful
- ☐ Doubtful
- ☐ Embarrassed
- ☐ Hesitant
- ☐ Indecisive
- ☐ Lost
- ☐ Misgiving
- ☐ Perplexed
- ☐ Pessimistic
- ☐ Shy
- ☐ Skeptical
- ☐ Stupefied
- ☐ Tense
- ☐ Unbelieving
- ☐ Uncertain
- ☐ Uneasy
- ☐ Unsure
- ☐ Upset

😞 DEPRESSED
- ☐ A Sense of Loss
- ☐ Abominable
- ☐ Ashamed
- ☐ Bad
- ☐ Despicable
- ☐ Detestable
- ☐ Diminished
- ☐ Disappointed
- ☐ Discouraged
- ☐ Disgusting
- ☐ Dissatisfied
- ☐ Guilty
- ☐ In Despair
- ☐ Lousy
- ☐ Miserable
- ☐ Powerless
- ☐ Repugnant
- ☐ Sulky
- ☐ Terrible

😠 ANGRY
- ☐ Aggressive
- ☐ Annoyed
- ☐ Bitter
- ☐ Boiling
- ☐ Cross
- ☐ Enraged
- ☐ Fuming
- ☐ Hateful
- ☐ Hostile
- ☐ Incensed
- ☐ Inflamed
- ☐ Infuriated
- ☐ Insulting
- ☐ Irritated
- ☐ Offensive
- ☐ Provoked
- ☐ Resentful
- ☐ Sore
- ☐ Unpleasant
- ☐ Upset
- ☐ Worked Up

😢 SAD
- ☐ Anguish
- ☐ Desolate
- ☐ Desperate
- ☐ Dismayed
- ☐ Grief
- ☐ Grieved
- ☐ Lonely
- ☐ Mournful
- ☐ Pained
- ☐ Pessimistic
- ☐ Sorrowful
- ☐ Tearful
- ☐ Unhappy

😐 INDIFFERENT
- ☐ Bored
- ☐ Cold
- ☐ Disinterested
- ☐ Dull
- ☐ Insensitive
- ☐ Lifeless
- ☐ Neutral
- ☐ Nonchalant
- ☐ Preoccupied
- ☐ Reserved
- ☐ Weary

😨 AFRAID
- ☐ Alarmed
- ☐ Anxious
- ☐ Cowardly
- ☐ Doubtful
- ☐ Fearful
- ☐ Frightened
- ☐ Menaced
- ☐ Nervous
- ☐ Panic
- ☐ Quaking
- ☐ Restless
- ☐ Scared
- ☐ Shaky
- ☐ Suspicious
- ☐ Terrified
- ☐ Threatened
- ☐ Timid
- ☐ Wary
- ☐ Worried

😣 HURT
- ☐ Aching
- ☐ Afflicted
- ☐ Agonized
- ☐ Alienated
- ☐ Appalled
- ☐ Crushed
- ☐ Dejected
- ☐ Deprived
- ☐ Heartbroken
- ☐ Humiliated
- ☐ Injured
- ☐ Offended
- ☐ Pained
- ☐ Rejected
- ☐ Tormented
- ☐ Tortured
- ☐ Victimized
- ☐ Wronged

Notes: _____
_____
_____
_____

8 Pitfalls to avoid
- ☐ Me-too-ism. Don't start telling your story, or comparing your story to theirs.
- ☐ Moralizing, preaching, being judgmental
- ☐ Asking a direct question to satisfy your own curiosity
- ☐ Being an interviewer rather then a listener
- ☐ Giving advice (try fixing it)
- ☐ Cheap consolation. *"Oh, that's not to bad"*
- ☐ Arguing or disagreeing with the speaker
- ☐ Analyzing or interpreting
- ☐ Ignoring obvious heavy emotions

Date: _____

PLEASANT FEELINGS

OPEN
- ☐ Accepting
- ☐ Amazed
- ☐ Confident
- ☐ Easy
- ☐ Free
- ☐ Interested
- ☐ Kind
- ☐ Receptive
- ☐ Reliable
- ☐ Satisfied
- ☐ Sympathetic
- ☐ Understanding

INTERESTED
- ☐ Absorbed
- ☐ Affected
- ☐ Concerned
- ☐ Curious
- ☐ Engrossed
- ☐ Fascinated
- ☐ Inquisitive
- ☐ Intrigued
- ☐ Nosy
- ☐ Snoopy

ALIVE
- ☐ Animated
- ☐ Courageous
- ☐ Energetic
- ☐ Free
- ☐ Frisky
- ☐ Impulsive
- ☐ Liberated
- ☐ Optimistic
- ☐ Playful
- ☐ Provocative
- ☐ Spirited
- ☐ Thrilled
- ☐ Wonderful

STRONG
- ☐ Certain
- ☐ Dynamic
- ☐ Free
- ☐ Hardy
- ☐ Impulsive
- ☐ Rebellious
- ☐ Secure
- ☐ Sure
- ☐ Tenacious
- ☐ Unique

LOVE
- ☐ Admiration
- ☐ Affectionate
- ☐ Attracted
- ☐ Close
- ☐ Comforted
- ☐ Considerate
- ☐ Devoted
- ☐ Drawn toward
- ☐ Loved
- ☐ Loving
- ☐ Passionate
- ☐ Sensitive
- ☐ Sympathy
- ☐ Tender
- ☐ Touched
- ☐ Warm

POSITIVE
- ☐ Anxious
- ☐ Bold
- ☐ Brave
- ☐ Challenged
- ☐ Confident
- ☐ Daring
- ☐ Determined
- ☐ Eager
- ☐ Earnest
- ☐ Enthusiastic
- ☐ Excited
- ☐ Hopeful
- ☐ Inspired
- ☐ Intent
- ☐ Keen
- ☐ Optimistic
- ☐ Re-enforced

GOOD
- ☐ At ease
- ☐ Blessed
- ☐ Bright
- ☐ Calm
- ☐ Certain
- ☐ Clever
- ☐ Comfortable
- ☐ Content
- ☐ Encouraged
- ☐ Free and easy
- ☐ Peaceful
- ☐ Pleased
- ☐ Quiet
- ☐ Reassured
- ☐ Relaxed
- ☐ Serene
- ☐ Surprised

HAPPY
- ☐ Cheerful
- ☐ Delighted
- ☐ Ecstatic
- ☐ Elated
- ☐ Festive
- ☐ Fortunate
- ☐ Glad
- ☐ Gleeful
- ☐ Great
- ☐ Important
- ☐ Joyous
- ☐ Jubilant
- ☐ Lucky
- ☐ Merry
- ☐ Overjoyed
- ☐ Satisfied
- ☐ Sunny
- ☐ Thankful

Read and check off
✓

Preparing to listen
- ☐ Remember to put your mind and feelings in neutral gear.
- ☐ Your body posture must say, *"I am open, very interested, affirmative, attentive."*
- ☐ Maintain good eye contact.
- ☐ Give the speaker a verbal door opening, showing your readiness to listen.

While Listening
- ☐ Track what the speaker is saying in both content and feeling levels
- ☐ Stay with the content of communication
- ☐ Listen for and identify the basic general feeling; anger, fear, joy, resentment, etc.
- ☐ Suspend judgment; open yourself to the presence of their heart.

Responding
- ☐ Use oral responses, which are affirming, which say, *"I am with you"*, *"I understand."*
- ☐ Feed general feelings back to the speaker. *"You seem to feel this has been a good experience for you"*
- ☐ Stay an inch ahead of the speaker, not a mile.

UNPLEASANT FEELINGS

😢 HELPLESS
- [ ] Alone
- [ ] Despair
- [ ] Distressed
- [ ] Dominated
- [ ] Empty
- [ ] Fatigued
- [ ] Forced
- [ ] Frustrated
- [ ] Hesitant
- [ ] In A Stew
- [ ] Incapable
- [ ] Inferior
- [ ] Paralyzed
- [ ] Pathetic
- [ ] Tragic
- [ ] Useless
- [ ] Vulnerable
- [ ] Woeful

😕 CONFUSED
- [ ] Disillusioned
- [ ] Distrustful
- [ ] Doubtful
- [ ] Embarrassed
- [ ] Hesitant
- [ ] Indecisive
- [ ] Lost
- [ ] Misgiving
- [ ] Perplexed
- [ ] Pessimistic
- [ ] Shy
- [ ] Skeptical
- [ ] Stupefied
- [ ] Tense
- [ ] Unbelieving
- [ ] Uncertain
- [ ] Uneasy
- [ ] Unsure
- [ ] Upset

😞 DEPRESSED
- [ ] A Sense of Loss
- [ ] Abominable
- [ ] Ashamed
- [ ] Bad
- [ ] Despicable
- [ ] Detestable
- [ ] Diminished
- [ ] Disappointed
- [ ] Discouraged
- [ ] Disgusting
- [ ] Dissatisfied
- [ ] Guilty
- [ ] In Despair
- [ ] Lousy
- [ ] Miserable
- [ ] Powerless
- [ ] Repugnant
- [ ] Sulky
- [ ] Terrible

😠 ANGRY
- [ ] Aggressive
- [ ] Annoyed
- [ ] Bitter
- [ ] Boiling
- [ ] Cross
- [ ] Enraged
- [ ] Fuming
- [ ] Hateful
- [ ] Hostile
- [ ] Incensed
- [ ] Inflamed
- [ ] Infuriated
- [ ] Insulting
- [ ] Irritated
- [ ] Offensive
- [ ] Provoked
- [ ] Resentful
- [ ] Sore
- [ ] Unpleasant
- [ ] Upset
- [ ] Worked Up

😢 SAD
- [ ] Anguish
- [ ] Desolate
- [ ] Desperate
- [ ] Dismayed
- [ ] Grief
- [ ] Grieved
- [ ] Lonely
- [ ] Mournful
- [ ] Pained
- [ ] Pessimistic
- [ ] Sorrowful
- [ ] Tearful
- [ ] Unhappy

😐 INDIFFERENT
- [ ] Bored
- [ ] Cold
- [ ] Disinterested
- [ ] Dull
- [ ] Insensitive
- [ ] Lifeless
- [ ] Neutral
- [ ] Nonchalant
- [ ] Preoccupied
- [ ] Reserved
- [ ] Weary

😨 AFRAID
- [ ] Alarmed
- [ ] Anxious
- [ ] Cowardly
- [ ] Doubtful
- [ ] Fearful
- [ ] Frightened
- [ ] Menaced
- [ ] Nervous
- [ ] Panic
- [ ] Quaking
- [ ] Restless
- [ ] Scared
- [ ] Shaky
- [ ] Suspicious
- [ ] Terrified
- [ ] Threatened
- [ ] Timid
- [ ] Wary
- [ ] Worried

😟 HURT
- [ ] Aching
- [ ] Afflicted
- [ ] Agonized
- [ ] Alienated
- [ ] Appalled
- [ ] Crushed
- [ ] Dejected
- [ ] Deprived
- [ ] Heartbroken
- [ ] Humiliated
- [ ] Injured
- [ ] Offended
- [ ] Pained
- [ ] Rejected
- [ ] Tormented
- [ ] Tortured
- [ ] Victimized
- [ ] Wronged

Notes: _____
_____
_____
_____

8 Pitfalls to avoid
- [ ] Me-too-ism. Don't start telling your story, or comparing your story to theirs.
- [ ] Moralizing, preaching, being judgmental
- [ ] Asking a direct question to satisfy your own curiosity
- [ ] Being an interviewer rather then a listener
- [ ] Giving advice (try fixing it)
- [ ] Cheap consolation. *"Oh, that's not to bad"*
- [ ] Arguing or disagreeing with the speaker
- [ ] Analyzing or interpreting
- [ ] Ignoring obvious heavy emotions

Date: _____

PLEASANT FEELINGS

OPEN
- ☐ Accepting
- ☐ Amazed
- ☐ Confident
- ☐ Easy
- ☐ Free
- ☐ Interested
- ☐ Kind
- ☐ Receptive
- ☐ Reliable
- ☐ Satisfied
- ☐ Sympathetic
- ☐ Understanding

INTERESTED
- ☐ Absorbed
- ☐ Affected
- ☐ Concerned
- ☐ Curious
- ☐ Engrossed
- ☐ Fascinated
- ☐ Inquisitive
- ☐ Intrigued
- ☐ Nosy
- ☐ Snoopy

ALIVE
- ☐ Animated
- ☐ Courageous
- ☐ Energetic
- ☐ Free
- ☐ Frisky
- ☐ Impulsive
- ☐ Liberated
- ☐ Optimistic
- ☐ Playful
- ☐ Provocative
- ☐ Spirited
- ☐ Thrilled
- ☐ Wonderful

STRONG
- ☐ Certain
- ☐ Dynamic
- ☐ Free
- ☐ Hardy
- ☐ Impulsive
- ☐ Rebellious
- ☐ Secure
- ☐ Sure
- ☐ Tenacious
- ☐ Unique

LOVE
- ☐ Admiration
- ☐ Affectionate
- ☐ Attracted
- ☐ Close
- ☐ Comforted
- ☐ Considerate
- ☐ Devoted
- ☐ Drawn toward
- ☐ Loved
- ☐ Loving
- ☐ Passionate
- ☐ Sensitive
- ☐ Sympathy
- ☐ Tender
- ☐ Touched
- ☐ Warm

POSITIVE
- ☐ Anxious
- ☐ Bold
- ☐ Brave
- ☐ Challenged
- ☐ Confident
- ☐ Daring
- ☐ Determined
- ☐ Eager
- ☐ Earnest
- ☐ Enthusiastic
- ☐ Excited
- ☐ Hopeful
- ☐ Inspired
- ☐ Intent
- ☐ Keen
- ☐ Optimistic
- ☐ Re-enforced

GOOD
- ☐ At ease
- ☐ Blessed
- ☐ Bright
- ☐ Calm
- ☐ Certain
- ☐ Clever
- ☐ Comfortable
- ☐ Content
- ☐ Encouraged
- ☐ Free and easy
- ☐ Peaceful
- ☐ Pleased
- ☐ Quiet
- ☐ Reassured
- ☐ Relaxed
- ☐ Serene
- ☐ Surprised

HAPPY
- ☐ Cheerful
- ☐ Delighted
- ☐ Ecstatic
- ☐ Elated
- ☐ Festive
- ☐ Fortunate
- ☐ Glad
- ☐ Gleeful
- ☐ Great
- ☐ Important
- ☐ Joyous
- ☐ Jubilant
- ☐ Lucky
- ☐ Merry
- ☐ Overjoyed
- ☐ Satisfied
- ☐ Sunny
- ☐ Thankful

Read and check off
✓

Preparing to listen
- ☐ Remember to put your mind and feelings in neutral gear.
- ☐ Your body posture must say, *"I am open, very interested, affirmative, attentive."*
- ☐ Maintain good eye contact.
- ☐ Give the speaker a verbal door opening, showing your readiness to listen.

While Listening
- ☐ Track what the speaker is saying in both content and feeling levels
- ☐ Stay with the content of communication
- ☐ Listen for and identify the basic general feeling; anger, fear, joy, resentment, etc.
- ☐ Suspend judgment; open yourself to the presence of their heart.

Responding
- ☐ Use oral responses, which are affirming, which say, *"I am with you", "I understand."*
- ☐ Feed general feelings back to the speaker. *"You seem to feel this has been a good experience for you"*
- ☐ Stay an inch ahead of the speaker, not a mile.

UNPLEASANT FEELINGS

HELPLESS
- [ ] Alone
- [ ] Despair
- [ ] Distressed
- [ ] Dominated
- [ ] Empty
- [ ] Fatigued
- [ ] Forced
- [ ] Frustrated
- [ ] Hesitant
- [ ] In A Stew
- [ ] Incapable
- [ ] Inferior
- [ ] Paralyzed
- [ ] Pathetic
- [ ] Tragic
- [ ] Useless
- [ ] Vulnerable
- [ ] Woeful

SAD
- [ ] Anguish
- [ ] Desolate
- [ ] Desperate
- [ ] Dismayed
- [ ] Grief
- [ ] Grieved
- [ ] Lonely
- [ ] Mournful
- [ ] Pained
- [ ] Pessimistic
- [ ] Sorrowful
- [ ] Tearful
- [ ] Unhappy

CONFUSED
- [ ] Disillusioned
- [ ] Distrustful
- [ ] Doubtful
- [ ] Embarrassed
- [ ] Hesitant
- [ ] Indecisive
- [ ] Lost
- [ ] Misgiving
- [ ] Perplexed
- [ ] Pessimistic
- [ ] Shy
- [ ] Skeptical
- [ ] Stupefied
- [ ] Tense
- [ ] Unbelieving
- [ ] Uncertain
- [ ] Uneasy
- [ ] Unsure
- [ ] Upset

INDIFFERENT
- [ ] Bored
- [ ] Cold
- [ ] Disinterested
- [ ] Dull
- [ ] Insensitive
- [ ] Lifeless
- [ ] Neutral
- [ ] Nonchalant
- [ ] Preoccupied
- [ ] Reserved
- [ ] Weary

DEPRESSED
- [ ] A Sense of Loss
- [ ] Abominable
- [ ] Ashamed
- [ ] Bad
- [ ] Despicable
- [ ] Detestable
- [ ] Diminished
- [ ] Disappointed
- [ ] Discouraged
- [ ] Disgusting
- [ ] Dissatisfied
- [ ] Guilty
- [ ] In Despair
- [ ] Lousy
- [ ] Miserable
- [ ] Powerless
- [ ] Repugnant
- [ ] Sulky
- [ ] Terrible

AFRAID
- [ ] Alarmed
- [ ] Anxious
- [ ] Cowardly
- [ ] Doubtful
- [ ] Fearful
- [ ] Frightened
- [ ] Menaced
- [ ] Nervous
- [ ] Panic
- [ ] Quaking
- [ ] Restless
- [ ] Scared
- [ ] Shaky
- [ ] Suspicious
- [ ] Terrified
- [ ] Threatened
- [ ] Timid
- [ ] Wary
- [ ] Worried

ANGRY
- [ ] Aggressive
- [ ] Annoyed
- [ ] Bitter
- [ ] Boiling
- [ ] Cross
- [ ] Enraged
- [ ] Fuming
- [ ] Hateful
- [ ] Hostile
- [ ] Incensed
- [ ] Inflamed
- [ ] Infuriated
- [ ] Insulting
- [ ] Irritated
- [ ] Offensive
- [ ] Provoked
- [ ] Resentful
- [ ] Sore
- [ ] Unpleasant
- [ ] Upset
- [ ] Worked Up

HURT
- [ ] Aching
- [ ] Afflicted
- [ ] Agonized
- [ ] Alienated
- [ ] Appalled
- [ ] Crushed
- [ ] Dejected
- [ ] Deprived
- [ ] Heartbroken
- [ ] Humiliated
- [ ] Injured
- [ ] Offended
- [ ] Pained
- [ ] Rejected
- [ ] Tormented
- [ ] Tortured
- [ ] Victimized
- [ ] Wronged

Notes:
_____
_____
_____
_____

8 Pitfalls to avoid
- [ ] Me-too-ism. Don't start telling your story, or comparing your story to theirs.
- [ ] Moralizing, preaching, being judgmental
- [ ] Asking a direct question to satisfy your own curiosity
- [ ] Being an interviewer rather then a listener
- [ ] Giving advice (try fixing it)
- [ ] Cheap consolation. *"Oh, that's not to bad"*
- [ ] Arguing or disagreeing with the speaker
- [ ] Analyzing or interpreting
- [ ] Ignoring obvious heavy emotions

Date: _____

PLEASANT FEELINGS

OPEN
- [ ] Accepting
- [ ] Amazed
- [ ] Confident
- [ ] Easy
- [ ] Free
- [ ] Interested
- [ ] Kind
- [ ] Receptive
- [ ] Reliable
- [ ] Satisfied
- [ ] Sympathetic
- [ ] Understanding

INTERESTED
- [ ] Absorbed
- [ ] Affected
- [ ] Concerned
- [ ] Curious
- [ ] Engrossed
- [ ] Fascinated
- [ ] Inquisitive
- [ ] Intrigued
- [ ] Nosy
- [ ] Snoopy

ALIVE
- [ ] Animated
- [ ] Courageous
- [ ] Energetic
- [ ] Free
- [ ] Frisky
- [ ] Impulsive
- [ ] Liberated
- [ ] Optimistic
- [ ] Playful
- [ ] Provocative
- [ ] Spirited
- [ ] Thrilled
- [ ] Wonderful

STRONG
- [ ] Certain
- [ ] Dynamic
- [ ] Free
- [ ] Hardy
- [ ] Impulsive
- [ ] Rebellious
- [ ] Secure
- [ ] Sure
- [ ] Tenacious
- [ ] Unique

LOVE
- [ ] Admiration
- [ ] Affectionate
- [ ] Attracted
- [ ] Close
- [ ] Comforted
- [ ] Considerate
- [ ] Devoted
- [ ] Drawn toward
- [ ] Loved
- [ ] Loving
- [ ] Passionate
- [ ] Sensitive
- [ ] Sympathy
- [ ] Tender
- [ ] Touched
- [ ] Warm

POSITIVE
- [ ] Anxious
- [ ] Bold
- [ ] Brave
- [ ] Challenged
- [ ] Confident
- [ ] Daring
- [ ] Determined
- [ ] Eager
- [ ] Earnest
- [ ] Enthusiastic
- [ ] Excited
- [ ] Hopeful
- [ ] Inspired
- [ ] Intent
- [ ] Keen
- [ ] Optimistic
- [ ] Re-enforced

GOOD
- [ ] At ease
- [ ] Blessed
- [ ] Bright
- [ ] Calm
- [ ] Certain
- [ ] Clever
- [ ] Comfortable
- [ ] Content
- [ ] Encouraged
- [ ] Free and easy
- [ ] Peaceful
- [ ] Pleased
- [ ] Quiet
- [ ] Reassured
- [ ] Relaxed
- [ ] Serene
- [ ] Surprised

HAPPY
- [ ] Cheerful
- [ ] Delighted
- [ ] Ecstatic
- [ ] Elated
- [ ] Festive
- [ ] Fortunate
- [ ] Glad
- [ ] Gleeful
- [ ] Great
- [ ] Important
- [ ] Joyous
- [ ] Jubilant
- [ ] Lucky
- [ ] Merry
- [ ] Overjoyed
- [ ] Satisfied
- [ ] Sunny
- [ ] Thankful

Read and check off ✓

Preparing to listen
- [ ] Remember to put your mind and feelings in neutral gear.
- [ ] Your body posture must say, *"I am open, very interested, affirmative, attentive."*
- [ ] Maintain good eye contact.
- [ ] Give the speaker a verbal door opening, showing your readiness to listen.

While Listening
- [ ] Track what the speaker is saying in both content and feeling levels
- [ ] Stay with the content of communication
- [ ] Listen for and identify the basic general feeling; anger, fear, joy, resentment, etc.
- [ ] Suspend judgment; open yourself to the presence of their heart.

Responding
- [ ] Use oral responses, which are affirming, which say, *"I am with you"*, *"I understand."*
- [ ] Feed general feelings back to the speaker. *"You seem to feel this has been a good experience for you"*
- [ ] Stay an inch ahead of the speaker, not a mile.

UNPLEASANT FEELINGS

😦 HELPLESS
- ☐ Alone
- ☐ Despair
- ☐ Distressed
- ☐ Dominated
- ☐ Empty
- ☐ Fatigued
- ☐ Forced
- ☐ Frustrated
- ☐ Hesitant
- ☐ In A Stew
- ☐ Incapable
- ☐ Inferior
- ☐ Paralyzed
- ☐ Pathetic
- ☐ Tragic
- ☐ Useless
- ☐ Vulnerable
- ☐ Woeful

😕 CONFUSED
- ☐ Disillusioned
- ☐ Distrustful
- ☐ Doubtful
- ☐ Embarrassed
- ☐ Hesitant
- ☐ Indecisive
- ☐ Lost
- ☐ Misgiving
- ☐ Perplexed
- ☐ Pessimistic
- ☐ Shy
- ☐ Skeptical
- ☐ Stupefied
- ☐ Tense
- ☐ Unbelieving
- ☐ Uncertain
- ☐ Uneasy
- ☐ Unsure
- ☐ Upset

😞 DEPRESSED
- ☐ A Sense of Loss
- ☐ Abominable
- ☐ Ashamed
- ☐ Bad
- ☐ Despicable
- ☐ Detestable
- ☐ Diminished
- ☐ Disappointed
- ☐ Discouraged
- ☐ Disgusting
- ☐ Dissatisfied
- ☐ Guilty
- ☐ In Despair
- ☐ Lousy
- ☐ Miserable
- ☐ Powerless
- ☐ Repugnant
- ☐ Sulky
- ☐ Terrible

😠 ANGRY
- ☐ Aggressive
- ☐ Annoyed
- ☐ Bitter
- ☐ Boiling
- ☐ Cross
- ☐ Enraged
- ☐ Fuming
- ☐ Hateful
- ☐ Hostile
- ☐ Incensed
- ☐ Inflamed
- ☐ Infuriated
- ☐ Insulting
- ☐ Irritated
- ☐ Offensive
- ☐ Provoked
- ☐ Resentful
- ☐ Sore
- ☐ Unpleasant
- ☐ Upset
- ☐ Worked Up

🙁 SAD
- ☐ Anguish
- ☐ Desolate
- ☐ Desperate
- ☐ Dismayed
- ☐ Grief
- ☐ Grieved
- ☐ Lonely
- ☐ Mournful
- ☐ Pained
- ☐ Pessimistic
- ☐ Sorrowful
- ☐ Tearful
- ☐ Unhappy

😐 INDIFFERENT
- ☐ Bored
- ☐ Cold
- ☐ Disinterested
- ☐ Dull
- ☐ Insensitive
- ☐ Lifeless
- ☐ Neutral
- ☐ Nonchalant
- ☐ Preoccupied
- ☐ Reserved
- ☐ Weary

😨 AFRAID
- ☐ Alarmed
- ☐ Anxious
- ☐ Cowardly
- ☐ Doubtful
- ☐ Fearful
- ☐ Frightened
- ☐ Menaced
- ☐ Nervous
- ☐ Panic
- ☐ Quaking
- ☐ Restless
- ☐ Scared
- ☐ Shaky
- ☐ Suspicious
- ☐ Terrified
- ☐ Threatened
- ☐ Timid
- ☐ Wary
- ☐ Worried

🙁 HURT
- ☐ Aching
- ☐ Afflicted
- ☐ Agonized
- ☐ Alienated
- ☐ Appalled
- ☐ Crushed
- ☐ Dejected
- ☐ Deprived
- ☐ Heartbroken
- ☐ Humiliated
- ☐ Injured
- ☐ Offended
- ☐ Pained
- ☐ Rejected
- ☐ Tormented
- ☐ Tortured
- ☐ Victimized
- ☐ Wronged

Notes: _____
_____
_____
_____

8 Pitfalls to avoid
- ☐ Me-too-ism. Don't start telling your story, or comparing your story to theirs.
- ☐ Moralizing, preaching, being judgmental
- ☐ Asking a direct question to satisfy your own curiosity
- ☐ Being an interviewer rather then a listener
- ☐ Giving advice (try fixing it)
- ☐ Cheap consolation. *"Oh, that's not to bad"*
- ☐ Arguing or disagreeing with the speaker
- ☐ Analyzing or interpreting
- ☐ Ignoring obvious heavy emotions

Date: _____

PLEASANT FEELINGS

OPEN	INTERESTED	ALIVE	STRONG
☐ Accepting	☐ Absorbed	☐ Animated	☐ Certain
☐ Amazed	☐ Affected	☐ Courageous	☐ Dynamic
☐ Confident	☐ Concerned	☐ Energetic	☐ Free
☐ Easy	☐ Curious	☐ Free	☐ Hardy
☐ Free	☐ Engrossed	☐ Frisky	☐ Impulsive
☐ Interested	☐ Fascinated	☐ Impulsive	☐ Rebellious
☐ Kind	☐ Inquisitive	☐ Liberated	☐ Secure
☐ Receptive	☐ Intrigued	☐ Optimistic	☐ Sure
☐ Reliable	☐ Nosy	☐ Playful	☐ Tenacious
☐ Satisfied	☐ Snoopy	☐ Provocative	☐ Unique
☐ Sympathetic		☐ Spirited	
☐ Understanding		☐ Thrilled	
		☐ Wonderful	

LOVE	POSITIVE	GOOD	HAPPY
☐ Admiration	☐ Anxious	☐ At ease	☐ Cheerful
☐ Affectionate	☐ Bold	☐ Blessed	☐ Delighted
☐ Attracted	☐ Brave	☐ Bright	☐ Ecstatic
☐ Close	☐ Challenged	☐ Calm	☐ Elated
☐ Comforted	☐ Confident	☐ Certain	☐ Festive
☐ Considerate	☐ Daring	☐ Clever	☐ Fortunate
☐ Devoted	☐ Determined	☐ Comfortable	☐ Glad
☐ Drawn toward	☐ Eager	☐ Content	☐ Gleeful
☐ Loved	☐ Earnest	☐ Encouraged	☐ Great
☐ Loving	☐ Enthusiastic	☐ Free and easy	☐ Important
☐ Passionate	☐ Excited	☐ Peaceful	☐ Joyous
☐ Sensitive	☐ Hopeful	☐ Pleased	☐ Jubilant
☐ Sympathy	☐ Inspired	☐ Quiet	☐ Lucky
☐ Tender	☐ Intent	☐ Reassured	☐ Merry
☐ Touched	☐ Keen	☐ Relaxed	☐ Overjoyed
☐ Warm	☐ Optimistic	☐ Serene	☐ Satisfied
	☐ Re-enforced	☐ Surprised	☐ Sunny
			☐ Thankful

Read and check off
✓

Preparing to listen
- ☐ Remember to put your mind and feelings in neutral gear.
- ☐ Your body posture must say, *"I am open, very interested, affirmative, attentive."*
- ☐ Maintain good eye contact.
- ☐ Give the speaker a verbal door opening, showing your readiness to listen.

While Listening
- ☐ Track what the speaker is saying in both content and feeling levels
- ☐ Stay with the content of communication
- ☐ Listen for and identify the basic general feeling; anger, fear, joy, resentment, etc.
- ☐ Suspend judgment; open yourself to the presence of their heart.

Responding
- ☐ Use oral responses, which are affirming, which say, *"I am with you", "I understand."*
- ☐ Feed general feelings back to the speaker. *"You seem to feel this has been a good experience for you"*
- ☐ Stay an inch ahead of the speaker, not a mile.

UNPLEASANT FEELINGS

HELPLESS
- ☐ Alone
- ☐ Despair
- ☐ Distressed
- ☐ Dominated
- ☐ Empty
- ☐ Fatigued
- ☐ Forced
- ☐ Frustrated
- ☐ Hesitant
- ☐ In A Stew
- ☐ Incapable
- ☐ Inferior
- ☐ Paralyzed
- ☐ Pathetic
- ☐ Tragic
- ☐ Useless
- ☐ Vulnerable
- ☐ Woeful

CONFUSED
- ☐ Disillusioned
- ☐ Distrustful
- ☐ Doubtful
- ☐ Embarrassed
- ☐ Hesitant
- ☐ Indecisive
- ☐ Lost
- ☐ Misgiving
- ☐ Perplexed
- ☐ Pessimistic
- ☐ Shy
- ☐ Skeptical
- ☐ Stupefied
- ☐ Tense
- ☐ Unbelieving
- ☐ Uncertain
- ☐ Uneasy
- ☐ Unsure
- ☐ Upset

DEPRESSED
- ☐ A Sense of Loss
- ☐ Abominable
- ☐ Ashamed
- ☐ Bad
- ☐ Despicable
- ☐ Detestable
- ☐ Diminished
- ☐ Disappointed
- ☐ Discouraged
- ☐ Disgusting
- ☐ Dissatisfied
- ☐ Guilty
- ☐ In Despair
- ☐ Lousy
- ☐ Miserable
- ☐ Powerless
- ☐ Repugnant
- ☐ Sulky
- ☐ Terrible

ANGRY
- ☐ Aggressive
- ☐ Annoyed
- ☐ Bitter
- ☐ Boiling
- ☐ Cross
- ☐ Enraged
- ☐ Fuming
- ☐ Hateful
- ☐ Hostile
- ☐ Incensed
- ☐ Inflamed
- ☐ Infuriated
- ☐ Insulting
- ☐ Irritated
- ☐ Offensive
- ☐ Provoked
- ☐ Resentful
- ☐ Sore
- ☐ Unpleasant
- ☐ Upset
- ☐ Worked Up

SAD
- ☐ Anguish
- ☐ Desolate
- ☐ Desperate
- ☐ Dismayed
- ☐ Grief
- ☐ Grieved
- ☐ Lonely
- ☐ Mournful
- ☐ Pained
- ☐ Pessimistic
- ☐ Sorrowful
- ☐ Tearful
- ☐ Unhappy

INDIFFERENT
- ☐ Bored
- ☐ Cold
- ☐ Disinterested
- ☐ Dull
- ☐ Insensitive
- ☐ Lifeless
- ☐ Neutral
- ☐ Nonchalant
- ☐ Preoccupied
- ☐ Reserved
- ☐ Weary

AFRAID
- ☐ Alarmed
- ☐ Anxious
- ☐ Cowardly
- ☐ Doubtful
- ☐ Fearful
- ☐ Frightened
- ☐ Menaced
- ☐ Nervous
- ☐ Panic
- ☐ Quaking
- ☐ Restless
- ☐ Scared
- ☐ Shaky
- ☐ Suspicious
- ☐ Terrified
- ☐ Threatened
- ☐ Timid
- ☐ Wary
- ☐ Worried

HURT
- ☐ Aching
- ☐ Afflicted
- ☐ Agonized
- ☐ Alienated
- ☐ Appalled
- ☐ Crushed
- ☐ Dejected
- ☐ Deprived
- ☐ Heartbroken
- ☐ Humiliated
- ☐ Injured
- ☐ Offended
- ☐ Pained
- ☐ Rejected
- ☐ Tormented
- ☐ Tortured
- ☐ Victimized
- ☐ Wronged

Notes: _____
_____
_____
_____

8 Pitfalls to avoid

- ☐ Me-too-ism. Don't start telling your story, or comparing your story to theirs.
- ☐ Moralizing, preaching, being judgmental
- ☐ Asking a direct question to satisfy your own curiosity
- ☐ Being an interviewer rather then a listener
- ☐ Giving advice (try fixing it)
- ☐ Cheap consolation. *"Oh, that's not to bad"*
- ☐ Arguing or disagreeing with the speaker
- ☐ Analyzing or interpreting
- ☐ Ignoring obvious heavy emotions

Date: _____

PLEASANT FEELINGS

OPEN
- ☐ Accepting
- ☐ Amazed
- ☐ Confident
- ☐ Easy
- ☐ Free
- ☐ Interested
- ☐ Kind
- ☐ Receptive
- ☐ Reliable
- ☐ Satisfied
- ☐ Sympathetic
- ☐ Understanding

INTERESTED
- ☐ Absorbed
- ☐ Affected
- ☐ Concerned
- ☐ Curious
- ☐ Engrossed
- ☐ Fascinated
- ☐ Inquisitive
- ☐ Intrigued
- ☐ Nosy
- ☐ Snoopy

ALIVE
- ☐ Animated
- ☐ Courageous
- ☐ Energetic
- ☐ Free
- ☐ Frisky
- ☐ Impulsive
- ☐ Liberated
- ☐ Optimistic
- ☐ Playful
- ☐ Provocative
- ☐ Spirited
- ☐ Thrilled
- ☐ Wonderful

STRONG
- ☐ Certain
- ☐ Dynamic
- ☐ Free
- ☐ Hardy
- ☐ Impulsive
- ☐ Rebellious
- ☐ Secure
- ☐ Sure
- ☐ Tenacious
- ☐ Unique

LOVE
- ☐ Admiration
- ☐ Affectionate
- ☐ Attracted
- ☐ Close
- ☐ Comforted
- ☐ Considerate
- ☐ Devoted
- ☐ Drawn toward
- ☐ Loved
- ☐ Loving
- ☐ Passionate
- ☐ Sensitive
- ☐ Sympathy
- ☐ Tender
- ☐ Touched
- ☐ Warm

POSITIVE
- ☐ Anxious
- ☐ Bold
- ☐ Brave
- ☐ Challenged
- ☐ Confident
- ☐ Daring
- ☐ Determined
- ☐ Eager
- ☐ Earnest
- ☐ Enthusiastic
- ☐ Excited
- ☐ Hopeful
- ☐ Inspired
- ☐ Intent
- ☐ Keen
- ☐ Optimistic
- ☐ Re-enforced

GOOD
- ☐ At ease
- ☐ Blessed
- ☐ Bright
- ☐ Calm
- ☐ Certain
- ☐ Clever
- ☐ Comfortable
- ☐ Content
- ☐ Encouraged
- ☐ Free and easy
- ☐ Peaceful
- ☐ Pleased
- ☐ Quiet
- ☐ Reassured
- ☐ Relaxed
- ☐ Serene
- ☐ Surprised

HAPPY
- ☐ Cheerful
- ☐ Delighted
- ☐ Ecstatic
- ☐ Elated
- ☐ Festive
- ☐ Fortunate
- ☐ Glad
- ☐ Gleeful
- ☐ Great
- ☐ Important
- ☐ Joyous
- ☐ Jubilant
- ☐ Lucky
- ☐ Merry
- ☐ Overjoyed
- ☐ Satisfied
- ☐ Sunny
- ☐ Thankful

Read and check off
✓

Preparing to listen
- ☐ Remember to put your mind and feelings in neutral gear.
- ☐ Your body posture must say, *"I' am open, very interested, affirmative, attentive."*
- ☐ Maintain good eye contact.
- ☐ Give the speaker a verbal door opening, showing your readiness to listen.

While Listening
- ☐ Track what the speaker is saying in both content and feeling levels
- ☐ Stay with the content of communication
- ☐ Listen for and identify the basic general feeling; anger, fear, joy, resentment, etc.
- ☐ Suspend judgment; open yourself to the presence of their heart.

Responding
- ☐ Use oral responses, which are affirming, which say, *"I am with you"*, *"I understand."*
- ☐ Feed general feelings back to the speaker. *"You seem to feel this has been a good experience for you"*
- ☐ Stay an inch ahead of the speaker, not a mile.

(What is your favorite food and why?)

UNPLEASANT FEELINGS

☺ HELPLESS
- ☐ Alone
- ☐ Despair
- ☐ Distressed
- ☐ Dominated
- ☐ Empty
- ☐ Fatigued
- ☐ Forced
- ☐ Frustrated
- ☐ Hesitant
- ☐ In A Stew
- ☐ Incapable
- ☐ Inferior
- ☐ Paralyzed
- ☐ Pathetic
- ☐ Tragic
- ☐ Useless
- ☐ Vulnerable
- ☐ Woeful

☺ SAD
- ☐ Anguish
- ☐ Desolate
- ☐ Desperate
- ☐ Dismayed
- ☐ Grief
- ☐ Grieved
- ☐ Lonely
- ☐ Mournful
- ☐ Pained
- ☐ Pessimistic
- ☐ Sorrowful
- ☐ Tearful
- ☐ Unhappy

☺ CONFUSED
- ☐ Disillusioned
- ☐ Distrustful
- ☐ Doubtful
- ☐ Embarrassed
- ☐ Hesitant
- ☐ Indecisive
- ☐ Lost
- ☐ Misgiving
- ☐ Perplexed
- ☐ Pessimistic
- ☐ Shy
- ☐ Skeptical
- ☐ Stupefied
- ☐ Tense
- ☐ Unbelieving
- ☐ Uncertain
- ☐ Uneasy
- ☐ Unsure
- ☐ Upset

☺ INDIFFERENT
- ☐ Bored
- ☐ Cold
- ☐ Disinterested
- ☐ Dull
- ☐ Insensitive
- ☐ Lifeless
- ☐ Neutral
- ☐ Nonchalant
- ☐ Preoccupied
- ☐ Reserved
- ☐ Weary

☺ DEPRESSED
- ☐ A Sense of Loss
- ☐ Abominable
- ☐ Ashamed
- ☐ Bad
- ☐ Despicable
- ☐ Detestable
- ☐ Diminished
- ☐ Disappointed
- ☐ Discouraged
- ☐ Disgusting
- ☐ Dissatisfied
- ☐ Guilty
- ☐ In Despair
- ☐ Lousy
- ☐ Miserable
- ☐ Powerless
- ☐ Repugnant
- ☐ Sulky
- ☐ Terrible

☺ AFRAID
- ☐ Alarmed
- ☐ Anxious
- ☐ Cowardly
- ☐ Doubtful
- ☐ Fearful
- ☐ Frightened
- ☐ Menaced
- ☐ Nervous
- ☐ Panic
- ☐ Quaking
- ☐ Restless
- ☐ Scared
- ☐ Shaky
- ☐ Suspicious
- ☐ Terrified
- ☐ Threatened
- ☐ Timid
- ☐ Wary
- ☐ Worried

☺ ANGRY
- ☐ Aggressive
- ☐ Annoyed
- ☐ Bitter
- ☐ Boiling
- ☐ Cross
- ☐ Enraged
- ☐ Fuming
- ☐ Hateful
- ☐ Hostile
- ☐ Incensed
- ☐ Inflamed
- ☐ Infuriated
- ☐ Insulting
- ☐ Irritated
- ☐ Offensive
- ☐ Provoked
- ☐ Resentful
- ☐ Sore
- ☐ Unpleasant
- ☐ Upset
- ☐ Worked Up

☺ HURT
- ☐ Aching
- ☐ Afflicted
- ☐ Agonized
- ☐ Alienated
- ☐ Appalled
- ☐ Crushed
- ☐ Dejected
- ☐ Deprived
- ☐ Heartbroken
- ☐ Humiliated
- ☐ Injured
- ☐ Offended
- ☐ Pained
- ☐ Rejected
- ☐ Tormented
- ☐ Tortured
- ☐ Victimized
- ☐ Wronged

Notes: _____
_____
_____
_____

8 Pitfalls to avoid
- ☐ Me-too-ism. Don't start telling your story, or comparing your story to theirs.
- ☐ Moralizing, preaching, being judgmental
- ☐ Asking a direct question to satisfy your own curiosity
- ☐ Being an interviewer rather then a listener
- ☐ Giving advice (try fixing it)
- ☐ Cheap consolation. *"Oh, that's not to bad"*
- ☐ Arguing or disagreeing with the speaker
- ☐ Analyzing or interpreting
- ☐ Ignoring obvious heavy emotions

Date: _____

PLEASANT FEELINGS

OPEN
- [ ] Accepting
- [ ] Amazed
- [ ] Confident
- [ ] Easy
- [ ] Free
- [ ] Interested
- [ ] Kind
- [ ] Receptive
- [ ] Reliable
- [ ] Satisfied
- [ ] Sympathetic
- [ ] Understanding

INTERESTED
- [ ] Absorbed
- [ ] Affected
- [ ] Concerned
- [ ] Curious
- [ ] Engrossed
- [ ] Fascinated
- [ ] Inquisitive
- [ ] Intrigued
- [ ] Nosy
- [ ] Snoopy

ALIVE
- [ ] Animated
- [ ] Courageous
- [ ] Energetic
- [ ] Free
- [ ] Frisky
- [ ] Impulsive
- [ ] Liberated
- [ ] Optimistic
- [ ] Playful
- [ ] Provocative
- [ ] Spirited
- [ ] Thrilled
- [ ] Wonderful

STRONG
- [ ] Certain
- [ ] Dynamic
- [ ] Free
- [ ] Hardy
- [ ] Impulsive
- [ ] Rebellious
- [ ] Secure
- [ ] Sure
- [ ] Tenacious
- [ ] Unique

LOVE
- [ ] Admiration
- [ ] Affectionate
- [ ] Attracted
- [ ] Close
- [ ] Comforted
- [ ] Considerate
- [ ] Devoted
- [ ] Drawn toward
- [ ] Loved
- [ ] Loving
- [ ] Passionate
- [ ] Sensitive
- [ ] Sympathy
- [ ] Tender
- [ ] Touched
- [ ] Warm

POSITIVE
- [ ] Anxious
- [ ] Bold
- [ ] Brave
- [ ] Challenged
- [ ] Confident
- [ ] Daring
- [ ] Determined
- [ ] Eager
- [ ] Earnest
- [ ] Enthusiastic
- [ ] Excited
- [ ] Hopeful
- [ ] Inspired
- [ ] Intent
- [ ] Keen
- [ ] Optimistic
- [ ] Re-enforced

GOOD
- [ ] At ease
- [ ] Blessed
- [ ] Bright
- [ ] Calm
- [ ] Certain
- [ ] Clever
- [ ] Comfortable
- [ ] Content
- [ ] Encouraged
- [ ] Free and easy
- [ ] Peaceful
- [ ] Pleased
- [ ] Quiet
- [ ] Reassured
- [ ] Relaxed
- [ ] Serene
- [ ] Surprised

HAPPY
- [ ] Cheerful
- [ ] Delighted
- [ ] Ecstatic
- [ ] Elated
- [ ] Festive
- [ ] Fortunate
- [ ] Glad
- [ ] Gleeful
- [ ] Great
- [ ] Important
- [ ] Joyous
- [ ] Jubilant
- [ ] Lucky
- [ ] Merry
- [ ] Overjoyed
- [ ] Satisfied
- [ ] Sunny
- [ ] Thankful

Read and check off
✓

Preparing to listen
- [ ] Remember to put your mind and feelings in neutral gear.
- [ ] Your body posture must say, *"I am open, very interested, affirmative, attentive."*
- [ ] Maintain good eye contact.
- [ ] Give the speaker a verbal door opening, showing your readiness to listen.

While Listening
- [ ] Track what the speaker is saying in both content and feeling levels
- [ ] Stay with the content of communication
- [ ] Listen for and identify the basic general feeling; anger, fear, joy, resentment, etc.
- [ ] Suspend judgment; open yourself to the presence of their heart.

Responding
- [ ] Use oral responses, which are affirming, which say, *"I am with you", "I understand."*
- [ ] Feed general feelings back to the speaker. *"You seem to feel this has been a good experience for you"*
- [ ] Stay an inch ahead of the speaker, not a mile.

UNPLEASANT FEELINGS

HELPLESS
- ☐ Alone
- ☐ Despair
- ☐ Distressed
- ☐ Dominated
- ☐ Empty
- ☐ Fatigued
- ☐ Forced
- ☐ Frustrated
- ☐ Hesitant
- ☐ In A Stew
- ☐ Incapable
- ☐ Inferior
- ☐ Paralyzed
- ☐ Pathetic
- ☐ Tragic
- ☐ Useless
- ☐ Vulnerable
- ☐ Woeful

SAD
- ☐ Anguish
- ☐ Desolate
- ☐ Desperate
- ☐ Dismayed
- ☐ Grief
- ☐ Grieved
- ☐ Lonely
- ☐ Mournful
- ☐ Pained
- ☐ Pessimistic
- ☐ Sorrowful
- ☐ Tearful
- ☐ Unhappy

CONFUSED
- ☐ Disillusioned
- ☐ Distrustful
- ☐ Doubtful
- ☐ Embarrassed
- ☐ Hesitant
- ☐ Indecisive
- ☐ Lost
- ☐ Misgiving
- ☐ Perplexed
- ☐ Pessimistic
- ☐ Shy
- ☐ Skeptical
- ☐ Stupefied
- ☐ Tense
- ☐ Unbelieving
- ☐ Uncertain
- ☐ Uneasy
- ☐ Unsure
- ☐ Upset

INDIFFERENT
- ☐ Bored
- ☐ Cold
- ☐ Disinterested
- ☐ Dull
- ☐ Insensitive
- ☐ Lifeless
- ☐ Neutral
- ☐ Nonchalant
- ☐ Preoccupied
- ☐ Reserved
- ☐ Weary

DEPRESSED
- ☐ A Sense of Loss
- ☐ Abominable
- ☐ Ashamed
- ☐ Bad
- ☐ Despicable
- ☐ Detestable
- ☐ Diminished
- ☐ Disappointed
- ☐ Discouraged
- ☐ Disgusting
- ☐ Dissatisfied
- ☐ Guilty
- ☐ In Despair
- ☐ Lousy
- ☐ Miserable
- ☐ Powerless
- ☐ Repugnant
- ☐ Sulky
- ☐ Terrible

AFRAID
- ☐ Alarmed
- ☐ Anxious
- ☐ Cowardly
- ☐ Doubtful
- ☐ Fearful
- ☐ Frightened
- ☐ Menaced
- ☐ Nervous
- ☐ Panic
- ☐ Quaking
- ☐ Restless
- ☐ Scared
- ☐ Shaky
- ☐ Suspicious
- ☐ Terrified
- ☐ Threatened
- ☐ Timid
- ☐ Wary
- ☐ Worried

ANGRY
- ☐ Aggressive
- ☐ Annoyed
- ☐ Bitter
- ☐ Boiling
- ☐ Cross
- ☐ Enraged
- ☐ Fuming
- ☐ Hateful
- ☐ Hostile
- ☐ Incensed
- ☐ Inflamed
- ☐ Infuriated
- ☐ Insulting
- ☐ Irritated
- ☐ Offensive
- ☐ Provoked
- ☐ Resentful
- ☐ Sore
- ☐ Unpleasant
- ☐ Upset
- ☐ Worked Up

HURT
- ☐ Aching
- ☐ Afflicted
- ☐ Agonized
- ☐ Alienated
- ☐ Appalled
- ☐ Crushed
- ☐ Dejected
- ☐ Deprived
- ☐ Heartbroken
- ☐ Humiliated
- ☐ Injured
- ☐ Offended
- ☐ Pained
- ☐ Rejected
- ☐ Tormented
- ☐ Tortured
- ☐ Victimized
- ☐ Wronged

Notes: _____
_____
_____
_____

8 Pitfalls to avoid

- ☐ Me-too-ism. Don't start telling your story, or comparing your story to theirs.
- ☐ Moralizing, preaching, being judgmental
- ☐ Asking a direct question to satisfy your own curiosity
- ☐ Being an interviewer rather then a listener
- ☐ Giving advice (try fixing it)
- ☐ Cheap consolation. *"Oh, that's not to bad"*
- ☐ Arguing or disagreeing with the speaker
- ☐ Analyzing or interpreting
- ☐ Ignoring obvious heavy emotions

Date: _____

PLEASANT FEELINGS

OPEN	INTERESTED	ALIVE	STRONG
☐ Accepting	☐ Absorbed	☐ Animated	☐ Certain
☐ Amazed	☐ Affected	☐ Courageous	☐ Dynamic
☐ Confident	☐ Concerned	☐ Energetic	☐ Free
☐ Easy	☐ Curious	☐ Free	☐ Hardy
☐ Free	☐ Engrossed	☐ Frisky	☐ Impulsive
☐ Interested	☐ Fascinated	☐ Impulsive	☐ Rebellious
☐ Kind	☐ Inquisitive	☐ Liberated	☐ Secure
☐ Receptive	☐ Intrigued	☐ Optimistic	☐ Sure
☐ Reliable	☐ Nosy	☐ Playful	☐ Tenacious
☐ Satisfied	☐ Snoopy	☐ Provocative	☐ Unique
☐ Sympathetic		☐ Spirited	
☐ Understanding		☐ Thrilled	
		☐ Wonderful	

LOVE	POSITIVE	GOOD	HAPPY
☐ Admiration	☐ Anxious	☐ At ease	☐ Cheerful
☐ Affectionate	☐ Bold	☐ Blessed	☐ Delighted
☐ Attracted	☐ Brave	☐ Bright	☐ Ecstatic
☐ Close	☐ Challenged	☐ Calm	☐ Elated
☐ Comforted	☐ Confident	☐ Certain	☐ Festive
☐ Considerate	☐ Daring	☐ Clever	☐ Fortunate
☐ Devoted	☐ Determined	☐ Comfortable	☐ Glad
☐ Drawn toward	☐ Eager	☐ Content	☐ Gleeful
☐ Loved	☐ Earnest	☐ Encouraged	☐ Great
☐ Loving	☐ Enthusiastic	☐ Free and easy	☐ Important
☐ Passionate	☐ Excited	☐ Peaceful	☐ Joyous
☐ Sensitive	☐ Hopeful	☐ Pleased	☐ Jubilant
☐ Sympathy	☐ Inspired	☐ Quiet	☐ Lucky
☐ Tender	☐ Intent	☐ Reassured	☐ Merry
☐ Touched	☐ Keen	☐ Relaxed	☐ Overjoyed
☐ Warm	☐ Optimistic	☐ Serene	☐ Satisfied
	☐ Re-enforced	☐ Surprised	☐ Sunny
			☐ Thankful

Read and check off
✓

Preparing to listen

- ☐ Remember to put your mind and feelings in neutral gear.
- ☐ Your body posture must say, *"I' am open, very interested, affirmative, attentive."*
- ☐ Maintain good eye contact.
- ☐ Give the speaker a verbal door opening, showing your readiness to listen.

While Listening

- ☐ Track what the speaker is saying in both content and feeling levels
- ☐ Stay with the content of communication
- ☐ Listen for and identify the basic general feeling; anger, fear, joy, resentment, etc.
- ☐ Suspend judgment; open yourself to the presence of their heart.

Responding

- ☐ Use oral responses, which are affirming, which say, *"I am with you"*, *"I understand."*
- ☐ Feed general feelings back to the speaker. *"You seem to feel this has been a good experience for you"*
- ☐ Stay an inch ahead of the speaker, not a mile.

UNPLEASANT FEELINGS

HELPLESS
- ☐ Alone
- ☐ Despair
- ☐ Distressed
- ☐ Dominated
- ☐ Empty
- ☐ Fatigued
- ☐ Forced
- ☐ Frustrated
- ☐ Hesitant
- ☐ In A Stew
- ☐ Incapable
- ☐ Inferior
- ☐ Paralyzed
- ☐ Pathetic
- ☐ Tragic
- ☐ Useless
- ☐ Vulnerable
- ☐ Woeful

CONFUSED
- ☐ Disillusioned
- ☐ Distrustful
- ☐ Doubtful
- ☐ Embarrassed
- ☐ Hesitant
- ☐ Indecisive
- ☐ Lost
- ☐ Misgiving
- ☐ Perplexed
- ☐ Pessimistic
- ☐ Shy
- ☐ Skeptical
- ☐ Stupefied
- ☐ Tense
- ☐ Unbelieving
- ☐ Uncertain
- ☐ Uneasy
- ☐ Unsure
- ☐ Upset

DEPRESSED
- ☐ A Sense of Loss
- ☐ Abominable
- ☐ Ashamed
- ☐ Bad
- ☐ Despicable
- ☐ Detestable
- ☐ Diminished
- ☐ Disappointed
- ☐ Discouraged
- ☐ Disgusting
- ☐ Dissatisfied
- ☐ Guilty
- ☐ In Despair
- ☐ Lousy
- ☐ Miserable
- ☐ Powerless
- ☐ Repugnant
- ☐ Sulky
- ☐ Terrible

ANGRY
- ☐ Aggressive
- ☐ Annoyed
- ☐ Bitter
- ☐ Boiling
- ☐ Cross
- ☐ Enraged
- ☐ Fuming
- ☐ Hateful
- ☐ Hostile
- ☐ Incensed
- ☐ Inflamed
- ☐ Infuriated
- ☐ Insulting
- ☐ Irritated
- ☐ Offensive
- ☐ Provoked
- ☐ Resentful
- ☐ Sore
- ☐ Unpleasant
- ☐ Upset
- ☐ Worked Up

SAD
- ☐ Anguish
- ☐ Desolate
- ☐ Desperate
- ☐ Dismayed
- ☐ Grief
- ☐ Grieved
- ☐ Lonely
- ☐ Mournful
- ☐ Pained
- ☐ Pessimistic
- ☐ Sorrowful
- ☐ Tearful
- ☐ Unhappy

INDIFFERENT
- ☐ Bored
- ☐ Cold
- ☐ Disinterested
- ☐ Dull
- ☐ Insensitive
- ☐ Lifeless
- ☐ Neutral
- ☐ Nonchalant
- ☐ Preoccupied
- ☐ Reserved
- ☐ Weary

AFRAID
- ☐ Alarmed
- ☐ Anxious
- ☐ Cowardly
- ☐ Doubtful
- ☐ Fearful
- ☐ Frightened
- ☐ Menaced
- ☐ Nervous
- ☐ Panic
- ☐ Quaking
- ☐ Restless
- ☐ Scared
- ☐ Shaky
- ☐ Suspicious
- ☐ Terrified
- ☐ Threatened
- ☐ Timid
- ☐ Wary
- ☐ Worried

HURT
- ☐ Aching
- ☐ Afflicted
- ☐ Agonized
- ☐ Alienated
- ☐ Appalled
- ☐ Crushed
- ☐ Dejected
- ☐ Deprived
- ☐ Heartbroken
- ☐ Humiliated
- ☐ Injured
- ☐ Offended
- ☐ Pained
- ☐ Rejected
- ☐ Tormented
- ☐ Tortured
- ☐ Victimized
- ☐ Wronged

Notes: _____
_____
_____

8 Pitfalls to avoid
- ☐ Me-too-ism. Don't start telling your story, or comparing your story to theirs.
- ☐ Moralizing, preaching, being judgmental
- ☐ Asking a direct question to satisfy your own curiosity
- ☐ Being an interviewer rather then a listener
- ☐ Giving advice (try fixing it)
- ☐ Cheap consolation. *"Oh, that's not to bad"*
- ☐ Arguing or disagreeing with the speaker
- ☐ Analyzing or interpreting
- ☐ Ignoring obvious heavy emotions

Date: _____

PLEASANT FEELINGS

OPEN
- ☐ Accepting
- ☐ Amazed
- ☐ Confident
- ☐ Easy
- ☐ Free
- ☐ Interested
- ☐ Kind
- ☐ Receptive
- ☐ Reliable
- ☐ Satisfied
- ☐ Sympathetic
- ☐ Understanding

INTERESTED
- ☐ Absorbed
- ☐ Affected
- ☐ Concerned
- ☐ Curious
- ☐ Engrossed
- ☐ Fascinated
- ☐ Inquisitive
- ☐ Intrigued
- ☐ Nosy
- ☐ Snoopy

ALIVE
- ☐ Animated
- ☐ Courageous
- ☐ Energetic
- ☐ Free
- ☐ Frisky
- ☐ Impulsive
- ☐ Liberated
- ☐ Optimistic
- ☐ Playful
- ☐ Provocative
- ☐ Spirited
- ☐ Thrilled
- ☐ Wonderful

STRONG
- ☐ Certain
- ☐ Dynamic
- ☐ Free
- ☐ Hardy
- ☐ Impulsive
- ☐ Rebellious
- ☐ Secure
- ☐ Sure
- ☐ Tenacious
- ☐ Unique

LOVE
- ☐ Admiration
- ☐ Affectionate
- ☐ Attracted
- ☐ Close
- ☐ Comforted
- ☐ Considerate
- ☐ Devoted
- ☐ Drawn toward
- ☐ Loved
- ☐ Loving
- ☐ Passionate
- ☐ Sensitive
- ☐ Sympathy
- ☐ Tender
- ☐ Touched
- ☐ Warm

POSITIVE
- ☐ Anxious
- ☐ Bold
- ☐ Brave
- ☐ Challenged
- ☐ Confident
- ☐ Daring
- ☐ Determined
- ☐ Eager
- ☐ Earnest
- ☐ Enthusiastic
- ☐ Excited
- ☐ Hopeful
- ☐ Inspired
- ☐ Intent
- ☐ Keen
- ☐ Optimistic
- ☐ Re-enforced

GOOD
- ☐ At ease
- ☐ Blessed
- ☐ Bright
- ☐ Calm
- ☐ Certain
- ☐ Clever
- ☐ Comfortable
- ☐ Content
- ☐ Encouraged
- ☐ Free and easy
- ☐ Peaceful
- ☐ Pleased
- ☐ Quiet
- ☐ Reassured
- ☐ Relaxed
- ☐ Serene
- ☐ Surprised

HAPPY
- ☐ Cheerful
- ☐ Delighted
- ☐ Ecstatic
- ☐ Elated
- ☐ Festive
- ☐ Fortunate
- ☐ Glad
- ☐ Gleeful
- ☐ Great
- ☐ Important
- ☐ Joyous
- ☐ Jubilant
- ☐ Lucky
- ☐ Merry
- ☐ Overjoyed
- ☐ Satisfied
- ☐ Sunny
- ☐ Thankful

Read and check off
✓

Preparing to listen
- ☐ Remember to put your mind and feelings in neutral gear.
- ☐ Your body posture must say, *"I am open, very interested, affirmative, attentive."*
- ☐ Maintain good eye contact.
- ☐ Give the speaker a verbal door opening, showing your readiness to listen.

While Listening
- ☐ Track what the speaker is saying in both content and feeling levels
- ☐ Stay with the content of communication
- ☐ Listen for and identify the basic general feeling; anger, fear, joy, resentment, etc.
- ☐ Suspend judgment; open yourself to the presence of their heart.

Responding
- ☐ Use oral responses, which are affirming, which say, *"I am with you"*, *"I understand."*
- ☐ Feed general feelings back to the speaker. *"You seem to feel this has been a good experience for you"*
- ☐ Stay an inch ahead of the speaker, not a mile.

UNPLEASANT FEELINGS

😔 HELPLESS
- ☐ Alone
- ☐ Despair
- ☐ Distressed
- ☐ Dominated
- ☐ Empty
- ☐ Fatigued
- ☐ Forced
- ☐ Frustrated
- ☐ Hesitant
- ☐ In A Stew
- ☐ Incapable
- ☐ Inferior
- ☐ Paralyzed
- ☐ Pathetic
- ☐ Tragic
- ☐ Useless
- ☐ Vulnerable
- ☐ Woeful

😕 CONFUSED
- ☐ Disillusioned
- ☐ Distrustful
- ☐ Doubtful
- ☐ Embarrassed
- ☐ Hesitant
- ☐ Indecisive
- ☐ Lost
- ☐ Misgiving
- ☐ Perplexed
- ☐ Pessimistic
- ☐ Shy
- ☐ Skeptical
- ☐ Stupefied
- ☐ Tense
- ☐ Unbelieving
- ☐ Uncertain
- ☐ Uneasy
- ☐ Unsure
- ☐ Upset

😞 DEPRESSED
- ☐ A Sense of Loss
- ☐ Abominable
- ☐ Ashamed
- ☐ Bad
- ☐ Despicable
- ☐ Detestable
- ☐ Diminished
- ☐ Disappointed
- ☐ Discouraged
- ☐ Disgusting
- ☐ Dissatisfied
- ☐ Guilty
- ☐ In Despair
- ☐ Lousy
- ☐ Miserable
- ☐ Powerless
- ☐ Repugnant
- ☐ Sulky
- ☐ Terrible

😠 ANGRY
- ☐ Aggressive
- ☐ Annoyed
- ☐ Bitter
- ☐ Boiling
- ☐ Cross
- ☐ Enraged
- ☐ Fuming
- ☐ Hateful
- ☐ Hostile
- ☐ Incensed
- ☐ Inflamed
- ☐ Infuriated
- ☐ Insulting
- ☐ Irritated
- ☐ Offensive
- ☐ Provoked
- ☐ Resentful
- ☐ Sore
- ☐ Unpleasant
- ☐ Upset
- ☐ Worked Up

😢 SAD
- ☐ Anguish
- ☐ Desolate
- ☐ Desperate
- ☐ Dismayed
- ☐ Grief
- ☐ Grieved
- ☐ Lonely
- ☐ Mournful
- ☐ Pained
- ☐ Pessimistic
- ☐ Sorrowful
- ☐ Tearful
- ☐ Unhappy

😐 INDIFFERENT
- ☐ Bored
- ☐ Cold
- ☐ Disinterested
- ☐ Dull
- ☐ Insensitive
- ☐ Lifeless
- ☐ Neutral
- ☐ Nonchalant
- ☐ Preoccupied
- ☐ Reserved
- ☐ Weary

😨 AFRAID
- ☐ Alarmed
- ☐ Anxious
- ☐ Cowardly
- ☐ Doubtful
- ☐ Fearful
- ☐ Frightened
- ☐ Menaced
- ☐ Nervous
- ☐ Panic
- ☐ Quaking
- ☐ Restless
- ☐ Scared
- ☐ Shaky
- ☐ Suspicious
- ☐ Terrified
- ☐ Threatened
- ☐ Timid
- ☐ Wary
- ☐ Worried

😟 HURT
- ☐ Aching
- ☐ Afflicted
- ☐ Agonized
- ☐ Alienated
- ☐ Appalled
- ☐ Crushed
- ☐ Dejected
- ☐ Deprived
- ☐ Heartbroken
- ☐ Humiliated
- ☐ Injured
- ☐ Offended
- ☐ Pained
- ☐ Rejected
- ☐ Tormented
- ☐ Tortured
- ☐ Victimized
- ☐ Wronged

Notes: _____
_____
_____
_____

8 Pitfalls to avoid

- ☐ Me-too-ism. Don't start telling your story, or comparing your story to theirs.
- ☐ Moralizing, preaching, being judgmental
- ☐ Asking a direct question to satisfy your own curiosity
- ☐ Being an interviewer rather then a listener
- ☐ Giving advice (try fixing it)
- ☐ Cheap consolation. *"Oh, that's not to bad"*
- ☐ Arguing or disagreeing with the speaker
- ☐ Analyzing or interpreting
- ☐ Ignoring obvious heavy emotions

Date: _____

(What is your best childhood memory and why?)

PLEASANT FEELINGS

OPEN
- ☐ Accepting
- ☐ Amazed
- ☐ Confident
- ☐ Easy
- ☐ Free
- ☐ Interested
- ☐ Kind
- ☐ Receptive
- ☐ Reliable
- ☐ Satisfied
- ☐ Sympathetic
- ☐ Understanding

INTERESTED
- ☐ Absorbed
- ☐ Affected
- ☐ Concerned
- ☐ Curious
- ☐ Engrossed
- ☐ Fascinated
- ☐ Inquisitive
- ☐ Intrigued
- ☐ Nosy
- ☐ Snoopy

ALIVE
- ☐ Animated
- ☐ Courageous
- ☐ Energetic
- ☐ Free
- ☐ Frisky
- ☐ Impulsive
- ☐ Liberated
- ☐ Optimistic
- ☐ Playful
- ☐ Provocative
- ☐ Spirited
- ☐ Thrilled
- ☐ Wonderful

STRONG
- ☐ Certain
- ☐ Dynamic
- ☐ Free
- ☐ Hardy
- ☐ Impulsive
- ☐ Rebellious
- ☐ Secure
- ☐ Sure
- ☐ Tenacious
- ☐ Unique

LOVE
- ☐ Admiration
- ☐ Affectionate
- ☐ Attracted
- ☐ Close
- ☐ Comforted
- ☐ Considerate
- ☐ Devoted
- ☐ Drawn toward
- ☐ Loved
- ☐ Loving
- ☐ Passionate
- ☐ Sensitive
- ☐ Sympathy
- ☐ Tender
- ☐ Touched
- ☐ Warm

POSITIVE
- ☐ Anxious
- ☐ Bold
- ☐ Brave
- ☐ Challenged
- ☐ Confident
- ☐ Daring
- ☐ Determined
- ☐ Eager
- ☐ Earnest
- ☐ Enthusiastic
- ☐ Excited
- ☐ Hopeful
- ☐ Inspired
- ☐ Intent
- ☐ Keen
- ☐ Optimistic
- ☐ Re-enforced

GOOD
- ☐ At ease
- ☐ Blessed
- ☐ Bright
- ☐ Calm
- ☐ Certain
- ☐ Clever
- ☐ Comfortable
- ☐ Content
- ☐ Encouraged
- ☐ Free and easy
- ☐ Peaceful
- ☐ Pleased
- ☐ Quiet
- ☐ Reassured
- ☐ Relaxed
- ☐ Serene
- ☐ Surprised

HAPPY
- ☐ Cheerful
- ☐ Delighted
- ☐ Ecstatic
- ☐ Elated
- ☐ Festive
- ☐ Fortunate
- ☐ Glad
- ☐ Gleeful
- ☐ Great
- ☐ Important
- ☐ Joyous
- ☐ Jubilant
- ☐ Lucky
- ☐ Merry
- ☐ Overjoyed
- ☐ Satisfied
- ☐ Sunny
- ☐ Thankful

Read and check off
✓

Preparing to listen
- ☐ Remember to put your mind and feelings in neutral gear.
- ☐ Your body posture must say, *"I am open, very interested, affirmative, attentive."*
- ☐ Maintain good eye contact.
- ☐ Give the speaker a verbal door opening, showing your readiness to listen.

While Listening
- ☐ Track what the speaker is saying in both content and feeling levels
- ☐ Stay with the content of communication
- ☐ Listen for and identify the basic general feeling; anger, fear, joy, resentment, etc.
- ☐ Suspend judgment; open yourself to the presence of their heart.

Responding
- ☐ Use oral responses, which are affirming, which say, *"I am with you"*, *"I understand."*
- ☐ Feed general feelings back to the speaker. *"You seem to feel this has been a good experience for you"*
- ☐ Stay an inch ahead of the speaker, not a mile.

UNPLEASANT FEELINGS

HELPLESS
- ☐ Alone
- ☐ Despair
- ☐ Distressed
- ☐ Dominated
- ☐ Empty
- ☐ Fatigued
- ☐ Forced
- ☐ Frustrated
- ☐ Hesitant
- ☐ In A Stew
- ☐ Incapable
- ☐ Inferior
- ☐ Paralyzed
- ☐ Pathetic
- ☐ Tragic
- ☐ Useless
- ☐ Vulnerable
- ☐ Woeful

CONFUSED
- ☐ Disillusioned
- ☐ Distrustful
- ☐ Doubtful
- ☐ Embarrassed
- ☐ Hesitant
- ☐ Indecisive
- ☐ Lost
- ☐ Misgiving
- ☐ Perplexed
- ☐ Pessimistic
- ☐ Shy
- ☐ Skeptical
- ☐ Stupefied
- ☐ Tense
- ☐ Unbelieving
- ☐ Uncertain
- ☐ Uneasy
- ☐ Unsure
- ☐ Upset

DEPRESSED
- ☐ A Sense of Loss
- ☐ Abominable
- ☐ Ashamed
- ☐ Bad
- ☐ Despicable
- ☐ Detestable
- ☐ Diminished
- ☐ Disappointed
- ☐ Discouraged
- ☐ Disgusting
- ☐ Dissatisfied
- ☐ Guilty
- ☐ In Despair
- ☐ Lousy
- ☐ Miserable
- ☐ Powerless
- ☐ Repugnant
- ☐ Sulky
- ☐ Terrible

ANGRY
- ☐ Aggressive
- ☐ Annoyed
- ☐ Bitter
- ☐ Boiling
- ☐ Cross
- ☐ Enraged
- ☐ Fuming
- ☐ Hateful
- ☐ Hostile
- ☐ Incensed
- ☐ Inflamed
- ☐ Infuriated
- ☐ Insulting
- ☐ Irritated
- ☐ Offensive
- ☐ Provoked
- ☐ Resentful
- ☐ Sore
- ☐ Unpleasant
- ☐ Upset
- ☐ Worked Up

SAD
- ☐ Anguish
- ☐ Desolate
- ☐ Desperate
- ☐ Dismayed
- ☐ Grief
- ☐ Grieved
- ☐ Lonely
- ☐ Mournful
- ☐ Pained
- ☐ Pessimistic
- ☐ Sorrowful
- ☐ Tearful
- ☐ Unhappy

INDIFFERENT
- ☐ Bored
- ☐ Cold
- ☐ Disinterested
- ☐ Dull
- ☐ Insensitive
- ☐ Lifeless
- ☐ Neutral
- ☐ Nonchalant
- ☐ Preoccupied
- ☐ Reserved
- ☐ Weary

AFRAID
- ☐ Alarmed
- ☐ Anxious
- ☐ Cowardly
- ☐ Doubtful
- ☐ Fearful
- ☐ Frightened
- ☐ Menaced
- ☐ Nervous
- ☐ Panic
- ☐ Quaking
- ☐ Restless
- ☐ Scared
- ☐ Shaky
- ☐ Suspicious
- ☐ Terrified
- ☐ Threatened
- ☐ Timid
- ☐ Wary
- ☐ Worried

HURT
- ☐ Aching
- ☐ Afflicted
- ☐ Agonized
- ☐ Alienated
- ☐ Appalled
- ☐ Crushed
- ☐ Dejected
- ☐ Deprived
- ☐ Heartbroken
- ☐ Humiliated
- ☐ Injured
- ☐ Offended
- ☐ Pained
- ☐ Rejected
- ☐ Tormented
- ☐ Tortured
- ☐ Victimized
- ☐ Wronged

Notes: _____
_____
_____
_____

8 Pitfalls to avoid
- ☐ Me-too-ism. Don't start telling your story, or comparing your story to theirs.
- ☐ Moralizing, preaching, being judgmental
- ☐ Asking a direct question to satisfy your own curiosity
- ☐ Being an interviewer rather then a listener
- ☐ Giving advice (try fixing it)
- ☐ Cheap consolation. *"Oh, that's not to bad"*
- ☐ Arguing or disagreeing with the speaker
- ☐ Analyzing or interpreting
- ☐ Ignoring obvious heavy emotions

Date: _____

44.

PLEASANT FEELINGS

☺ OPEN	☺ INTERESTED	☺ ALIVE	☺ STRONG
☐ Accepting	☐ Absorbed	☐ Animated	☐ Certain
☐ Amazed	☐ Affected	☐ Courageous	☐ Dynamic
☐ Confident	☐ Concerned	☐ Energetic	☐ Free
☐ Easy	☐ Curious	☐ Free	☐ Hardy
☐ Free	☐ Engrossed	☐ Frisky	☐ Impulsive
☐ Interested	☐ Fascinated	☐ Impulsive	☐ Rebellious
☐ Kind	☐ Inquisitive	☐ Liberated	☐ Secure
☐ Receptive	☐ Intrigued	☐ Optimistic	☐ Sure
☐ Reliable	☐ Nosy	☐ Playful	☐ Tenacious
☐ Satisfied	☐ Snoopy	☐ Provocative	☐ Unique
☐ Sympathetic		☐ Spirited	
☐ Understanding		☐ Thrilled	
		☐ Wonderful	

☺ LOVE	☺ POSITIVE	☺ GOOD	☺ HAPPY
☐ Admiration	☐ Anxious	☐ At ease	☐ Cheerful
☐ Affectionate	☐ Bold	☐ Blessed	☐ Delighted
☐ Attracted	☐ Brave	☐ Bright	☐ Ecstatic
☐ Close	☐ Challenged	☐ Calm	☐ Elated
☐ Comforted	☐ Confident	☐ Certain	☐ Festive
☐ Considerate	☐ Daring	☐ Clever	☐ Fortunate
☐ Devoted	☐ Determined	☐ Comfortable	☐ Glad
☐ Drawn toward	☐ Eager	☐ Content	☐ Gleeful
☐ Loved	☐ Earnest	☐ Encouraged	☐ Great
☐ Loving	☐ Enthusiastic	☐ Free and easy	☐ Important
☐ Passionate	☐ Excited	☐ Peaceful	☐ Joyous
☐ Sensitive	☐ Hopeful	☐ Pleased	☐ Jubilant
☐ Sympathy	☐ Inspired	☐ Quiet	☐ Lucky
☐ Tender	☐ Intent	☐ Reassured	☐ Merry
☐ Touched	☐ Keen	☐ Relaxed	☐ Overjoyed
☐ Warm	☐ Optimistic	☐ Serene	☐ Satisfied
	☐ Re-enforced	☐ Surprised	☐ Sunny
			☐ Thankful

Read and check off
✓

Preparing to listen
☐ Remember to put your mind and feelings in neutral gear.
☐ Your body posture must say, *"I' am open, very interested, affirmative, attentive."*
☐ Maintain good eye contact.
☐ Give the speaker a verbal door opening, showing your readiness to listen.

While Listening
☐ Track what the speaker is saying in both content and feeling levels
☐ Stay with the content of communication
☐ Listen for and identify the basic general feeling; anger, fear, joy, resentment, etc.
☐ Suspend judgment; open yourself to the presence of their heart.

Responding
☐ Use oral responses, which are affirming, which say, *"I am with you", "I understand."*
☐ Feed general feelings back to the speaker. *"You seem to feel this has been a good experience for you"*
☐ Stay an inch ahead of the speaker, not a mile.

UNPLEASANT FEELINGS

☺ HELPLESS
- ☐ Alone
- ☐ Despair
- ☐ Distressed
- ☐ Dominated
- ☐ Empty
- ☐ Fatigued
- ☐ Forced
- ☐ Frustrated
- ☐ Hesitant
- ☐ In A Stew
- ☐ Incapable
- ☐ Inferior
- ☐ Paralyzed
- ☐ Pathetic
- ☐ Tragic
- ☐ Useless
- ☐ Vulnerable
- ☐ Woeful

☺ CONFUSED
- ☐ Disillusioned
- ☐ Distrustful
- ☐ Doubtful
- ☐ Embarrassed
- ☐ Hesitant
- ☐ Indecisive
- ☐ Lost
- ☐ Misgiving
- ☐ Perplexed
- ☐ Pessimistic
- ☐ Shy
- ☐ Skeptical
- ☐ Stupefied
- ☐ Tense
- ☐ Unbelieving
- ☐ Uncertain
- ☐ Uneasy
- ☐ Unsure
- ☐ Upset

☺ DEPRESSED
- ☐ A Sense of Loss
- ☐ Abominable
- ☐ Ashamed
- ☐ Bad
- ☐ Despicable
- ☐ Detestable
- ☐ Diminished
- ☐ Disappointed
- ☐ Discouraged
- ☐ Disgusting
- ☐ Dissatisfied
- ☐ Guilty
- ☐ In Despair
- ☐ Lousy
- ☐ Miserable
- ☐ Powerless
- ☐ Repugnant
- ☐ Sulky
- ☐ Terrible

☺ ANGRY
- ☐ Aggressive
- ☐ Annoyed
- ☐ Bitter
- ☐ Boiling
- ☐ Cross
- ☐ Enraged
- ☐ Fuming
- ☐ Hateful
- ☐ Hostile
- ☐ Incensed
- ☐ Inflamed
- ☐ Infuriated
- ☐ Insulting
- ☐ Irritated
- ☐ Offensive
- ☐ Provoked
- ☐ Resentful
- ☐ Sore
- ☐ Unpleasant
- ☐ Upset
- ☐ Worked Up

☺ SAD
- ☐ Anguish
- ☐ Desolate
- ☐ Desperate
- ☐ Dismayed
- ☐ Grief
- ☐ Grieved
- ☐ Lonely
- ☐ Mournful
- ☐ Pained
- ☐ Pessimistic
- ☐ Sorrowful
- ☐ Tearful
- ☐ Unhappy

☺ INDIFFERENT
- ☐ Bored
- ☐ Cold
- ☐ Disinterested
- ☐ Dull
- ☐ Insensitive
- ☐ Lifeless
- ☐ Neutral
- ☐ Nonchalant
- ☐ Preoccupied
- ☐ Reserved
- ☐ Weary

☺ AFRAID
- ☐ Alarmed
- ☐ Anxious
- ☐ Cowardly
- ☐ Doubtful
- ☐ Fearful
- ☐ Frightened
- ☐ Menaced
- ☐ Nervous
- ☐ Panic
- ☐ Quaking
- ☐ Restless
- ☐ Scared
- ☐ Shaky
- ☐ Suspicious
- ☐ Terrified
- ☐ Threatened
- ☐ Timid
- ☐ Wary
- ☐ Worried

☺ HURT
- ☐ Aching
- ☐ Afflicted
- ☐ Agonized
- ☐ Alienated
- ☐ Appalled
- ☐ Crushed
- ☐ Dejected
- ☐ Deprived
- ☐ Heartbroken
- ☐ Humiliated
- ☐ Injured
- ☐ Offended
- ☐ Pained
- ☐ Rejected
- ☐ Tormented
- ☐ Tortured
- ☐ Victimized
- ☐ Wronged

Notes: _____
_____
_____

8 Pitfalls to avoid

- ☐ Me-too-ism. Don't start telling your story, or comparing your story to theirs.
- ☐ Moralizing, preaching, being judgmental
- ☐ Asking a direct question to satisfy your own curiosity
- ☐ Being an interviewer rather then a listener
- ☐ Giving advice (try fixing it)
- ☐ Cheap consolation. *"Oh, that's not to bad"*
- ☐ Arguing or disagreeing with the speaker
- ☐ Analyzing or interpreting
- ☐ Ignoring obvious heavy emotions

Date: _____

PLEASANT FEELINGS

OPEN
- ☐ Accepting
- ☐ Amazed
- ☐ Confident
- ☐ Easy
- ☐ Free
- ☐ Interested
- ☐ Kind
- ☐ Receptive
- ☐ Reliable
- ☐ Satisfied
- ☐ Sympathetic
- ☐ Understanding

INTERESTED
- ☐ Absorbed
- ☐ Affected
- ☐ Concerned
- ☐ Curious
- ☐ Engrossed
- ☐ Fascinated
- ☐ Inquisitive
- ☐ Intrigued
- ☐ Nosy
- ☐ Snoopy

ALIVE
- ☐ Animated
- ☐ Courageous
- ☐ Energetic
- ☐ Free
- ☐ Frisky
- ☐ Impulsive
- ☐ Liberated
- ☐ Optimistic
- ☐ Playful
- ☐ Provocative
- ☐ Spirited
- ☐ Thrilled
- ☐ Wonderful

STRONG
- ☐ Certain
- ☐ Dynamic
- ☐ Free
- ☐ Hardy
- ☐ Impulsive
- ☐ Rebellious
- ☐ Secure
- ☐ Sure
- ☐ Tenacious
- ☐ Unique

LOVE
- ☐ Admiration
- ☐ Affectionate
- ☐ Attracted
- ☐ Close
- ☐ Comforted
- ☐ Considerate
- ☐ Devoted
- ☐ Drawn toward
- ☐ Loved
- ☐ Loving
- ☐ Passionate
- ☐ Sensitive
- ☐ Sympathy
- ☐ Tender
- ☐ Touched
- ☐ Warm

POSITIVE
- ☐ Anxious
- ☐ Bold
- ☐ Brave
- ☐ Challenged
- ☐ Confident
- ☐ Daring
- ☐ Determined
- ☐ Eager
- ☐ Earnest
- ☐ Enthusiastic
- ☐ Excited
- ☐ Hopeful
- ☐ Inspired
- ☐ Intent
- ☐ Keen
- ☐ Optimistic
- ☐ Re-enforced

GOOD
- ☐ At ease
- ☐ Blessed
- ☐ Bright
- ☐ Calm
- ☐ Certain
- ☐ Clever
- ☐ Comfortable
- ☐ Content
- ☐ Encouraged
- ☐ Free and easy
- ☐ Peaceful
- ☐ Pleased
- ☐ Quiet
- ☐ Reassured
- ☐ Relaxed
- ☐ Serene
- ☐ Surprised

HAPPY
- ☐ Cheerful
- ☐ Delighted
- ☐ Ecstatic
- ☐ Elated
- ☐ Festive
- ☐ Fortunate
- ☐ Glad
- ☐ Gleeful
- ☐ Great
- ☐ Important
- ☐ Joyous
- ☐ Jubilant
- ☐ Lucky
- ☐ Merry
- ☐ Overjoyed
- ☐ Satisfied
- ☐ Sunny
- ☐ Thankful

Read and check off ✓

Preparing to listen
- ☐ Remember to put your mind and feelings in neutral gear.
- ☐ Your body posture must say, *"I am open, very interested, affirmative, attentive."*
- ☐ Maintain good eye contact.
- ☐ Give the speaker a verbal door opening, showing your readiness to listen.

While Listening
- ☐ Track what the speaker is saying in both content and feeling levels
- ☐ Stay with the content of communication
- ☐ Listen for and identify the basic general feeling; anger, fear, joy, resentment, etc.
- ☐ Suspend judgment; open yourself to the presence of their heart.

Responding
- ☐ Use oral responses, which are affirming, which say, *"I am with you"*, *"I understand."*
- ☐ Feed general feelings back to the speaker. *"You seem to feel this has been a good experience for you"*
- ☐ Stay an inch ahead of the speaker, not a mile.

UNPLEASANT FEELINGS

😟 HELPLESS
- ☐ Alone
- ☐ Despair
- ☐ Distressed
- ☐ Dominated
- ☐ Empty
- ☐ Fatigued
- ☐ Forced
- ☐ Frustrated
- ☐ Hesitant
- ☐ In A Stew
- ☐ Incapable
- ☐ Inferior
- ☐ Paralyzed
- ☐ Pathetic
- ☐ Tragic
- ☐ Useless
- ☐ Vulnerable
- ☐ Woeful

😕 CONFUSED
- ☐ Disillusioned
- ☐ Distrustful
- ☐ Doubtful
- ☐ Embarrassed
- ☐ Hesitant
- ☐ Indecisive
- ☐ Lost
- ☐ Misgiving
- ☐ Perplexed
- ☐ Pessimistic
- ☐ Shy
- ☐ Skeptical
- ☐ Stupefied
- ☐ Tense
- ☐ Unbelieving
- ☐ Uncertain
- ☐ Uneasy
- ☐ Unsure
- ☐ Upset

😞 DEPRESSED
- ☐ A Sense of Loss
- ☐ Abominable
- ☐ Ashamed
- ☐ Bad
- ☐ Despicable
- ☐ Detestable
- ☐ Diminished
- ☐ Disappointed
- ☐ Discouraged
- ☐ Disgusting
- ☐ Dissatisfied
- ☐ Guilty
- ☐ In Despair
- ☐ Lousy
- ☐ Miserable
- ☐ Powerless
- ☐ Repugnant
- ☐ Sulky
- ☐ Terrible

😠 ANGRY
- ☐ Aggressive
- ☐ Annoyed
- ☐ Bitter
- ☐ Boiling
- ☐ Cross
- ☐ Enraged
- ☐ Fuming
- ☐ Hateful
- ☐ Hostile
- ☐ Incensed
- ☐ Inflamed
- ☐ Infuriated
- ☐ Insulting
- ☐ Irritated
- ☐ Offensive
- ☐ Provoked
- ☐ Resentful
- ☐ Sore
- ☐ Unpleasant
- ☐ Upset
- ☐ Worked Up

😢 SAD
- ☐ Anguish
- ☐ Desolate
- ☐ Desperate
- ☐ Dismayed
- ☐ Grief
- ☐ Grieved
- ☐ Lonely
- ☐ Mournful
- ☐ Pained
- ☐ Pessimistic
- ☐ Sorrowful
- ☐ Tearful
- ☐ Unhappy

😐 INDIFFERENT
- ☐ Bored
- ☐ Cold
- ☐ Disinterested
- ☐ Dull
- ☐ Insensitive
- ☐ Lifeless
- ☐ Neutral
- ☐ Nonchalant
- ☐ Preoccupied
- ☐ Reserved
- ☐ Weary

😨 AFRAID
- ☐ Alarmed
- ☐ Anxious
- ☐ Cowardly
- ☐ Doubtful
- ☐ Fearful
- ☐ Frightened
- ☐ Menaced
- ☐ Nervous
- ☐ Panic
- ☐ Quaking
- ☐ Restless
- ☐ Scared
- ☐ Shaky
- ☐ Suspicious
- ☐ Terrified
- ☐ Threatened
- ☐ Timid
- ☐ Wary
- ☐ Worried

😣 HURT
- ☐ Aching
- ☐ Afflicted
- ☐ Agonized
- ☐ Alienated
- ☐ Appalled
- ☐ Crushed
- ☐ Dejected
- ☐ Deprived
- ☐ Heartbroken
- ☐ Humiliated
- ☐ Injured
- ☐ Offended
- ☐ Pained
- ☐ Rejected
- ☐ Tormented
- ☐ Tortured
- ☐ Victimized
- ☐ Wronged

Notes: _____
_____
_____
_____

8 Pitfalls to avoid
- ☐ Me-too-ism. Don't start telling your story, or comparing your story to theirs.
- ☐ Moralizing, preaching, being judgmental
- ☐ Asking a direct question to satisfy your own curiosity
- ☐ Being an interviewer rather then a listener
- ☐ Giving advice (try fixing it)
- ☐ Cheap consolation. *"Oh, that's not to bad"*
- ☐ Arguing or disagreeing with the speaker
- ☐ Analyzing or interpreting
- ☐ Ignoring obvious heavy emotions

Date: _____

48.

PLEASANT FEELINGS

OPEN
- [ ] Accepting
- [ ] Amazed
- [ ] Confident
- [ ] Easy
- [ ] Free
- [ ] Interested
- [ ] Kind
- [ ] Receptive
- [ ] Reliable
- [ ] Satisfied
- [ ] Sympathetic
- [ ] Understanding

INTERESTED
- [ ] Absorbed
- [ ] Affected
- [ ] Concerned
- [ ] Curious
- [ ] Engrossed
- [ ] Fascinated
- [ ] Inquisitive
- [ ] Intrigued
- [ ] Nosy
- [ ] Snoopy

ALIVE
- [ ] Animated
- [ ] Courageous
- [ ] Energetic
- [ ] Free
- [ ] Frisky
- [ ] Impulsive
- [ ] Liberated
- [ ] Optimistic
- [ ] Playful
- [ ] Provocative
- [ ] Spirited
- [ ] Thrilled
- [ ] Wonderful

STRONG
- [ ] Certain
- [ ] Dynamic
- [ ] Free
- [ ] Hardy
- [ ] Impulsive
- [ ] Rebellious
- [ ] Secure
- [ ] Sure
- [ ] Tenacious
- [ ] Unique

LOVE
- [ ] Admiration
- [ ] Affectionate
- [ ] Attracted
- [ ] Close
- [ ] Comforted
- [ ] Considerate
- [ ] Devoted
- [ ] Drawn toward
- [ ] Loved
- [ ] Loving
- [ ] Passionate
- [ ] Sensitive
- [ ] Sympathy
- [ ] Tender
- [ ] Touched
- [ ] Warm

POSITIVE
- [ ] Anxious
- [ ] Bold
- [ ] Brave
- [ ] Challenged
- [ ] Confident
- [ ] Daring
- [ ] Determined
- [ ] Eager
- [ ] Earnest
- [ ] Enthusiastic
- [ ] Excited
- [ ] Hopeful
- [ ] Inspired
- [ ] Intent
- [ ] Keen
- [ ] Optimistic
- [ ] Re-enforced

GOOD
- [ ] At ease
- [ ] Blessed
- [ ] Bright
- [ ] Calm
- [ ] Certain
- [ ] Clever
- [ ] Comfortable
- [ ] Content
- [ ] Encouraged
- [ ] Free and easy
- [ ] Peaceful
- [ ] Pleased
- [ ] Quiet
- [ ] Reassured
- [ ] Relaxed
- [ ] Serene
- [ ] Surprised

HAPPY
- [ ] Cheerful
- [ ] Delighted
- [ ] Ecstatic
- [ ] Elated
- [ ] Festive
- [ ] Fortunate
- [ ] Glad
- [ ] Gleeful
- [ ] Great
- [ ] Important
- [ ] Joyous
- [ ] Jubilant
- [ ] Lucky
- [ ] Merry
- [ ] Overjoyed
- [ ] Satisfied
- [ ] Sunny
- [ ] Thankful

Read and check off
✓

Preparing to listen
- [ ] Remember to put your mind and feelings in neutral gear.
- [ ] Your body posture must say, *"I' am open, very interested, affirmative, attentive."*
- [ ] Maintain good eye contact.
- [ ] Give the speaker a verbal door opening, showing your readiness to listen.

While Listening
- [ ] Track what the speaker is saying in both content and feeling levels
- [ ] Stay with the content of communication
- [ ] Listen for and identify the basic general feeling; anger, fear, joy, resentment, etc.
- [ ] Suspend judgment; open yourself to the presence of their heart.

Responding
- [ ] Use oral responses, which are affirming, which say, *"I am with you"*, *"I understand."*
- [ ] Feed general feelings back to the speaker. *"You seem to feel this has been a good experience for you"*
- [ ] Stay an inch ahead of the speaker, not a mile.

UNPLEASANT FEELINGS

HELPLESS
- ☐ Alone
- ☐ Despair
- ☐ Distressed
- ☐ Dominated
- ☐ Empty
- ☐ Fatigued
- ☐ Forced
- ☐ Frustrated
- ☐ Hesitant
- ☐ In A Stew
- ☐ Incapable
- ☐ Inferior
- ☐ Paralyzed
- ☐ Pathetic
- ☐ Tragic
- ☐ Useless
- ☐ Vulnerable
- ☐ Woeful

CONFUSED
- ☐ Disillusioned
- ☐ Distrustful
- ☐ Doubtful
- ☐ Embarrassed
- ☐ Hesitant
- ☐ Indecisive
- ☐ Lost
- ☐ Misgiving
- ☐ Perplexed
- ☐ Pessimistic
- ☐ Shy
- ☐ Skeptical
- ☐ Stupefied
- ☐ Tense
- ☐ Unbelieving
- ☐ Uncertain
- ☐ Uneasy
- ☐ Unsure
- ☐ Upset

DEPRESSED
- ☐ A Sense of Loss
- ☐ Abominable
- ☐ Ashamed
- ☐ Bad
- ☐ Despicable
- ☐ Detestable
- ☐ Diminished
- ☐ Disappointed
- ☐ Discouraged
- ☐ Disgusting
- ☐ Dissatisfied
- ☐ Guilty
- ☐ In Despair
- ☐ Lousy
- ☐ Miserable
- ☐ Powerless
- ☐ Repugnant
- ☐ Sulky
- ☐ Terrible

ANGRY
- ☐ Aggressive
- ☐ Annoyed
- ☐ Bitter
- ☐ Boiling
- ☐ Cross
- ☐ Enraged
- ☐ Fuming
- ☐ Hateful
- ☐ Hostile
- ☐ Incensed
- ☐ Inflamed
- ☐ Infuriated
- ☐ Insulting
- ☐ Irritated
- ☐ Offensive
- ☐ Provoked
- ☐ Resentful
- ☐ Sore
- ☐ Unpleasant
- ☐ Upset
- ☐ Worked Up

SAD
- ☐ Anguish
- ☐ Desolate
- ☐ Desperate
- ☐ Dismayed
- ☐ Grief
- ☐ Grieved
- ☐ Lonely
- ☐ Mournful
- ☐ Pained
- ☐ Pessimistic
- ☐ Sorrowful
- ☐ Tearful
- ☐ Unhappy

INDIFFERENT
- ☐ Bored
- ☐ Cold
- ☐ Disinterested
- ☐ Dull
- ☐ Insensitive
- ☐ Lifeless
- ☐ Neutral
- ☐ Nonchalant
- ☐ Preoccupied
- ☐ Reserved
- ☐ Weary

AFRAID
- ☐ Alarmed
- ☐ Anxious
- ☐ Cowardly
- ☐ Doubtful
- ☐ Fearful
- ☐ Frightened
- ☐ Menaced
- ☐ Nervous
- ☐ Panic
- ☐ Quaking
- ☐ Restless
- ☐ Scared
- ☐ Shaky
- ☐ Suspicious
- ☐ Terrified
- ☐ Threatened
- ☐ Timid
- ☐ Wary
- ☐ Worried

HURT
- ☐ Aching
- ☐ Afflicted
- ☐ Agonized
- ☐ Alienated
- ☐ Appalled
- ☐ Crushed
- ☐ Dejected
- ☐ Deprived
- ☐ Heartbroken
- ☐ Humiliated
- ☐ Injured
- ☐ Offended
- ☐ Pained
- ☐ Rejected
- ☐ Tormented
- ☐ Tortured
- ☐ Victimized
- ☐ Wronged

Notes: _____
_____
_____

8 Pitfalls to avoid
- ☐ Me-too-ism. Don't start telling your story, or comparing your story to theirs.
- ☐ Moralizing, preaching, being judgmental
- ☐ Asking a direct question to satisfy your own curiosity
- ☐ Being an interviewer rather then a listener
- ☐ Giving advice (try fixing it)
- ☐ Cheap consolation. *"Oh, that's not to bad"*
- ☐ Arguing or disagreeing with the speaker
- ☐ Analyzing or interpreting
- ☐ Ignoring obvious heavy emotions

Date: _____

50.

PLEASANT FEELINGS

OPEN
- Accepting
- Amazed
- Confident
- Easy
- Free
- Interested
- Kind
- Receptive
- Reliable
- Satisfied
- Sympathetic
- Understanding

INTERESTED
- Absorbed
- Affected
- Concerned
- Curious
- Engrossed
- Fascinated
- Inquisitive
- Intrigued
- Nosy
- Snoopy

ALIVE
- Animated
- Courageous
- Energetic
- Free
- Frisky
- Impulsive
- Liberated
- Optimistic
- Playful
- Provocative
- Spirited
- Thrilled
- Wonderful

STRONG
- Certain
- Dynamic
- Free
- Hardy
- Impulsive
- Rebellious
- Secure
- Sure
- Tenacious
- Unique

LOVE
- Admiration
- Affectionate
- Attracted
- Close
- Comforted
- Considerate
- Devoted
- Drawn toward
- Loved
- Loving
- Passionate
- Sensitive
- Sympathy
- Tender
- Touched
- Warm

POSITIVE
- Anxious
- Bold
- Brave
- Challenged
- Confident
- Daring
- Determined
- Eager
- Earnest
- Enthusiastic
- Excited
- Hopeful
- Inspired
- Intent
- Keen
- Optimistic
- Re-enforced

GOOD
- At ease
- Blessed
- Bright
- Calm
- Certain
- Clever
- Comfortable
- Content
- Encouraged
- Free and easy
- Peaceful
- Pleased
- Quiet
- Reassured
- Relaxed
- Serene
- Surprised

HAPPY
- Cheerful
- Delighted
- Ecstatic
- Elated
- Festive
- Fortunate
- Glad
- Gleeful
- Great
- Important
- Joyous
- Jubilant
- Lucky
- Merry
- Overjoyed
- Satisfied
- Sunny
- Thankful

Read and check off ✓

Preparing to listen
- [ ] Remember to put your mind and feelings in neutral gear.
- [ ] Your body posture must say, *"I' am open, very interested, affirmative, attentive."*
- [ ] Maintain good eye contact.
- [ ] Give the speaker a verbal door opening, showing your readiness to listen.

While Listening
- [ ] Track what the speaker is saying in both content and feeling levels
- [ ] Stay with the content of communication
- [ ] Listen for and identify the basic general feeling; anger, fear, joy, resentment, etc.
- [ ] Suspend judgment; open yourself to the presence of their heart.

Responding
- [ ] Use oral responses, which are affirming, which say, *"I am with you"*, *"I understand."*
- [ ] Feed general feelings back to the speaker. *"You seem to feel this has been a good experience for you"*
- [ ] Stay an inch ahead of the speaker, not a mile.

UNPLEASANT FEELINGS

😳 HELPLESS
- ☐ Alone
- ☐ Despair
- ☐ Distressed
- ☐ Dominated
- ☐ Empty
- ☐ Fatigued
- ☐ Forced
- ☐ Frustrated
- ☐ Hesitant
- ☐ In A Stew
- ☐ Incapable
- ☐ Inferior
- ☐ Paralyzed
- ☐ Pathetic
- ☐ Tragic
- ☐ Useless
- ☐ Vulnerable
- ☐ Woeful

😕 SAD
- ☐ Anguish
- ☐ Desolate
- ☐ Desperate
- ☐ Dismayed
- ☐ Grief
- ☐ Grieved
- ☐ Lonely
- ☐ Mournful
- ☐ Pained
- ☐ Pessimistic
- ☐ Sorrowful
- ☐ Tearful
- ☐ Unhappy

😟 CONFUSED
- ☐ Disillusioned
- ☐ Distrustful
- ☐ Doubtful
- ☐ Embarrassed
- ☐ Hesitant
- ☐ Indecisive
- ☐ Lost
- ☐ Misgiving
- ☐ Perplexed
- ☐ Pessimistic
- ☐ Shy
- ☐ Skeptical
- ☐ Stupefied
- ☐ Tense
- ☐ Unbelieving
- ☐ Uncertain
- ☐ Uneasy
- ☐ Unsure
- ☐ Upset

😐 INDIFFERENT
- ☐ Bored
- ☐ Cold
- ☐ Disinterested
- ☐ Dull
- ☐ Insensitive
- ☐ Lifeless
- ☐ Neutral
- ☐ Nonchalant
- ☐ Preoccupied
- ☐ Reserved
- ☐ Weary

😞 DEPRESSED
- ☐ A Sense of Loss
- ☐ Abominable
- ☐ Ashamed
- ☐ Bad
- ☐ Despicable
- ☐ Detestable
- ☐ Diminished
- ☐ Disappointed
- ☐ Discouraged
- ☐ Disgusting
- ☐ Dissatisfied
- ☐ Guilty
- ☐ In Despair
- ☐ Lousy
- ☐ Miserable
- ☐ Powerless
- ☐ Repugnant
- ☐ Sulky
- ☐ Terrible

😨 AFRAID
- ☐ Alarmed
- ☐ Anxious
- ☐ Cowardly
- ☐ Doubtful
- ☐ Fearful
- ☐ Frightened
- ☐ Menaced
- ☐ Nervous
- ☐ Panic
- ☐ Quaking
- ☐ Restless
- ☐ Scared
- ☐ Shaky
- ☐ Suspicious
- ☐ Terrified
- ☐ Threatened
- ☐ Timid
- ☐ Wary
- ☐ Worried

😠 ANGRY
- ☐ Aggressive
- ☐ Annoyed
- ☐ Bitter
- ☐ Boiling
- ☐ Cross
- ☐ Enraged
- ☐ Fuming
- ☐ Hateful
- ☐ Hostile
- ☐ Incensed
- ☐ Inflamed
- ☐ Infuriated
- ☐ Insulting
- ☐ Irritated
- ☐ Offensive
- ☐ Provoked
- ☐ Resentful
- ☐ Sore
- ☐ Unpleasant
- ☐ Upset
- ☐ Worked Up

😟 HURT
- ☐ Aching
- ☐ Afflicted
- ☐ Agonized
- ☐ Alienated
- ☐ Appalled
- ☐ Crushed
- ☐ Dejected
- ☐ Deprived
- ☐ Heartbroken
- ☐ Humiliated
- ☐ Injured
- ☐ Offended
- ☐ Pained
- ☐ Rejected
- ☐ Tormented
- ☐ Tortured
- ☐ Victimized
- ☐ Wronged

Notes:
_____
_____
_____

8 Pitfalls to avoid
- ☐ Me-too-ism. Don't start telling your story, or comparing your story to theirs.
- ☐ Moralizing, preaching, being judgmental
- ☐ Asking a direct question to satisfy your own curiosity
- ☐ Being an interviewer rather then a listener
- ☐ Giving advice (try fixing it)
- ☐ Cheap consolation. *"Oh, that's not to bad"*
- ☐ Arguing or disagreeing with the speaker
- ☐ Analyzing or interpreting
- ☐ Ignoring obvious heavy emotions

Date: _____

PLEASANT FEELINGS

OPEN
- ☐ Accepting
- ☐ Amazed
- ☐ Confident
- ☐ Easy
- ☐ Free
- ☐ Interested
- ☐ Kind
- ☐ Receptive
- ☐ Reliable
- ☐ Satisfied
- ☐ Sympathetic
- ☐ Understanding

INTERESTED
- ☐ Absorbed
- ☐ Affected
- ☐ Concerned
- ☐ Curious
- ☐ Engrossed
- ☐ Fascinated
- ☐ Inquisitive
- ☐ Intrigued
- ☐ Nosy
- ☐ Snoopy

ALIVE
- ☐ Animated
- ☐ Courageous
- ☐ Energetic
- ☐ Free
- ☐ Frisky
- ☐ Impulsive
- ☐ Liberated
- ☐ Optimistic
- ☐ Playful
- ☐ Provocative
- ☐ Spirited
- ☐ Thrilled
- ☐ Wonderful

STRONG
- ☐ Certain
- ☐ Dynamic
- ☐ Free
- ☐ Hardy
- ☐ Impulsive
- ☐ Rebellious
- ☐ Secure
- ☐ Sure
- ☐ Tenacious
- ☐ Unique

LOVE
- ☐ Admiration
- ☐ Affectionate
- ☐ Attracted
- ☐ Close
- ☐ Comforted
- ☐ Considerate
- ☐ Devoted
- ☐ Drawn toward
- ☐ Loved
- ☐ Loving
- ☐ Passionate
- ☐ Sensitive
- ☐ Sympathy
- ☐ Tender
- ☐ Touched
- ☐ Warm

POSITIVE
- ☐ Anxious
- ☐ Bold
- ☐ Brave
- ☐ Challenged
- ☐ Confident
- ☐ Daring
- ☐ Determined
- ☐ Eager
- ☐ Earnest
- ☐ Enthusiastic
- ☐ Excited
- ☐ Hopeful
- ☐ Inspired
- ☐ Intent
- ☐ Keen
- ☐ Optimistic
- ☐ Re-enforced

GOOD
- ☐ At ease
- ☐ Blessed
- ☐ Bright
- ☐ Calm
- ☐ Certain
- ☐ Clever
- ☐ Comfortable
- ☐ Content
- ☐ Encouraged
- ☐ Free and easy
- ☐ Peaceful
- ☐ Pleased
- ☐ Quiet
- ☐ Reassured
- ☐ Relaxed
- ☐ Serene
- ☐ Surprised

HAPPY
- ☐ Cheerful
- ☐ Delighted
- ☐ Ecstatic
- ☐ Elated
- ☐ Festive
- ☐ Fortunate
- ☐ Glad
- ☐ Gleeful
- ☐ Great
- ☐ Important
- ☐ Joyous
- ☐ Jubilant
- ☐ Lucky
- ☐ Merry
- ☐ Overjoyed
- ☐ Satisfied
- ☐ Sunny
- ☐ Thankful

Read and check off ✓

Preparing to listen
- ☐ Remember to put your mind and feelings in neutral gear.
- ☐ Your body posture must say, *"I am open, very interested, affirmative, attentive."*
- ☐ Maintain good eye contact.
- ☐ Give the speaker a verbal door opening, showing your readiness to listen.

While Listening
- ☐ Track what the speaker is saying in both content and feeling levels
- ☐ Stay with the content of communication
- ☐ Listen for and identify the basic general feeling; anger, fear, joy, resentment, etc.
- ☐ Suspend judgment; open yourself to the presence of their heart.

Responding
- ☐ Use oral responses, which are affirming, which say, *"I am with you"*, *"I understand."*
- ☐ Feed general feelings back to the speaker. *"You seem to feel this has been a good experience for you"*
- ☐ Stay an inch ahead of the speaker, not a mile.

UNPLEASANT FEELINGS

😳 HELPLESS
- ☐ Alone
- ☐ Despair
- ☐ Distressed
- ☐ Dominated
- ☐ Empty
- ☐ Fatigued
- ☐ Forced
- ☐ Frustrated
- ☐ Hesitant
- ☐ In A Stew
- ☐ Incapable
- ☐ Inferior
- ☐ Paralyzed
- ☐ Pathetic
- ☐ Tragic
- ☐ Useless
- ☐ Vulnerable
- ☐ Woeful

😕 CONFUSED
- ☐ Disillusioned
- ☐ Distrustful
- ☐ Doubtful
- ☐ Embarrassed
- ☐ Hesitant
- ☐ Indecisive
- ☐ Lost
- ☐ Misgiving
- ☐ Perplexed
- ☐ Pessimistic
- ☐ Shy
- ☐ Skeptical
- ☐ Stupefied
- ☐ Tense
- ☐ Unbelieving
- ☐ Uncertain
- ☐ Uneasy
- ☐ Unsure
- ☐ Upset

😞 DEPRESSED
- ☐ A Sense of Loss
- ☐ Abominable
- ☐ Ashamed
- ☐ Bad
- ☐ Despicable
- ☐ Detestable
- ☐ Diminished
- ☐ Disappointed
- ☐ Discouraged
- ☐ Disgusting
- ☐ Dissatisfied
- ☐ Guilty
- ☐ In Despair
- ☐ Lousy
- ☐ Miserable
- ☐ Powerless
- ☐ Repugnant
- ☐ Sulky
- ☐ Terrible

😠 ANGRY
- ☐ Aggressive
- ☐ Annoyed
- ☐ Bitter
- ☐ Boiling
- ☐ Cross
- ☐ Enraged
- ☐ Fuming
- ☐ Hateful
- ☐ Hostile
- ☐ Incensed
- ☐ Inflamed
- ☐ Infuriated
- ☐ Insulting
- ☐ Irritated
- ☐ Offensive
- ☐ Provoked
- ☐ Resentful
- ☐ Sore
- ☐ Unpleasant
- ☐ Upset
- ☐ Worked Up

😢 SAD
- ☐ Anguish
- ☐ Desolate
- ☐ Desperate
- ☐ Dismayed
- ☐ Grief
- ☐ Grieved
- ☐ Lonely
- ☐ Mournful
- ☐ Pained
- ☐ Pessimistic
- ☐ Sorrowful
- ☐ Tearful
- ☐ Unhappy

😐 INDIFFERENT
- ☐ Bored
- ☐ Cold
- ☐ Disinterested
- ☐ Dull
- ☐ Insensitive
- ☐ Lifeless
- ☐ Neutral
- ☐ Nonchalant
- ☐ Preoccupied
- ☐ Reserved
- ☐ Weary

😨 AFRAID
- ☐ Alarmed
- ☐ Anxious
- ☐ Cowardly
- ☐ Doubtful
- ☐ Fearful
- ☐ Frightened
- ☐ Menaced
- ☐ Nervous
- ☐ Panic
- ☐ Quaking
- ☐ Restless
- ☐ Scared
- ☐ Shaky
- ☐ Suspicious
- ☐ Terrified
- ☐ Threatened
- ☐ Timid
- ☐ Wary
- ☐ Worried

🙁 HURT
- ☐ Aching
- ☐ Afflicted
- ☐ Agonized
- ☐ Alienated
- ☐ Appalled
- ☐ Crushed
- ☐ Dejected
- ☐ Deprived
- ☐ Heartbroken
- ☐ Humiliated
- ☐ Injured
- ☐ Offended
- ☐ Pained
- ☐ Rejected
- ☐ Tormented
- ☐ Tortured
- ☐ Victimized
- ☐ Wronged

Notes: _____
_____
_____
_____

8 Pitfalls to avoid
- ☐ Me-too-ism. Don't start telling your story, or comparing your story to theirs.
- ☐ Moralizing, preaching, being judgmental
- ☐ Asking a direct question to satisfy your own curiosity
- ☐ Being an interviewer rather then a listener
- ☐ Giving advice (try fixing it)
- ☐ Cheap consolation. *"Oh, that's not to bad"*
- ☐ Arguing or disagreeing with the speaker
- ☐ Analyzing or interpreting
- ☐ Ignoring obvious heavy emotions

Date: _____

PLEASANT FEELINGS

OPEN
- ☐ Accepting
- ☐ Amazed
- ☐ Confident
- ☐ Easy
- ☐ Free
- ☐ Interested
- ☐ Kind
- ☐ Receptive
- ☐ Reliable
- ☐ Satisfied
- ☐ Sympathetic
- ☐ Understanding

INTERESTED
- ☐ Absorbed
- ☐ Affected
- ☐ Concerned
- ☐ Curious
- ☐ Engrossed
- ☐ Fascinated
- ☐ Inquisitive
- ☐ Intrigued
- ☐ Nosy
- ☐ Snoopy

ALIVE
- ☐ Animated
- ☐ Courageous
- ☐ Energetic
- ☐ Free
- ☐ Frisky
- ☐ Impulsive
- ☐ Liberated
- ☐ Optimistic
- ☐ Playful
- ☐ Provocative
- ☐ Spirited
- ☐ Thrilled
- ☐ Wonderful

STRONG
- ☐ Certain
- ☐ Dynamic
- ☐ Free
- ☐ Hardy
- ☐ Impulsive
- ☐ Rebellious
- ☐ Secure
- ☐ Sure
- ☐ Tenacious
- ☐ Unique

LOVE
- ☐ Admiration
- ☐ Affectionate
- ☐ Attracted
- ☐ Close
- ☐ Comforted
- ☐ Considerate
- ☐ Devoted
- ☐ Drawn toward
- ☐ Loved
- ☐ Loving
- ☐ Passionate
- ☐ Sensitive
- ☐ Sympathy
- ☐ Tender
- ☐ Touched
- ☐ Warm

POSITIVE
- ☐ Anxious
- ☐ Bold
- ☐ Brave
- ☐ Challenged
- ☐ Confident
- ☐ Daring
- ☐ Determined
- ☐ Eager
- ☐ Earnest
- ☐ Enthusiastic
- ☐ Excited
- ☐ Hopeful
- ☐ Inspired
- ☐ Intent
- ☐ Keen
- ☐ Optimistic
- ☐ Re-enforced

GOOD
- ☐ At ease
- ☐ Blessed
- ☐ Bright
- ☐ Calm
- ☐ Certain
- ☐ Clever
- ☐ Comfortable
- ☐ Content
- ☐ Encouraged
- ☐ Free and easy
- ☐ Peaceful
- ☐ Pleased
- ☐ Quiet
- ☐ Reassured
- ☐ Relaxed
- ☐ Serene
- ☐ Surprised

HAPPY
- ☐ Cheerful
- ☐ Delighted
- ☐ Ecstatic
- ☐ Elated
- ☐ Festive
- ☐ Fortunate
- ☐ Glad
- ☐ Gleeful
- ☐ Great
- ☐ Important
- ☐ Joyous
- ☐ Jubilant
- ☐ Lucky
- ☐ Merry
- ☐ Overjoyed
- ☐ Satisfied
- ☐ Sunny
- ☐ Thankful

Read and check off
✓

Preparing to listen
- ☐ Remember to put your mind and feelings in neutral gear.
- ☐ Your body posture must say, *"I' am open, very interested, affirmative, attentive."*
- ☐ Maintain good eye contact.
- ☐ Give the speaker a verbal door opening, showing your readiness to listen.

While Listening
- ☐ Track what the speaker is saying in both content and feeling levels
- ☐ Stay with the content of communication
- ☐ Listen for and identify the basic general feeling; anger, fear, joy, resentment, etc.
- ☐ Suspend judgment; open yourself to the presence of their heart.

Responding
- ☐ Use oral responses, which are affirming, which say, *"I am with you"*, *"I understand."*
- ☐ Feed general feelings back to the speaker. *"You seem to feel this has been a good experience for you"*
- ☐ Stay an inch ahead of the speaker, not a mile.

UNPLEASANT FEELINGS

😖 HELPLESS
- ☐ Alone
- ☐ Despair
- ☐ Distressed
- ☐ Dominated
- ☐ Empty
- ☐ Fatigued
- ☐ Forced
- ☐ Frustrated
- ☐ Hesitant
- ☐ In A Stew
- ☐ Incapable
- ☐ Inferior
- ☐ Paralyzed
- ☐ Pathetic
- ☐ Tragic
- ☐ Useless
- ☐ Vulnerable
- ☐ Woeful

😕 CONFUSED
- ☐ Disillusioned
- ☐ Distrustful
- ☐ Doubtful
- ☐ Embarrassed
- ☐ Hesitant
- ☐ Indecisive
- ☐ Lost
- ☐ Misgiving
- ☐ Perplexed
- ☐ Pessimistic
- ☐ Shy
- ☐ Skeptical
- ☐ Stupefied
- ☐ Tense
- ☐ Unbelieving
- ☐ Uncertain
- ☐ Uneasy
- ☐ Unsure
- ☐ Upset

😔 DEPRESSED
- ☐ A Sense of Loss
- ☐ Abominable
- ☐ Ashamed
- ☐ Bad
- ☐ Despicable
- ☐ Detestable
- ☐ Diminished
- ☐ Disappointed
- ☐ Discouraged
- ☐ Disgusting
- ☐ Dissatisfied
- ☐ Guilty
- ☐ In Despair
- ☐ Lousy
- ☐ Miserable
- ☐ Powerless
- ☐ Repugnant
- ☐ Sulky
- ☐ Terrible

😡 ANGRY
- ☐ Aggressive
- ☐ Annoyed
- ☐ Bitter
- ☐ Boiling
- ☐ Cross
- ☐ Enraged
- ☐ Fuming
- ☐ Hateful
- ☐ Hostile
- ☐ Incensed
- ☐ Inflamed
- ☐ Infuriated
- ☐ Insulting
- ☐ Irritated
- ☐ Offensive
- ☐ Provoked
- ☐ Resentful
- ☐ Sore
- ☐ Unpleasant
- ☐ Upset
- ☐ Worked Up

😢 SAD
- ☐ Anguish
- ☐ Desolate
- ☐ Desperate
- ☐ Dismayed
- ☐ Grief
- ☐ Grieved
- ☐ Lonely
- ☐ Mournful
- ☐ Pained
- ☐ Pessimistic
- ☐ Sorrowful
- ☐ Tearful
- ☐ Unhappy

😐 INDIFFERENT
- ☐ Bored
- ☐ Cold
- ☐ Disinterested
- ☐ Dull
- ☐ Insensitive
- ☐ Lifeless
- ☐ Neutral
- ☐ Nonchalant
- ☐ Preoccupied
- ☐ Reserved
- ☐ Weary

😨 AFRAID
- ☐ Alarmed
- ☐ Anxious
- ☐ Cowardly
- ☐ Doubtful
- ☐ Fearful
- ☐ Frightened
- ☐ Menaced
- ☐ Nervous
- ☐ Panic
- ☐ Quaking
- ☐ Restless
- ☐ Scared
- ☐ Shaky
- ☐ Suspicious
- ☐ Terrified
- ☐ Threatened
- ☐ Timid
- ☐ Wary
- ☐ Worried

😟 HURT
- ☐ Aching
- ☐ Afflicted
- ☐ Agonized
- ☐ Alienated
- ☐ Appalled
- ☐ Crushed
- ☐ Dejected
- ☐ Deprived
- ☐ Heartbroken
- ☐ Humiliated
- ☐ Injured
- ☐ Offended
- ☐ Pained
- ☐ Rejected
- ☐ Tormented
- ☐ Tortured
- ☐ Victimized
- ☐ Wronged

Notes:
_____
_____
_____
_____

8 Pitfalls to avoid

- ☐ Me-too-ism. Don't start telling your story, or comparing your story to theirs.
- ☐ Moralizing, preaching, being judgmental
- ☐ Asking a direct question to satisfy your own curiosity
- ☐ Being an interviewer rather then a listener
- ☐ Giving advice (try fixing it)
- ☐ Cheap consolation. *"Oh, that's not to bad"*
- ☐ Arguing or disagreeing with the speaker
- ☐ Analyzing or interpreting
- ☐ Ignoring obvious heavy emotions

Date: _____

PLEASANT FEELINGS

OPEN
- ☐ Accepting
- ☐ Amazed
- ☐ Confident
- ☐ Easy
- ☐ Free
- ☐ Interested
- ☐ Kind
- ☐ Receptive
- ☐ Reliable
- ☐ Satisfied
- ☐ Sympathetic
- ☐ Understanding

INTERESTED
- ☐ Absorbed
- ☐ Affected
- ☐ Concerned
- ☐ Curious
- ☐ Engrossed
- ☐ Fascinated
- ☐ Inquisitive
- ☐ Intrigued
- ☐ Nosy
- ☐ Snoopy

ALIVE
- ☐ Animated
- ☐ Courageous
- ☐ Energetic
- ☐ Free
- ☐ Frisky
- ☐ Impulsive
- ☐ Liberated
- ☐ Optimistic
- ☐ Playful
- ☐ Provocative
- ☐ Spirited
- ☐ Thrilled
- ☐ Wonderful

STRONG
- ☐ Certain
- ☐ Dynamic
- ☐ Free
- ☐ Hardy
- ☐ Impulsive
- ☐ Rebellious
- ☐ Secure
- ☐ Sure
- ☐ Tenacious
- ☐ Unique

LOVE
- ☐ Admiration
- ☐ Affectionate
- ☐ Attracted
- ☐ Close
- ☐ Comforted
- ☐ Considerate
- ☐ Devoted
- ☐ Drawn toward
- ☐ Loved
- ☐ Loving
- ☐ Passionate
- ☐ Sensitive
- ☐ Sympathy
- ☐ Tender
- ☐ Touched
- ☐ Warm

POSITIVE
- ☐ Anxious
- ☐ Bold
- ☐ Brave
- ☐ Challenged
- ☐ Confident
- ☐ Daring
- ☐ Determined
- ☐ Eager
- ☐ Earnest
- ☐ Enthusiastic
- ☐ Excited
- ☐ Hopeful
- ☐ Inspired
- ☐ Intent
- ☐ Keen
- ☐ Optimistic
- ☐ Re-enforced

GOOD
- ☐ At ease
- ☐ Blessed
- ☐ Bright
- ☐ Calm
- ☐ Certain
- ☐ Clever
- ☐ Comfortable
- ☐ Content
- ☐ Encouraged
- ☐ Free and easy
- ☐ Peaceful
- ☐ Pleased
- ☐ Quiet
- ☐ Reassured
- ☐ Relaxed
- ☐ Serene
- ☐ Surprised

HAPPY
- ☐ Cheerful
- ☐ Delighted
- ☐ Ecstatic
- ☐ Elated
- ☐ Festive
- ☐ Fortunate
- ☐ Glad
- ☐ Gleeful
- ☐ Great
- ☐ Important
- ☐ Joyous
- ☐ Jubilant
- ☐ Lucky
- ☐ Merry
- ☐ Overjoyed
- ☐ Satisfied
- ☐ Sunny
- ☐ Thankful

Read and check off ✓

Preparing to listen
- ☐ Remember to put your mind and feelings in neutral gear.
- ☐ Your body posture must say, *"I' am open, very interested, affirmative, attentive."*
- ☐ Maintain good eye contact.
- ☐ Give the speaker a verbal door opening, showing your readiness to listen.

While Listening
- ☐ Track what the speaker is saying in both content and feeling levels
- ☐ Stay with the content of communication
- ☐ Listen for and identify the basic general feeling; anger, fear, joy, resentment, etc.
- ☐ Suspend judgment; open yourself to the presence of their heart.

Responding
- ☐ Use oral responses, which are affirming, which say, *"I am with you", "I understand."*
- ☐ Feed general feelings back to the speaker. *"You seem to feel this has been a good experience for you"*
- ☐ Stay an inch ahead of the speaker, not a mile.

UNPLEASANT FEELINGS

HELPLESS
- ☐ Alone
- ☐ Despair
- ☐ Distressed
- ☐ Dominated
- ☐ Empty
- ☐ Fatigued
- ☐ Forced
- ☐ Frustrated
- ☐ Hesitant
- ☐ In A Stew
- ☐ Incapable
- ☐ Inferior
- ☐ Paralyzed
- ☐ Pathetic
- ☐ Tragic
- ☐ Useless
- ☐ Vulnerable
- ☐ Woeful

CONFUSED
- ☐ Disillusioned
- ☐ Distrustful
- ☐ Doubtful
- ☐ Embarrassed
- ☐ Hesitant
- ☐ Indecisive
- ☐ Lost
- ☐ Misgiving
- ☐ Perplexed
- ☐ Pessimistic
- ☐ Shy
- ☐ Skeptical
- ☐ Stupefied
- ☐ Tense
- ☐ Unbelieving
- ☐ Uncertain
- ☐ Uneasy
- ☐ Unsure
- ☐ Upset

DEPRESSED
- ☐ A Sense of Loss
- ☐ Abominable
- ☐ Ashamed
- ☐ Bad
- ☐ Despicable
- ☐ Detestable
- ☐ Diminished
- ☐ Disappointed
- ☐ Discouraged
- ☐ Disgusting
- ☐ Dissatisfied
- ☐ Guilty
- ☐ In Despair
- ☐ Lousy
- ☐ Miserable
- ☐ Powerless
- ☐ Repugnant
- ☐ Sulky
- ☐ Terrible

ANGRY
- ☐ Aggressive
- ☐ Annoyed
- ☐ Bitter
- ☐ Boiling
- ☐ Cross
- ☐ Enraged
- ☐ Fuming
- ☐ Hateful
- ☐ Hostile
- ☐ Incensed
- ☐ Inflamed
- ☐ Infuriated
- ☐ Insulting
- ☐ Irritated
- ☐ Offensive
- ☐ Provoked
- ☐ Resentful
- ☐ Sore
- ☐ Unpleasant
- ☐ Upset
- ☐ Worked Up

SAD
- ☐ Anguish
- ☐ Desolate
- ☐ Desperate
- ☐ Dismayed
- ☐ Grief
- ☐ Grieved
- ☐ Lonely
- ☐ Mournful
- ☐ Pained
- ☐ Pessimistic
- ☐ Sorrowful
- ☐ Tearful
- ☐ Unhappy

INDIFFERENT
- ☐ Bored
- ☐ Cold
- ☐ Disinterested
- ☐ Dull
- ☐ Insensitive
- ☐ Lifeless
- ☐ Neutral
- ☐ Nonchalant
- ☐ Preoccupied
- ☐ Reserved
- ☐ Weary

AFRAID
- ☐ Alarmed
- ☐ Anxious
- ☐ Cowardly
- ☐ Doubtful
- ☐ Fearful
- ☐ Frightened
- ☐ Menaced
- ☐ Nervous
- ☐ Panic
- ☐ Quaking
- ☐ Restless
- ☐ Scared
- ☐ Shaky
- ☐ Suspicious
- ☐ Terrified
- ☐ Threatened
- ☐ Timid
- ☐ Wary
- ☐ Worried

HURT
- ☐ Aching
- ☐ Afflicted
- ☐ Agonized
- ☐ Alienated
- ☐ Appalled
- ☐ Crushed
- ☐ Dejected
- ☐ Deprived
- ☐ Heartbroken
- ☐ Humiliated
- ☐ Injured
- ☐ Offended
- ☐ Pained
- ☐ Rejected
- ☐ Tormented
- ☐ Tortured
- ☐ Victimized
- ☐ Wronged

Notes: _____
_____
_____

8 Pitfalls to avoid
- ☐ Me-too-ism. Don't start telling your story, or comparing your story to theirs.
- ☐ Moralizing, preaching, being judgmental
- ☐ Asking a direct question to satisfy your own curiosity
- ☐ Being an interviewer rather then a listener
- ☐ Giving advice (try fixing it)
- ☐ Cheap consolation. *"Oh, that's not to bad"*
- ☐ Arguing or disagreeing with the speaker
- ☐ Analyzing or interpreting
- ☐ Ignoring obvious heavy emotions

Date: _____

PLEASANT FEELINGS

OPEN
- ☐ Accepting
- ☐ Amazed
- ☐ Confident
- ☐ Easy
- ☐ Free
- ☐ Interested
- ☐ Kind
- ☐ Receptive
- ☐ Reliable
- ☐ Satisfied
- ☐ Sympathetic
- ☐ Understanding

INTERESTED
- ☐ Absorbed
- ☐ Affected
- ☐ Concerned
- ☐ Curious
- ☐ Engrossed
- ☐ Fascinated
- ☐ Inquisitive
- ☐ Intrigued
- ☐ Nosy
- ☐ Snoopy

ALIVE
- ☐ Animated
- ☐ Courageous
- ☐ Energetic
- ☐ Free
- ☐ Frisky
- ☐ Impulsive
- ☐ Liberated
- ☐ Optimistic
- ☐ Playful
- ☐ Provocative
- ☐ Spirited
- ☐ Thrilled
- ☐ Wonderful

STRONG
- ☐ Certain
- ☐ Dynamic
- ☐ Free
- ☐ Hardy
- ☐ Impulsive
- ☐ Rebellious
- ☐ Secure
- ☐ Sure
- ☐ Tenacious
- ☐ Unique

LOVE
- ☐ Admiration
- ☐ Affectionate
- ☐ Attracted
- ☐ Close
- ☐ Comforted
- ☐ Considerate
- ☐ Devoted
- ☐ Drawn toward
- ☐ Loved
- ☐ Loving
- ☐ Passionate
- ☐ Sensitive
- ☐ Sympathy
- ☐ Tender
- ☐ Touched
- ☐ Warm

POSITIVE
- ☐ Anxious
- ☐ Bold
- ☐ Brave
- ☐ Challenged
- ☐ Confident
- ☐ Daring
- ☐ Determined
- ☐ Eager
- ☐ Earnest
- ☐ Enthusiastic
- ☐ Excited
- ☐ Hopeful
- ☐ Inspired
- ☐ Intent
- ☐ Keen
- ☐ Optimistic
- ☐ Re-enforced

GOOD
- ☐ At ease
- ☐ Blessed
- ☐ Bright
- ☐ Calm
- ☐ Certain
- ☐ Clever
- ☐ Comfortable
- ☐ Content
- ☐ Encouraged
- ☐ Free and easy
- ☐ Peaceful
- ☐ Pleased
- ☐ Quiet
- ☐ Reassured
- ☐ Relaxed
- ☐ Serene
- ☐ Surprised

HAPPY
- ☐ Cheerful
- ☐ Delighted
- ☐ Ecstatic
- ☐ Elated
- ☐ Festive
- ☐ Fortunate
- ☐ Glad
- ☐ Gleeful
- ☐ Great
- ☐ Important
- ☐ Joyous
- ☐ Jubilant
- ☐ Lucky
- ☐ Merry
- ☐ Overjoyed
- ☐ Satisfied
- ☐ Sunny
- ☐ Thankful

Read and check off
✓

Preparing to listen
- ☐ Remember to put your mind and feelings in neutral gear.
- ☐ Your body posture must say, *"I' am open, very interested, affirmative, attentive."*
- ☐ Maintain good eye contact.
- ☐ Give the speaker a verbal door opening, showing your readiness to listen.

While Listening
- ☐ Track what the speaker is saying in both content and feeling levels
- ☐ Stay with the content of communication
- ☐ Listen for and identify the basic general feeling; anger, fear, joy, resentment, etc.
- ☐ Suspend judgment; open yourself to the presence of their heart.

Responding
- ☐ Use oral responses, which are affirming, which say, *"I am with you"*, *"I understand."*
- ☐ Feed general feelings back to the speaker. *"You seem to feel this has been a good experience for you"*
- ☐ Stay an inch ahead of the speaker, not a mile.

UNPLEASANT FEELINGS

😞 HELPLESS
- ☐ Alone
- ☐ Despair
- ☐ Distressed
- ☐ Dominated
- ☐ Empty
- ☐ Fatigued
- ☐ Forced
- ☐ Frustrated
- ☐ Hesitant
- ☐ In A Stew
- ☐ Incapable
- ☐ Inferior
- ☐ Paralyzed
- ☐ Pathetic
- ☐ Tragic
- ☐ Useless
- ☐ Vulnerable
- ☐ Woeful

😕 CONFUSED
- ☐ Disillusioned
- ☐ Distrustful
- ☐ Doubtful
- ☐ Embarrassed
- ☐ Hesitant
- ☐ Indecisive
- ☐ Lost
- ☐ Misgiving
- ☐ Perplexed
- ☐ Pessimistic
- ☐ Shy
- ☐ Skeptical
- ☐ Stupefied
- ☐ Tense
- ☐ Unbelieving
- ☐ Uncertain
- ☐ Uneasy
- ☐ Unsure
- ☐ Upset

😔 DEPRESSED
- ☐ A Sense of Loss
- ☐ Abominable
- ☐ Ashamed
- ☐ Bad
- ☐ Despicable
- ☐ Detestable
- ☐ Diminished
- ☐ Disappointed
- ☐ Discouraged
- ☐ Disgusting
- ☐ Dissatisfied
- ☐ Guilty
- ☐ In Despair
- ☐ Lousy
- ☐ Miserable
- ☐ Powerless
- ☐ Repugnant
- ☐ Sulky
- ☐ Terrible

😠 ANGRY
- ☐ Aggressive
- ☐ Annoyed
- ☐ Bitter
- ☐ Boiling
- ☐ Cross
- ☐ Enraged
- ☐ Fuming
- ☐ Hateful
- ☐ Hostile
- ☐ Incensed
- ☐ Inflamed
- ☐ Infuriated
- ☐ Insulting
- ☐ Irritated
- ☐ Offensive
- ☐ Provoked
- ☐ Resentful
- ☐ Sore
- ☐ Unpleasant
- ☐ Upset
- ☐ Worked Up

😢 SAD
- ☐ Anguish
- ☐ Desolate
- ☐ Desperate
- ☐ Dismayed
- ☐ Grief
- ☐ Grieved
- ☐ Lonely
- ☐ Mournful
- ☐ Pained
- ☐ Pessimistic
- ☐ Sorrowful
- ☐ Tearful
- ☐ Unhappy

😐 INDIFFERENT
- ☐ Bored
- ☐ Cold
- ☐ Disinterested
- ☐ Dull
- ☐ Insensitive
- ☐ Lifeless
- ☐ Neutral
- ☐ Nonchalant
- ☐ Preoccupied
- ☐ Reserved
- ☐ Weary

😨 AFRAID
- ☐ Alarmed
- ☐ Anxious
- ☐ Cowardly
- ☐ Doubtful
- ☐ Fearful
- ☐ Frightened
- ☐ Menaced
- ☐ Nervous
- ☐ Panic
- ☐ Quaking
- ☐ Restless
- ☐ Scared
- ☐ Shaky
- ☐ Suspicious
- ☐ Terrified
- ☐ Threatened
- ☐ Timid
- ☐ Wary
- ☐ Worried

😟 HURT
- ☐ Aching
- ☐ Afflicted
- ☐ Agonized
- ☐ Alienated
- ☐ Appalled
- ☐ Crushed
- ☐ Dejected
- ☐ Deprived
- ☐ Heartbroken
- ☐ Humiliated
- ☐ Injured
- ☐ Offended
- ☐ Pained
- ☐ Rejected
- ☐ Tormented
- ☐ Tortured
- ☐ Victimized
- ☐ Wronged

Notes: _____
_____
_____
_____

8 Pitfalls to avoid
- ☐ Me-too-ism. Don't start telling your story, or comparing your story to theirs.
- ☐ Moralizing, preaching, being judgmental
- ☐ Asking a direct question to satisfy your own curiosity
- ☐ Being an interviewer rather then a listener
- ☐ Giving advice (try fixing it)
- ☐ Cheap consolation. *"Oh, that's not to bad"*
- ☐ Arguing or disagreeing with the speaker
- ☐ Analyzing or interpreting
- ☐ Ignoring obvious heavy emotions

Date: _____

After completing this, go back to page 10 and re-evaluate your intimacy.

PLEASANT FEELINGS

OPEN
- ☐ Accepting
- ☐ Amazed
- ☐ Confident
- ☐ Easy
- ☐ Free
- ☐ Interested
- ☐ Kind
- ☐ Receptive
- ☐ Reliable
- ☐ Satisfied
- ☐ Sympathetic
- ☐ Understanding

INTERESTED
- ☐ Absorbed
- ☐ Affected
- ☐ Concerned
- ☐ Curious
- ☐ Engrossed
- ☐ Fascinated
- ☐ Inquisitive
- ☐ Intrigued
- ☐ Nosy
- ☐ Snoopy

ALIVE
- ☐ Animated
- ☐ Courageous
- ☐ Energetic
- ☐ Free
- ☐ Frisky
- ☐ Impulsive
- ☐ Liberated
- ☐ Optimistic
- ☐ Playful
- ☐ Provocative
- ☐ Spirited
- ☐ Thrilled
- ☐ Wonderful

STRONG
- ☐ Certain
- ☐ Dynamic
- ☐ Free
- ☐ Hardy
- ☐ Impulsive
- ☐ Rebellious
- ☐ Secure
- ☐ Sure
- ☐ Tenacious
- ☐ Unique

LOVE
- ☐ Admiration
- ☐ Affectionate
- ☐ Attracted
- ☐ Close
- ☐ Comforted
- ☐ Considerate
- ☐ Devoted
- ☐ Drawn toward
- ☐ Loved
- ☐ Loving
- ☐ Passionate
- ☐ Sensitive
- ☐ Sympathy
- ☐ Tender
- ☐ Touched
- ☐ Warm

POSITIVE
- ☐ Anxious
- ☐ Bold
- ☐ Brave
- ☐ Challenged
- ☐ Confident
- ☐ Daring
- ☐ Determined
- ☐ Eager
- ☐ Earnest
- ☐ Enthusiastic
- ☐ Excited
- ☐ Hopeful
- ☐ Inspired
- ☐ Intent
- ☐ Keen
- ☐ Optimistic
- ☐ Re-enforced

GOOD
- ☐ At ease
- ☐ Blessed
- ☐ Bright
- ☐ Calm
- ☐ Certain
- ☐ Clever
- ☐ Comfortable
- ☐ Content
- ☐ Encouraged
- ☐ Free and easy
- ☐ Peaceful
- ☐ Pleased
- ☐ Quiet
- ☐ Reassured
- ☐ Relaxed
- ☐ Serene
- ☐ Surprised

HAPPY
- ☐ Cheerful
- ☐ Delighted
- ☐ Ecstatic
- ☐ Elated
- ☐ Festive
- ☐ Fortunate
- ☐ Glad
- ☐ Gleeful
- ☐ Great
- ☐ Important
- ☐ Joyous
- ☐ Jubilant
- ☐ Lucky
- ☐ Merry
- ☐ Overjoyed
- ☐ Satisfied
- ☐ Sunny
- ☐ Thankful

Read and check off ✓

Preparing to listen
- ☐ Remember to put your mind and feelings in neutral gear.
- ☐ Your body posture must say, *"I am open, very interested, affirmative, attentive."*
- ☐ Maintain good eye contact.
- ☐ Give the speaker a verbal door opening, showing your readiness to listen.

While Listening
- ☐ Track what the speaker is saying in both content and feeling levels
- ☐ Stay with the content of communication
- ☐ Listen for and identify the basic general feeling; anger, fear, joy, resentment, etc.
- ☐ Suspend judgment; open yourself to the presence of their heart.

Responding
- ☐ Use oral responses, which are affirming, which say, *"I am with you"*, *"I understand."*
- ☐ Feed general feelings back to the speaker. *"You seem to feel this has been a good experience for you"*
- ☐ Stay an inch ahead of the speaker, not a mile.

After completing this, go back to page 10 and re-evaluate your intimacy.

UNPLEASANT FEELINGS

😞 HELPLESS
- ☐ Alone
- ☐ Despair
- ☐ Distressed
- ☐ Dominated
- ☐ Empty
- ☐ Fatigued
- ☐ Forced
- ☐ Frustrated
- ☐ Hesitant
- ☐ In A Stew
- ☐ Incapable
- ☐ Inferior
- ☐ Paralyzed
- ☐ Pathetic
- ☐ Tragic
- ☐ Useless
- ☐ Vulnerable
- ☐ Woeful

😕 CONFUSED
- ☐ Disillusioned
- ☐ Distrustful
- ☐ Doubtful
- ☐ Embarrassed
- ☐ Hesitant
- ☐ Indecisive
- ☐ Lost
- ☐ Misgiving
- ☐ Perplexed
- ☐ Pessimistic
- ☐ Shy
- ☐ Skeptical
- ☐ Stupefied
- ☐ Tense
- ☐ Unbelieving
- ☐ Uncertain
- ☐ Uneasy
- ☐ Unsure
- ☐ Upset

😔 DEPRESSED
- ☐ A Sense of Loss
- ☐ Abominable
- ☐ Ashamed
- ☐ Bad
- ☐ Despicable
- ☐ Detestable
- ☐ Diminished
- ☐ Disappointed
- ☐ Discouraged
- ☐ Disgusting
- ☐ Dissatisfied
- ☐ Guilty
- ☐ In Despair
- ☐ Lousy
- ☐ Miserable
- ☐ Powerless
- ☐ Repugnant
- ☐ Sulky
- ☐ Terrible

😠 ANGRY
- ☐ Aggressive
- ☐ Annoyed
- ☐ Bitter
- ☐ Boiling
- ☐ Cross
- ☐ Enraged
- ☐ Fuming
- ☐ Hateful
- ☐ Hostile
- ☐ Incensed
- ☐ Inflamed
- ☐ Infuriated
- ☐ Insulting
- ☐ Irritated
- ☐ Offensive
- ☐ Provoked
- ☐ Resentful
- ☐ Sore
- ☐ Unpleasant
- ☐ Upset
- ☐ Worked Up

😢 SAD
- ☐ Anguish
- ☐ Desolate
- ☐ Desperate
- ☐ Dismayed
- ☐ Grief
- ☐ Grieved
- ☐ Lonely
- ☐ Mournful
- ☐ Pained
- ☐ Pessimistic
- ☐ Sorrowful
- ☐ Tearful
- ☐ Unhappy

😐 INDIFFERENT
- ☐ Bored
- ☐ Cold
- ☐ Disinterested
- ☐ Dull
- ☐ Insensitive
- ☐ Lifeless
- ☐ Neutral
- ☐ Nonchalant
- ☐ Preoccupied
- ☐ Reserved
- ☐ Weary

😨 AFRAID
- ☐ Alarmed
- ☐ Anxious
- ☐ Cowardly
- ☐ Doubtful
- ☐ Fearful
- ☐ Frightened
- ☐ Menaced
- ☐ Nervous
- ☐ Panic
- ☐ Quaking
- ☐ Restless
- ☐ Scared
- ☐ Shaky
- ☐ Suspicious
- ☐ Terrified
- ☐ Threatened
- ☐ Timid
- ☐ Wary
- ☐ Worried

😞 HURT
- ☐ Aching
- ☐ Afflicted
- ☐ Agonized
- ☐ Alienated
- ☐ Appalled
- ☐ Crushed
- ☐ Dejected
- ☐ Deprived
- ☐ Heartbroken
- ☐ Humiliated
- ☐ Injured
- ☐ Offended
- ☐ Pained
- ☐ Rejected
- ☐ Tormented
- ☐ Tortured
- ☐ Victimized
- ☐ Wronged

Notes: _____
_____
_____
_____

8 Pitfalls to avoid
- ☐ Me-too-ism. Don't start telling your story, or comparing your story to theirs.
- ☐ Moralizing, preaching, being judgmental
- ☐ Asking a direct question to satisfy your own curiosity
- ☐ Being an interviewer rather then a listener
- ☐ Giving advice (try fixing it)
- ☐ Cheap consolation. *"Oh, that's not to bad"*
- ☐ Arguing or disagreeing with the speaker
- ☐ Analyzing or interpreting
- ☐ Ignoring obvious heavy emotions

Date: _____

PLEASANT FEELINGS

OPEN
- ☐ Accepting
- ☐ Amazed
- ☐ Confident
- ☐ Easy
- ☐ Free
- ☐ Interested
- ☐ Kind
- ☐ Receptive
- ☐ Reliable
- ☐ Satisfied
- ☐ Sympathetic
- ☐ Understanding

INTERESTED
- ☐ Absorbed
- ☐ Affected
- ☐ Concerned
- ☐ Curious
- ☐ Engrossed
- ☐ Fascinated
- ☐ Inquisitive
- ☐ Intrigued
- ☐ Nosy
- ☐ Snoopy

ALIVE
- ☐ Animated
- ☐ Courageous
- ☐ Energetic
- ☐ Free
- ☐ Frisky
- ☐ Impulsive
- ☐ Liberated
- ☐ Optimistic
- ☐ Playful
- ☐ Provocative
- ☐ Spirited
- ☐ Thrilled
- ☐ Wonderful

STRONG
- ☐ Certain
- ☐ Dynamic
- ☐ Free
- ☐ Hardy
- ☐ Impulsive
- ☐ Rebellious
- ☐ Secure
- ☐ Sure
- ☐ Tenacious
- ☐ Unique

LOVE
- ☐ Admiration
- ☐ Affectionate
- ☐ Attracted
- ☐ Close
- ☐ Comforted
- ☐ Considerate
- ☐ Devoted
- ☐ Drawn toward
- ☐ Loved
- ☐ Loving
- ☐ Passionate
- ☐ Sensitive
- ☐ Sympathy
- ☐ Tender
- ☐ Touched
- ☐ Warm

POSITIVE
- ☐ Anxious
- ☐ Bold
- ☐ Brave
- ☐ Challenged
- ☐ Confident
- ☐ Daring
- ☐ Determined
- ☐ Eager
- ☐ Earnest
- ☐ Enthusiastic
- ☐ Excited
- ☐ Hopeful
- ☐ Inspired
- ☐ Intent
- ☐ Keen
- ☐ Optimistic
- ☐ Re-enforced

GOOD
- ☐ At ease
- ☐ Blessed
- ☐ Bright
- ☐ Calm
- ☐ Certain
- ☐ Clever
- ☐ Comfortable
- ☐ Content
- ☐ Encouraged
- ☐ Free and easy
- ☐ Peaceful
- ☐ Pleased
- ☐ Quiet
- ☐ Reassured
- ☐ Relaxed
- ☐ Serene
- ☐ Surprised

HAPPY
- ☐ Cheerful
- ☐ Delighted
- ☐ Ecstatic
- ☐ Elated
- ☐ Festive
- ☐ Fortunate
- ☐ Glad
- ☐ Gleeful
- ☐ Great
- ☐ Important
- ☐ Joyous
- ☐ Jubilant
- ☐ Lucky
- ☐ Merry
- ☐ Overjoyed
- ☐ Satisfied
- ☐ Sunny
- ☐ Thankful

Read and check off
✓

Preparing to listen
- ☐ Remember to put your mind and feelings in neutral gear.
- ☐ Your body posture must say, *"I am open, very interested, affirmative, attentive."*
- ☐ Maintain good eye contact.
- ☐ Give the speaker a verbal door opening, showing your readiness to listen.

While Listening
- ☐ Track what the speaker is saying in both content and feeling levels
- ☐ Stay with the content of communication
- ☐ Listen for and identify the basic general feeling; anger, fear, joy, resentment, etc.
- ☐ Suspend judgment; open yourself to the presence of their heart.

Responding
- ☐ Use oral responses, which are affirming, which say, *"I am with you"*, *"I understand."*
- ☐ Feed general feelings back to the speaker. *"You seem to feel this has been a good experience for you"*
- ☐ Stay an inch ahead of the speaker, not a mile.

UNPLEASANT FEELINGS

😕 HELPLESS
- ☐ Alone
- ☐ Despair
- ☐ Distressed
- ☐ Dominated
- ☐ Empty
- ☐ Fatigued
- ☐ Forced
- ☐ Frustrated
- ☐ Hesitant
- ☐ In A Stew
- ☐ Incapable
- ☐ Inferior
- ☐ Paralyzed
- ☐ Pathetic
- ☐ Tragic
- ☐ Useless
- ☐ Vulnerable
- ☐ Woeful

😕 CONFUSED
- ☐ Disillusioned
- ☐ Distrustful
- ☐ Doubtful
- ☐ Embarrassed
- ☐ Hesitant
- ☐ Indecisive
- ☐ Lost
- ☐ Misgiving
- ☐ Perplexed
- ☐ Pessimistic
- ☐ Shy
- ☐ Skeptical
- ☐ Stupefied
- ☐ Tense
- ☐ Unbelieving
- ☐ Uncertain
- ☐ Uneasy
- ☐ Unsure
- ☐ Upset

😞 DEPRESSED
- ☐ A Sense of Loss
- ☐ Abominable
- ☐ Ashamed
- ☐ Bad
- ☐ Despicable
- ☐ Detestable
- ☐ Diminished
- ☐ Disappointed
- ☐ Discouraged
- ☐ Disgusting
- ☐ Dissatisfied
- ☐ Guilty
- ☐ In Despair
- ☐ Lousy
- ☐ Miserable
- ☐ Powerless
- ☐ Repugnant
- ☐ Sulky
- ☐ Terrible

😠 ANGRY
- ☐ Aggressive
- ☐ Annoyed
- ☐ Bitter
- ☐ Boiling
- ☐ Cross
- ☐ Enraged
- ☐ Fuming
- ☐ Hateful
- ☐ Hostile
- ☐ Incensed
- ☐ Inflamed
- ☐ Infuriated
- ☐ Insulting
- ☐ Irritated
- ☐ Offensive
- ☐ Provoked
- ☐ Resentful
- ☐ Sore
- ☐ Unpleasant
- ☐ Upset
- ☐ Worked Up

😢 SAD
- ☐ Anguish
- ☐ Desolate
- ☐ Desperate
- ☐ Dismayed
- ☐ Grief
- ☐ Grieved
- ☐ Lonely
- ☐ Mournful
- ☐ Pained
- ☐ Pessimistic
- ☐ Sorrowful
- ☐ Tearful
- ☐ Unhappy

😐 INDIFFERENT
- ☐ Bored
- ☐ Cold
- ☐ Disinterested
- ☐ Dull
- ☐ Insensitive
- ☐ Lifeless
- ☐ Neutral
- ☐ Nonchalant
- ☐ Preoccupied
- ☐ Reserved
- ☐ Weary

😨 AFRAID
- ☐ Alarmed
- ☐ Anxious
- ☐ Cowardly
- ☐ Doubtful
- ☐ Fearful
- ☐ Frightened
- ☐ Menaced
- ☐ Nervous
- ☐ Panic
- ☐ Quaking
- ☐ Restless
- ☐ Scared
- ☐ Shaky
- ☐ Suspicious
- ☐ Terrified
- ☐ Threatened
- ☐ Timid
- ☐ Wary
- ☐ Worried

😟 HURT
- ☐ Aching
- ☐ Afflicted
- ☐ Agonized
- ☐ Alienated
- ☐ Appalled
- ☐ Crushed
- ☐ Dejected
- ☐ Deprived
- ☐ Heartbroken
- ☐ Humiliated
- ☐ Injured
- ☐ Offended
- ☐ Pained
- ☐ Rejected
- ☐ Tormented
- ☐ Tortured
- ☐ Victimized
- ☐ Wronged

Notes:
_____
_____
_____
_____

8 Pitfalls to avoid
- ☐ Me-too-ism. Don't start telling your story, or comparing your story to theirs.
- ☐ Moralizing, preaching, being judgmental
- ☐ Asking a direct question to satisfy your own curiosity
- ☐ Being an interviewer rather then a listener
- ☐ Giving advice (try fixing it)
- ☐ Cheap consolation. *"Oh, that's not to bad"*
- ☐ Arguing or disagreeing with the speaker
- ☐ Analyzing or interpreting
- ☐ Ignoring obvious heavy emotions

NOTE: Do the Opposite of good listening!
(What is your biggest fear and why?)

PLEASANT FEELINGS

😀 OPEN
- ☐ Accepting
- ☐ Amazed
- ☐ Confident
- ☐ Easy
- ☐ Free
- ☐ Interested
- ☐ Kind
- ☐ Receptive
- ☐ Reliable
- ☐ Satisfied
- ☐ Sympathetic
- ☐ Understanding

🤔 INTERESTED
- ☐ Absorbed
- ☐ Affected
- ☐ Concerned
- ☐ Curious
- ☐ Engrossed
- ☐ Fascinated
- ☐ Inquisitive
- ☐ Intrigued
- ☐ Nosy
- ☐ Snoopy

😊 ALIVE
- ☐ Animated
- ☐ Courageous
- ☐ Energetic
- ☐ Free
- ☐ Frisky
- ☐ Impulsive
- ☐ Liberated
- ☐ Optimistic
- ☐ Playful
- ☐ Provocative
- ☐ Spirited
- ☐ Thrilled
- ☐ Wonderful

😠 STRONG
- ☐ Certain
- ☐ Dynamic
- ☐ Free
- ☐ Hardy
- ☐ Impulsive
- ☐ Rebellious
- ☐ Secure
- ☐ Sure
- ☐ Tenacious
- ☐ Unique

👶 LOVE
- ☐ Admiration
- ☐ Affectionate
- ☐ Attracted
- ☐ Close
- ☐ Comforted
- ☐ Considerate
- ☐ Devoted
- ☐ Drawn toward
- ☐ Loved
- ☐ Loving
- ☐ Passionate
- ☐ Sensitive
- ☐ Sympathy
- ☐ Tender
- ☐ Touched
- ☐ Warm

🙂 POSITIVE
- ☐ Anxious
- ☐ Bold
- ☐ Brave
- ☐ Challenged
- ☐ Confident
- ☐ Daring
- ☐ Determined
- ☐ Eager
- ☐ Earnest
- ☐ Enthusiastic
- ☐ Excited
- ☐ Hopeful
- ☐ Inspired
- ☐ Intent
- ☐ Keen
- ☐ Optimistic
- ☐ Re-enforced

🙂 GOOD
- ☐ At ease
- ☐ Blessed
- ☐ Bright
- ☐ Calm
- ☐ Certain
- ☐ Clever
- ☐ Comfortable
- ☐ Content
- ☐ Encouraged
- ☐ Free and easy
- ☐ Peaceful
- ☐ Pleased
- ☐ Quiet
- ☐ Reassured
- ☐ Relaxed
- ☐ Serene
- ☐ Surprised

😊 HAPPY
- ☐ Cheerful
- ☐ Delighted
- ☐ Ecstatic
- ☐ Elated
- ☐ Festive
- ☐ Fortunate
- ☐ Glad
- ☐ Gleeful
- ☐ Great
- ☐ Important
- ☐ Joyous
- ☐ Jubilant
- ☐ Lucky
- ☐ Merry
- ☐ Overjoyed
- ☐ Satisfied
- ☐ Sunny
- ☐ Thankful

Read and check off
✓

Preparing to listen
- ☐ Remember to put your mind and feelings in neutral gear.
- ☐ Your body posture must say, *"I am open, very interested, affirmative, attentive."*
- ☐ Maintain good eye contact.
- ☐ Give the speaker a verbal door opening, showing your readiness to listen.

While Listening
- ☐ Track what the speaker is saying in both content and feeling levels
- ☐ Stay with the content of communication
- ☐ Listen for and identify the basic general feeling; anger, fear, joy, resentment, etc.
- ☐ Suspend judgment; open yourself to the presence of their heart.

Responding
- ☐ Use oral responses, which are affirming, which say, *"I am with you", "I understand."*
- ☐ Feed general feelings back to the speaker. *"You seem to feel this has been a good experience for you"*
- ☐ Stay an inch ahead of the speaker, not a mile.

UNPLEASANT FEELINGS

HELPLESS
- ☐ Alone
- ☐ Despair
- ☐ Distressed
- ☐ Dominated
- ☐ Empty
- ☐ Fatigued
- ☐ Forced
- ☐ Frustrated
- ☐ Hesitant
- ☐ In A Stew
- ☐ Incapable
- ☐ Inferior
- ☐ Paralyzed
- ☐ Pathetic
- ☐ Tragic
- ☐ Useless
- ☐ Vulnerable
- ☐ Woeful

CONFUSED
- ☐ Disillusioned
- ☐ Distrustful
- ☐ Doubtful
- ☐ Embarrassed
- ☐ Hesitant
- ☐ Indecisive
- ☐ Lost
- ☐ Misgiving
- ☐ Perplexed
- ☐ Pessimistic
- ☐ Shy
- ☐ Skeptical
- ☐ Stupefied
- ☐ Tense
- ☐ Unbelieving
- ☐ Uncertain
- ☐ Uneasy
- ☐ Unsure
- ☐ Upset

DEPRESSED
- ☐ A Sense of Loss
- ☐ Abominable
- ☐ Ashamed
- ☐ Bad
- ☐ Despicable
- ☐ Detestable
- ☐ Diminished
- ☐ Disappointed
- ☐ Discouraged
- ☐ Disgusting
- ☐ Dissatisfied
- ☐ Guilty
- ☐ In Despair
- ☐ Lousy
- ☐ Miserable
- ☐ Powerless
- ☐ Repugnant
- ☐ Sulky
- ☐ Terrible

ANGRY
- ☐ Aggressive
- ☐ Annoyed
- ☐ Bitter
- ☐ Boiling
- ☐ Cross
- ☐ Enraged
- ☐ Fuming
- ☐ Hateful
- ☐ Hostile
- ☐ Incensed
- ☐ Inflamed
- ☐ Infuriated
- ☐ Insulting
- ☐ Irritated
- ☐ Offensive
- ☐ Provoked
- ☐ Resentful
- ☐ Sore
- ☐ Unpleasant
- ☐ Upset
- ☐ Worked Up

SAD
- ☐ Anguish
- ☐ Desolate
- ☐ Desperate
- ☐ Dismayed
- ☐ Grief
- ☐ Grieved
- ☐ Lonely
- ☐ Mournful
- ☐ Pained
- ☐ Pessimistic
- ☐ Sorrowful
- ☐ Tearful
- ☐ Unhappy

INDIFFERENT
- ☐ Bored
- ☐ Cold
- ☐ Disinterested
- ☐ Dull
- ☐ Insensitive
- ☐ Lifeless
- ☐ Neutral
- ☐ Nonchalant
- ☐ Preoccupied
- ☐ Reserved
- ☐ Weary

AFRAID
- ☐ Alarmed
- ☐ Anxious
- ☐ Cowardly
- ☐ Doubtful
- ☐ Fearful
- ☐ Frightened
- ☐ Menaced
- ☐ Nervous
- ☐ Panic
- ☐ Quaking
- ☐ Restless
- ☐ Scared
- ☐ Shaky
- ☐ Suspicious
- ☐ Terrified
- ☐ Threatened
- ☐ Timid
- ☐ Wary
- ☐ Worried

HURT
- ☐ Aching
- ☐ Afflicted
- ☐ Agonized
- ☐ Alienated
- ☐ Appalled
- ☐ Crushed
- ☐ Dejected
- ☐ Deprived
- ☐ Heartbroken
- ☐ Humiliated
- ☐ Injured
- ☐ Offended
- ☐ Pained
- ☐ Rejected
- ☐ Tormented
- ☐ Tortured
- ☐ Victimized
- ☐ Wronged

Notes: _____
_____
_____
_____

8 Pitfalls to avoid
- ☐ Me-too-ism. Don't start telling your story, or comparing your story to theirs.
- ☐ Moralizing, preaching, being judgmental
- ☐ Asking a direct question to satisfy your own curiosity
- ☐ Being an interviewer rather then a listener
- ☐ Giving advice (try fixing it)
- ☐ Cheap consolation. *"Oh, that's not to bad"*
- ☐ Arguing or disagreeing with the speaker
- ☐ Analyzing or interpreting
- ☐ Ignoring obvious heavy emotions

Date: _____

PLEASANT FEELINGS

OPEN
- ☐ Accepting
- ☐ Amazed
- ☐ Confident
- ☐ Easy
- ☐ Free
- ☐ Interested
- ☐ Kind
- ☐ Receptive
- ☐ Reliable
- ☐ Satisfied
- ☐ Sympathetic
- ☐ Understanding

INTERESTED
- ☐ Absorbed
- ☐ Affected
- ☐ Concerned
- ☐ Curious
- ☐ Engrossed
- ☐ Fascinated
- ☐ Inquisitive
- ☐ Intrigued
- ☐ Nosy
- ☐ Snoopy

ALIVE
- ☐ Animated
- ☐ Courageous
- ☐ Energetic
- ☐ Free
- ☐ Frisky
- ☐ Impulsive
- ☐ Liberated
- ☐ Optimistic
- ☐ Playful
- ☐ Provocative
- ☐ Spirited
- ☐ Thrilled
- ☐ Wonderful

STRONG
- ☐ Certain
- ☐ Dynamic
- ☐ Free
- ☐ Hardy
- ☐ Impulsive
- ☐ Rebellious
- ☐ Secure
- ☐ Sure
- ☐ Tenacious
- ☐ Unique

LOVE
- ☐ Admiration
- ☐ Affectionate
- ☐ Attracted
- ☐ Close
- ☐ Comforted
- ☐ Considerate
- ☐ Devoted
- ☐ Drawn toward
- ☐ Loved
- ☐ Loving
- ☐ Passionate
- ☐ Sensitive
- ☐ Sympathy
- ☐ Tender
- ☐ Touched
- ☐ Warm

POSITIVE
- ☐ Anxious
- ☐ Bold
- ☐ Brave
- ☐ Challenged
- ☐ Confident
- ☐ Daring
- ☐ Determined
- ☐ Eager
- ☐ Earnest
- ☐ Enthusiastic
- ☐ Excited
- ☐ Hopeful
- ☐ Inspired
- ☐ Intent
- ☐ Keen
- ☐ Optimistic
- ☐ Re-enforced

GOOD
- ☐ At ease
- ☐ Blessed
- ☐ Bright
- ☐ Calm
- ☐ Certain
- ☐ Clever
- ☐ Comfortable
- ☐ Content
- ☐ Encouraged
- ☐ Free and easy
- ☐ Peaceful
- ☐ Pleased
- ☐ Quiet
- ☐ Reassured
- ☐ Relaxed
- ☐ Serene
- ☐ Surprised

HAPPY
- ☐ Cheerful
- ☐ Delighted
- ☐ Ecstatic
- ☐ Elated
- ☐ Festive
- ☐ Fortunate
- ☐ Glad
- ☐ Gleeful
- ☐ Great
- ☐ Important
- ☐ Joyous
- ☐ Jubilant
- ☐ Lucky
- ☐ Merry
- ☐ Overjoyed
- ☐ Satisfied
- ☐ Sunny
- ☐ Thankful

Read and check off
✓

Preparing to listen
- ☐ Remember to put your mind and feelings in neutral gear.
- ☐ Your body posture must say, *"I am open, very interested, affirmative, attentive."*
- ☐ Maintain good eye contact.
- ☐ Give the speaker a verbal door opening, showing your readiness to listen.

While Listening
- ☐ Track what the speaker is saying in both content and feeling levels
- ☐ Stay with the content of communication
- ☐ Listen for and identify the basic general feeling; anger, fear, joy, resentment, etc.
- ☐ Suspend judgment; open yourself to the presence of their heart.

Responding
- ☐ Use oral responses, which are affirming, which say, *"I am with you", "I understand."*
- ☐ Feed general feelings back to the speaker. *"You seem to feel this has been a good experience for you"*
- ☐ Stay an inch ahead of the speaker, not a mile.

UNPLEASANT FEELINGS

HELPLESS
- ☐ Alone
- ☐ Despair
- ☐ Distressed
- ☐ Dominated
- ☐ Empty
- ☐ Fatigued
- ☐ Forced
- ☐ Frustrated
- ☐ Hesitant
- ☐ In A Stew
- ☐ Incapable
- ☐ Inferior
- ☐ Paralyzed
- ☐ Pathetic
- ☐ Tragic
- ☐ Useless
- ☐ Vulnerable
- ☐ Woeful

CONFUSED
- ☐ Disillusioned
- ☐ Distrustful
- ☐ Doubtful
- ☐ Embarrassed
- ☐ Hesitant
- ☐ Indecisive
- ☐ Lost
- ☐ Misgiving
- ☐ Perplexed
- ☐ Pessimistic
- ☐ Shy
- ☐ Skeptical
- ☐ Stupefied
- ☐ Tense
- ☐ Unbelieving
- ☐ Uncertain
- ☐ Uneasy
- ☐ Unsure
- ☐ Upset

DEPRESSED
- ☐ A Sense of Loss
- ☐ Abominable
- ☐ Ashamed
- ☐ Bad
- ☐ Despicable
- ☐ Detestable
- ☐ Diminished
- ☐ Disappointed
- ☐ Discouraged
- ☐ Disgusting
- ☐ Dissatisfied
- ☐ Guilty
- ☐ In Despair
- ☐ Lousy
- ☐ Miserable
- ☐ Powerless
- ☐ Repugnant
- ☐ Sulky
- ☐ Terrible

ANGRY
- ☐ Aggressive
- ☐ Annoyed
- ☐ Bitter
- ☐ Boiling
- ☐ Cross
- ☐ Enraged
- ☐ Fuming
- ☐ Hateful
- ☐ Hostile
- ☐ Incensed
- ☐ Inflamed
- ☐ Infuriated
- ☐ Insulting
- ☐ Irritated
- ☐ Offensive
- ☐ Provoked
- ☐ Resentful
- ☐ Sore
- ☐ Unpleasant
- ☐ Upset
- ☐ Worked Up

SAD
- ☐ Anguish
- ☐ Desolate
- ☐ Desperate
- ☐ Dismayed
- ☐ Grief
- ☐ Grieved
- ☐ Lonely
- ☐ Mournful
- ☐ Pained
- ☐ Pessimistic
- ☐ Sorrowful
- ☐ Tearful
- ☐ Unhappy

INDIFFERENT
- ☐ Bored
- ☐ Cold
- ☐ Disinterested
- ☐ Dull
- ☐ Insensitive
- ☐ Lifeless
- ☐ Neutral
- ☐ Nonchalant
- ☐ Preoccupied
- ☐ Reserved
- ☐ Weary

AFRAID
- ☐ Alarmed
- ☐ Anxious
- ☐ Cowardly
- ☐ Doubtful
- ☐ Fearful
- ☐ Frightened
- ☐ Menaced
- ☐ Nervous
- ☐ Panic
- ☐ Quaking
- ☐ Restless
- ☐ Scared
- ☐ Shaky
- ☐ Suspicious
- ☐ Terrified
- ☐ Threatened
- ☐ Timid
- ☐ Wary
- ☐ Worried

HURT
- ☐ Aching
- ☐ Afflicted
- ☐ Agonized
- ☐ Alienated
- ☐ Appalled
- ☐ Crushed
- ☐ Dejected
- ☐ Deprived
- ☐ Heartbroken
- ☐ Humiliated
- ☐ Injured
- ☐ Offended
- ☐ Pained
- ☐ Rejected
- ☐ Tormented
- ☐ Tortured
- ☐ Victimized
- ☐ Wronged

Notes: _____
_____
_____
_____

8 Pitfalls to avoid

- ☐ Me-too-ism. Don't start telling your story, or comparing your story to theirs.
- ☐ Moralizing, preaching, being judgmental
- ☐ Asking a direct question to satisfy your own curiosity
- ☐ Being an interviewer rather then a listener
- ☐ Giving advice (try fixing it)
- ☐ Cheap consolation. *"Oh, that's not to bad"*
- ☐ Arguing or disagreeing with the speaker
- ☐ Analyzing or interpreting
- ☐ Ignoring obvious heavy emotions

Date: _____

PLEASANT FEELINGS

OPEN
- ☐ Accepting
- ☐ Amazed
- ☐ Confident
- ☐ Easy
- ☐ Free
- ☐ Interested
- ☐ Kind
- ☐ Receptive
- ☐ Reliable
- ☐ Satisfied
- ☐ Sympathetic
- ☐ Understanding

INTERESTED
- ☐ Absorbed
- ☐ Affected
- ☐ Concerned
- ☐ Curious
- ☐ Engrossed
- ☐ Fascinated
- ☐ Inquisitive
- ☐ Intrigued
- ☐ Nosy
- ☐ Snoopy

ALIVE
- ☐ Animated
- ☐ Courageous
- ☐ Energetic
- ☐ Free
- ☐ Frisky
- ☐ Impulsive
- ☐ Liberated
- ☐ Optimistic
- ☐ Playful
- ☐ Provocative
- ☐ Spirited
- ☐ Thrilled
- ☐ Wonderful

STRONG
- ☐ Certain
- ☐ Dynamic
- ☐ Free
- ☐ Hardy
- ☐ Impulsive
- ☐ Rebellious
- ☐ Secure
- ☐ Sure
- ☐ Tenacious
- ☐ Unique

LOVE
- ☐ Admiration
- ☐ Affectionate
- ☐ Attracted
- ☐ Close
- ☐ Comforted
- ☐ Considerate
- ☐ Devoted
- ☐ Drawn toward
- ☐ Loved
- ☐ Loving
- ☐ Passionate
- ☐ Sensitive
- ☐ Sympathy
- ☐ Tender
- ☐ Touched
- ☐ Warm

POSITIVE
- ☐ Anxious
- ☐ Bold
- ☐ Brave
- ☐ Challenged
- ☐ Confident
- ☐ Daring
- ☐ Determined
- ☐ Eager
- ☐ Earnest
- ☐ Enthusiastic
- ☐ Excited
- ☐ Hopeful
- ☐ Inspired
- ☐ Intent
- ☐ Keen
- ☐ Optimistic
- ☐ Re-enforced

GOOD
- ☐ At ease
- ☐ Blessed
- ☐ Bright
- ☐ Calm
- ☐ Certain
- ☐ Clever
- ☐ Comfortable
- ☐ Content
- ☐ Encouraged
- ☐ Free and easy
- ☐ Peaceful
- ☐ Pleased
- ☐ Quiet
- ☐ Reassured
- ☐ Relaxed
- ☐ Serene
- ☐ Surprised

HAPPY
- ☐ Cheerful
- ☐ Delighted
- ☐ Ecstatic
- ☐ Elated
- ☐ Festive
- ☐ Fortunate
- ☐ Glad
- ☐ Gleeful
- ☐ Great
- ☐ Important
- ☐ Joyous
- ☐ Jubilant
- ☐ Lucky
- ☐ Merry
- ☐ Overjoyed
- ☐ Satisfied
- ☐ Sunny
- ☐ Thankful

Read and check off
✓

Preparing to listen
- ☐ Remember to put your mind and feelings in neutral gear.
- ☐ Your body posture must say, *"I' am open, very interested, affirmative, attentive."*
- ☐ Maintain good eye contact.
- ☐ Give the speaker a verbal door opening, showing your readiness to listen.

While Listening
- ☐ Track what the speaker is saying in both content and feeling levels
- ☐ Stay with the content of communication
- ☐ Listen for and identify the basic general feeling; anger, fear, joy, resentment, etc.
- ☐ Suspend judgment; open yourself to the presence of their heart.

Responding
- ☐ Use oral responses, which are affirming, which say, *"I am with you"*, *"I understand."*
- ☐ Feed general feelings back to the speaker. *"You seem to feel this has been a good experience for you"*
- ☐ Stay an inch ahead of the speaker, not a mile.

UNPLEASANT FEELINGS

☺ HELPLESS
- ☐ Alone
- ☐ Despair
- ☐ Distressed
- ☐ Dominated
- ☐ Empty
- ☐ Fatigued
- ☐ Forced
- ☐ Frustrated
- ☐ Hesitant
- ☐ In A Stew
- ☐ Incapable
- ☐ Inferior
- ☐ Paralyzed
- ☐ Pathetic
- ☐ Tragic
- ☐ Useless
- ☐ Vulnerable
- ☐ Woeful

☺ CONFUSED
- ☐ Disillusioned
- ☐ Distrustful
- ☐ Doubtful
- ☐ Embarrassed
- ☐ Hesitant
- ☐ Indecisive
- ☐ Lost
- ☐ Misgiving
- ☐ Perplexed
- ☐ Pessimistic
- ☐ Shy
- ☐ Skeptical
- ☐ Stupefied
- ☐ Tense
- ☐ Unbelieving
- ☐ Uncertain
- ☐ Uneasy
- ☐ Unsure
- ☐ Upset

☺ DEPRESSED
- ☐ A Sense of Loss
- ☐ Abominable
- ☐ Ashamed
- ☐ Bad
- ☐ Despicable
- ☐ Detestable
- ☐ Diminished
- ☐ Disappointed
- ☐ Discouraged
- ☐ Disgusting
- ☐ Dissatisfied
- ☐ Guilty
- ☐ In Despair
- ☐ Lousy
- ☐ Miserable
- ☐ Powerless
- ☐ Repugnant
- ☐ Sulky
- ☐ Terrible

☺ ANGRY
- ☐ Aggressive
- ☐ Annoyed
- ☐ Bitter
- ☐ Boiling
- ☐ Cross
- ☐ Enraged
- ☐ Fuming
- ☐ Hateful
- ☐ Hostile
- ☐ Incensed
- ☐ Inflamed
- ☐ Infuriated
- ☐ Insulting
- ☐ Irritated
- ☐ Offensive
- ☐ Provoked
- ☐ Resentful
- ☐ Sore
- ☐ Unpleasant
- ☐ Upset
- ☐ Worked Up

☺ SAD
- ☐ Anguish
- ☐ Desolate
- ☐ Desperate
- ☐ Dismayed
- ☐ Grief
- ☐ Grieved
- ☐ Lonely
- ☐ Mournful
- ☐ Pained
- ☐ Pessimistic
- ☐ Sorrowful
- ☐ Tearful
- ☐ Unhappy

☺ INDIFFERENT
- ☐ Bored
- ☐ Cold
- ☐ Disinterested
- ☐ Dull
- ☐ Insensitive
- ☐ Lifeless
- ☐ Neutral
- ☐ Nonchalant
- ☐ Preoccupied
- ☐ Reserved
- ☐ Weary

☺ AFRAID
- ☐ Alarmed
- ☐ Anxious
- ☐ Cowardly
- ☐ Doubtful
- ☐ Fearful
- ☐ Frightened
- ☐ Menaced
- ☐ Nervous
- ☐ Panic
- ☐ Quaking
- ☐ Restless
- ☐ Scared
- ☐ Shaky
- ☐ Suspicious
- ☐ Terrified
- ☐ Threatened
- ☐ Timid
- ☐ Wary
- ☐ Worried

☺ HURT
- ☐ Aching
- ☐ Afflicted
- ☐ Agonized
- ☐ Alienated
- ☐ Appalled
- ☐ Crushed
- ☐ Dejected
- ☐ Deprived
- ☐ Heartbroken
- ☐ Humiliated
- ☐ Injured
- ☐ Offended
- ☐ Pained
- ☐ Rejected
- ☐ Tormented
- ☐ Tortured
- ☐ Victimized
- ☐ Wronged

Notes: _____
_____
_____

8 Pitfalls to avoid
- ☐ Me-too-ism. Don't start telling your story, or comparing your story to theirs.
- ☐ Moralizing, preaching, being judgmental
- ☐ Asking a direct question to satisfy your own curiosity
- ☐ Being an interviewer rather then a listener
- ☐ Giving advice (try fixing it)
- ☐ Cheap consolation. *"Oh, that's not to bad"*
- ☐ Arguing or disagreeing with the speaker
- ☐ Analyzing or interpreting
- ☐ Ignoring obvious heavy emotions

Date: _____

PLEASANT FEELINGS

OPEN	INTERESTED	ALIVE	STRONG
☐ Accepting	☐ Absorbed	☐ Animated	☐ Certain
☐ Amazed	☐ Affected	☐ Courageous	☐ Dynamic
☐ Confident	☐ Concerned	☐ Energetic	☐ Free
☐ Easy	☐ Curious	☐ Free	☐ Hardy
☐ Free	☐ Engrossed	☐ Frisky	☐ Impulsive
☐ Interested	☐ Fascinated	☐ Impulsive	☐ Rebellious
☐ Kind	☐ Inquisitive	☐ Liberated	☐ Secure
☐ Receptive	☐ Intrigued	☐ Optimistic	☐ Sure
☐ Reliable	☐ Nosy	☐ Playful	☐ Tenacious
☐ Satisfied	☐ Snoopy	☐ Provocative	☐ Unique
☐ Sympathetic		☐ Spirited	
☐ Understanding		☐ Thrilled	
		☐ Wonderful	

LOVE	POSITIVE	GOOD	HAPPY
☐ Admiration	☐ Anxious	☐ At ease	☐ Cheerful
☐ Affectionate	☐ Bold	☐ Blessed	☐ Delighted
☐ Attracted	☐ Brave	☐ Bright	☐ Ecstatic
☐ Close	☐ Challenged	☐ Calm	☐ Elated
☐ Comforted	☐ Confident	☐ Certain	☐ Festive
☐ Considerate	☐ Daring	☐ Clever	☐ Fortunate
☐ Devoted	☐ Determined	☐ Comfortable	☐ Glad
☐ Drawn toward	☐ Eager	☐ Content	☐ Gleeful
☐ Loved	☐ Earnest	☐ Encouraged	☐ Great
☐ Loving	☐ Enthusiastic	☐ Free and easy	☐ Important
☐ Passionate	☐ Excited	☐ Peaceful	☐ Joyous
☐ Sensitive	☐ Hopeful	☐ Pleased	☐ Jubilant
☐ Sympathy	☐ Inspired	☐ Quiet	☐ Lucky
☐ Tender	☐ Intent	☐ Reassured	☐ Merry
☐ Touched	☐ Keen	☐ Relaxed	☐ Overjoyed
☐ Warm	☐ Optimistic	☐ Serene	☐ Satisfied
	☐ Re-enforced	☐ Surprised	☐ Sunny
			☐ Thankful

Read and check off
✓

Preparing to listen
- ☐ Remember to put your mind and feelings in neutral gear.
- ☐ Your body posture must say, *"I' am open, very interested, affirmative, attentive."*
- ☐ Maintain good eye contact.
- ☐ Give the speaker a verbal door opening, showing your readiness to listen.

While Listening
- ☐ Track what the speaker is saying in both content and feeling levels
- ☐ Stay with the content of communication
- ☐ Listen for and identify the basic general feeling; anger, fear, joy, resentment, etc.
- ☐ Suspend judgment; open yourself to the presence of their heart.

Responding
- ☐ Use oral responses, which are affirming, which say, *"I am with you", "I understand."*
- ☐ Feed general feelings back to the speaker. *"You seem to feel this has been a good experience for you"*
- ☐ Stay an inch ahead of the speaker, not a mile.

UNPLEASANT FEELINGS

😳 HELPLESS
- ☐ Alone
- ☐ Despair
- ☐ Distressed
- ☐ Dominated
- ☐ Empty
- ☐ Fatigued
- ☐ Forced
- ☐ Frustrated
- ☐ Hesitant
- ☐ In A Stew
- ☐ Incapable
- ☐ Inferior
- ☐ Paralyzed
- ☐ Pathetic
- ☐ Tragic
- ☐ Useless
- ☐ Vulnerable
- ☐ Woeful

😕 CONFUSED
- ☐ Disillusioned
- ☐ Distrustful
- ☐ Doubtful
- ☐ Embarrassed
- ☐ Hesitant
- ☐ Indecisive
- ☐ Lost
- ☐ Misgiving
- ☐ Perplexed
- ☐ Pessimistic
- ☐ Shy
- ☐ Skeptical
- ☐ Stupefied
- ☐ Tense
- ☐ Unbelieving
- ☐ Uncertain
- ☐ Uneasy
- ☐ Unsure
- ☐ Upset

😞 DEPRESSED
- ☐ A Sense of Loss
- ☐ Abominable
- ☐ Ashamed
- ☐ Bad
- ☐ Despicable
- ☐ Detestable
- ☐ Diminished
- ☐ Disappointed
- ☐ Discouraged
- ☐ Disgusting
- ☐ Dissatisfied
- ☐ Guilty
- ☐ In Despair
- ☐ Lousy
- ☐ Miserable
- ☐ Powerless
- ☐ Repugnant
- ☐ Sulky
- ☐ Terrible

😠 ANGRY
- ☐ Aggressive
- ☐ Annoyed
- ☐ Bitter
- ☐ Boiling
- ☐ Cross
- ☐ Enraged
- ☐ Fuming
- ☐ Hateful
- ☐ Hostile
- ☐ Incensed
- ☐ Inflamed
- ☐ Infuriated
- ☐ Insulting
- ☐ Irritated
- ☐ Offensive
- ☐ Provoked
- ☐ Resentful
- ☐ Sore
- ☐ Unpleasant
- ☐ Upset
- ☐ Worked Up

😢 SAD
- ☐ Anguish
- ☐ Desolate
- ☐ Desperate
- ☐ Dismayed
- ☐ Grief
- ☐ Grieved
- ☐ Lonely
- ☐ Mournful
- ☐ Pained
- ☐ Pessimistic
- ☐ Sorrowful
- ☐ Tearful
- ☐ Unhappy

😑 INDIFFERENT
- ☐ Bored
- ☐ Cold
- ☐ Disinterested
- ☐ Dull
- ☐ Insensitive
- ☐ Lifeless
- ☐ Neutral
- ☐ Nonchalant
- ☐ Preoccupied
- ☐ Reserved
- ☐ Weary

😨 AFRAID
- ☐ Alarmed
- ☐ Anxious
- ☐ Cowardly
- ☐ Doubtful
- ☐ Fearful
- ☐ Frightened
- ☐ Menaced
- ☐ Nervous
- ☐ Panic
- ☐ Quaking
- ☐ Restless
- ☐ Scared
- ☐ Shaky
- ☐ Suspicious
- ☐ Terrified
- ☐ Threatened
- ☐ Timid
- ☐ Wary
- ☐ Worried

😟 HURT
- ☐ Aching
- ☐ Afflicted
- ☐ Agonized
- ☐ Alienated
- ☐ Appalled
- ☐ Crushed
- ☐ Dejected
- ☐ Deprived
- ☐ Heartbroken
- ☐ Humiliated
- ☐ Injured
- ☐ Offended
- ☐ Pained
- ☐ Rejected
- ☐ Tormented
- ☐ Tortured
- ☐ Victimized
- ☐ Wronged

Notes: _____
_____
_____

8 Pitfalls to avoid

- ☐ Me-too-ism. Don't start telling your story, or comparing your story to theirs.
- ☐ Moralizing, preaching, being judgmental
- ☐ Asking a direct question to satisfy your own curiosity
- ☐ Being an interviewer rather then a listener
- ☐ Giving advice (try fixing it)
- ☐ Cheap consolation. *"Oh, that's not to bad"*
- ☐ Arguing or disagreeing with the speaker
- ☐ Analyzing or interpreting
- ☐ Ignoring obvious heavy emotions

Date: _____

PLEASANT FEELINGS

☺☺ OPEN
- ☐ Accepting
- ☐ Amazed
- ☐ Confident
- ☐ Easy
- ☐ Free
- ☐ Interested
- ☐ Kind
- ☐ Receptive
- ☐ Reliable
- ☐ Satisfied
- ☐ Sympathetic
- ☐ Understanding

☺ INTERESTED
- ☐ Absorbed
- ☐ Affected
- ☐ Concerned
- ☐ Curious
- ☐ Engrossed
- ☐ Fascinated
- ☐ Inquisitive
- ☐ Intrigued
- ☐ Nosy
- ☐ Snoopy

☺ ALIVE
- ☐ Animated
- ☐ Courageous
- ☐ Energetic
- ☐ Free
- ☐ Frisky
- ☐ Impulsive
- ☐ Liberated
- ☐ Optimistic
- ☐ Playful
- ☐ Provocative
- ☐ Spirited
- ☐ Thrilled
- ☐ Wonderful

☺ STRONG
- ☐ Certain
- ☐ Dynamic
- ☐ Free
- ☐ Hardy
- ☐ Impulsive
- ☐ Rebellious
- ☐ Secure
- ☐ Sure
- ☐ Tenacious
- ☐ Unique

☺ LOVE
- ☐ Admiration
- ☐ Affectionate
- ☐ Attracted
- ☐ Close
- ☐ Comforted
- ☐ Considerate
- ☐ Devoted
- ☐ Drawn toward
- ☐ Loved
- ☐ Loving
- ☐ Passionate
- ☐ Sensitive
- ☐ Sympathy
- ☐ Tender
- ☐ Touched
- ☐ Warm

☺ POSITIVE
- ☐ Anxious
- ☐ Bold
- ☐ Brave
- ☐ Challenged
- ☐ Confident
- ☐ Daring
- ☐ Determined
- ☐ Eager
- ☐ Earnest
- ☐ Enthusiastic
- ☐ Excited
- ☐ Hopeful
- ☐ Inspired
- ☐ Intent
- ☐ Keen
- ☐ Optimistic
- ☐ Re-enforced

☺ GOOD
- ☐ At ease
- ☐ Blessed
- ☐ Bright
- ☐ Calm
- ☐ Certain
- ☐ Clever
- ☐ Comfortable
- ☐ Content
- ☐ Encouraged
- ☐ Free and easy
- ☐ Peaceful
- ☐ Pleased
- ☐ Quiet
- ☐ Reassured
- ☐ Relaxed
- ☐ Serene
- ☐ Surprised

☺ HAPPY
- ☐ Cheerful
- ☐ Delighted
- ☐ Ecstatic
- ☐ Elated
- ☐ Festive
- ☐ Fortunate
- ☐ Glad
- ☐ Gleeful
- ☐ Great
- ☐ Important
- ☐ Joyous
- ☐ Jubilant
- ☐ Lucky
- ☐ Merry
- ☐ Overjoyed
- ☐ Satisfied
- ☐ Sunny
- ☐ Thankful

Read and check off
✓

Preparing to listen
- ☐ Remember to put your mind and feelings in neutral gear.
- ☐ Your body posture must say, *"I am open, very interested, affirmative, attentive."*
- ☐ Maintain good eye contact.
- ☐ Give the speaker a verbal door opening, showing your readiness to listen.

While Listening
- ☐ Track what the speaker is saying in both content and feeling levels
- ☐ Stay with the content of communication
- ☐ Listen for and identify the basic general feeling; anger, fear, joy, resentment, etc.
- ☐ Suspend judgment; open yourself to the presence of their heart.

Responding
- ☐ Use oral responses, which are affirming, which say, *"I am with you"*, *"I understand."*
- ☐ Feed general feelings back to the speaker. *"You seem to feel this has been a good experience for you"*
- ☐ Stay an inch ahead of the speaker, not a mile.

UNPLEASANT FEELINGS

😮 HELPLESS
- ☐ Alone
- ☐ Despair
- ☐ Distressed
- ☐ Dominated
- ☐ Empty
- ☐ Fatigued
- ☐ Forced
- ☐ Frustrated
- ☐ Hesitant
- ☐ In A Stew
- ☐ Incapable
- ☐ Inferior
- ☐ Paralyzed
- ☐ Pathetic
- ☐ Tragic
- ☐ Useless
- ☐ Vulnerable
- ☐ Woeful

😕 CONFUSED
- ☐ Disillusioned
- ☐ Distrustful
- ☐ Doubtful
- ☐ Embarrassed
- ☐ Hesitant
- ☐ Indecisive
- ☐ Lost
- ☐ Misgiving
- ☐ Perplexed
- ☐ Pessimistic
- ☐ Shy
- ☐ Skeptical
- ☐ Stupefied
- ☐ Tense
- ☐ Unbelieving
- ☐ Uncertain
- ☐ Uneasy
- ☐ Unsure
- ☐ Upset

😞 DEPRESSED
- ☐ A Sense of Loss
- ☐ Abominable
- ☐ Ashamed
- ☐ Bad
- ☐ Despicable
- ☐ Detestable
- ☐ Diminished
- ☐ Disappointed
- ☐ Discouraged
- ☐ Disgusting
- ☐ Dissatisfied
- ☐ Guilty
- ☐ In Despair
- ☐ Lousy
- ☐ Miserable
- ☐ Powerless
- ☐ Repugnant
- ☐ Sulky
- ☐ Terrible

😠 ANGRY
- ☐ Aggressive
- ☐ Annoyed
- ☐ Bitter
- ☐ Boiling
- ☐ Cross
- ☐ Enraged
- ☐ Fuming
- ☐ Hateful
- ☐ Hostile
- ☐ Incensed
- ☐ Inflamed
- ☐ Infuriated
- ☐ Insulting
- ☐ Irritated
- ☐ Offensive
- ☐ Provoked
- ☐ Resentful
- ☐ Sore
- ☐ Unpleasant
- ☐ Upset
- ☐ Worked Up

😢 SAD
- ☐ Anguish
- ☐ Desolate
- ☐ Desperate
- ☐ Dismayed
- ☐ Grief
- ☐ Grieved
- ☐ Lonely
- ☐ Mournful
- ☐ Pained
- ☐ Pessimistic
- ☐ Sorrowful
- ☐ Tearful
- ☐ Unhappy

😐 INDIFFERENT
- ☐ Bored
- ☐ Cold
- ☐ Disinterested
- ☐ Dull
- ☐ Insensitive
- ☐ Lifeless
- ☐ Neutral
- ☐ Nonchalant
- ☐ Preoccupied
- ☐ Reserved
- ☐ Weary

😨 AFRAID
- ☐ Alarmed
- ☐ Anxious
- ☐ Cowardly
- ☐ Doubtful
- ☐ Fearful
- ☐ Frightened
- ☐ Menaced
- ☐ Nervous
- ☐ Panic
- ☐ Quaking
- ☐ Restless
- ☐ Scared
- ☐ Shaky
- ☐ Suspicious
- ☐ Terrified
- ☐ Threatened
- ☐ Timid
- ☐ Wary
- ☐ Worried

😟 HURT
- ☐ Aching
- ☐ Afflicted
- ☐ Agonized
- ☐ Alienated
- ☐ Appalled
- ☐ Crushed
- ☐ Dejected
- ☐ Deprived
- ☐ Heartbroken
- ☐ Humiliated
- ☐ Injured
- ☐ Offended
- ☐ Pained
- ☐ Rejected
- ☐ Tormented
- ☐ Tortured
- ☐ Victimized
- ☐ Wronged

Notes: _____
_____
_____

8 Pitfalls to avoid

- ☐ Me-too-ism. Don't start telling your story, or comparing your story to theirs.
- ☐ Moralizing, preaching, being judgmental
- ☐ Asking a direct question to satisfy your own curiosity
- ☐ Being an interviewer rather then a listener
- ☐ Giving advice (try fixing it)
- ☐ Cheap consolation. *"Oh, that's not to bad"*
- ☐ Arguing or disagreeing with the speaker
- ☐ Analyzing or interpreting
- ☐ Ignoring obvious heavy emotions

Date: _____

PLEASANT FEELINGS

OPEN
- ☐ Accepting
- ☐ Amazed
- ☐ Confident
- ☐ Easy
- ☐ Free
- ☐ Interested
- ☐ Kind
- ☐ Receptive
- ☐ Reliable
- ☐ Satisfied
- ☐ Sympathetic
- ☐ Understanding

INTERESTED
- ☐ Absorbed
- ☐ Affected
- ☐ Concerned
- ☐ Curious
- ☐ Engrossed
- ☐ Fascinated
- ☐ Inquisitive
- ☐ Intrigued
- ☐ Nosy
- ☐ Snoopy

ALIVE
- ☐ Animated
- ☐ Courageous
- ☐ Energetic
- ☐ Free
- ☐ Frisky
- ☐ Impulsive
- ☐ Liberated
- ☐ Optimistic
- ☐ Playful
- ☐ Provocative
- ☐ Spirited
- ☐ Thrilled
- ☐ Wonderful

STRONG
- ☐ Certain
- ☐ Dynamic
- ☐ Free
- ☐ Hardy
- ☐ Impulsive
- ☐ Rebellious
- ☐ Secure
- ☐ Sure
- ☐ Tenacious
- ☐ Unique

LOVE
- ☐ Admiration
- ☐ Affectionate
- ☐ Attracted
- ☐ Close
- ☐ Comforted
- ☐ Considerate
- ☐ Devoted
- ☐ Drawn toward
- ☐ Loved
- ☐ Loving
- ☐ Passionate
- ☐ Sensitive
- ☐ Sympathy
- ☐ Tender
- ☐ Touched
- ☐ Warm

POSITIVE
- ☐ Anxious
- ☐ Bold
- ☐ Brave
- ☐ Challenged
- ☐ Confident
- ☐ Daring
- ☐ Determined
- ☐ Eager
- ☐ Earnest
- ☐ Enthusiastic
- ☐ Excited
- ☐ Hopeful
- ☐ Inspired
- ☐ Intent
- ☐ Keen
- ☐ Optimistic
- ☐ Re-enforced

GOOD
- ☐ At ease
- ☐ Blessed
- ☐ Bright
- ☐ Calm
- ☐ Certain
- ☐ Clever
- ☐ Comfortable
- ☐ Content
- ☐ Encouraged
- ☐ Free and easy
- ☐ Peaceful
- ☐ Pleased
- ☐ Quiet
- ☐ Reassured
- ☐ Relaxed
- ☐ Serene
- ☐ Surprised

HAPPY
- ☐ Cheerful
- ☐ Delighted
- ☐ Ecstatic
- ☐ Elated
- ☐ Festive
- ☐ Fortunate
- ☐ Glad
- ☐ Gleeful
- ☐ Great
- ☐ Important
- ☐ Joyous
- ☐ Jubilant
- ☐ Lucky
- ☐ Merry
- ☐ Overjoyed
- ☐ Satisfied
- ☐ Sunny
- ☐ Thankful

Read and check off
✓

Preparing to listen
- ☐ Remember to put your mind and feelings in neutral gear.
- ☐ Your body posture must say, *"I' am open, very interested, affirmative, attentive."*
- ☐ Maintain good eye contact.
- ☐ Give the speaker a verbal door opening, showing your readiness to listen.

While Listening
- ☐ Track what the speaker is saying in both content and feeling levels
- ☐ Stay with the content of communication
- ☐ Listen for and identify the basic general feeling; anger, fear, joy, resentment, etc.
- ☐ Suspend judgment; open yourself to the presence of their heart.

Responding
- ☐ Use oral responses, which are affirming, which say, *"I am with you"*, *"I understand"*.
- ☐ Feed general feelings back to the speaker. *"You seem to feel this has been a good experience for you"*
- ☐ Stay an inch ahead of the speaker, not a mile.

UNPLEASANT FEELINGS

😔 HELPLESS
- ☐ Alone
- ☐ Despair
- ☐ Distressed
- ☐ Dominated
- ☐ Empty
- ☐ Fatigued
- ☐ Forced
- ☐ Frustrated
- ☐ Hesitant
- ☐ In A Stew
- ☐ Incapable
- ☐ Inferior
- ☐ Paralyzed
- ☐ Pathetic
- ☐ Tragic
- ☐ Useless
- ☐ Vulnerable
- ☐ Woeful

😕 CONFUSED
- ☐ Disillusioned
- ☐ Distrustful
- ☐ Doubtful
- ☐ Embarrassed
- ☐ Hesitant
- ☐ Indecisive
- ☐ Lost
- ☐ Misgiving
- ☐ Perplexed
- ☐ Pessimistic
- ☐ Shy
- ☐ Skeptical
- ☐ Stupefied
- ☐ Tense
- ☐ Unbelieving
- ☐ Uncertain
- ☐ Uneasy
- ☐ Unsure
- ☐ Upset

😟 DEPRESSED
- ☐ A Sense of Loss
- ☐ Abominable
- ☐ Ashamed
- ☐ Bad
- ☐ Despicable
- ☐ Detestable
- ☐ Diminished
- ☐ Disappointed
- ☐ Discouraged
- ☐ Disgusting
- ☐ Dissatisfied
- ☐ Guilty
- ☐ In Despair
- ☐ Lousy
- ☐ Miserable
- ☐ Powerless
- ☐ Repugnant
- ☐ Sulky
- ☐ Terrible

😠 ANGRY
- ☐ Aggressive
- ☐ Annoyed
- ☐ Bitter
- ☐ Boiling
- ☐ Cross
- ☐ Enraged
- ☐ Fuming
- ☐ Hateful
- ☐ Hostile
- ☐ Incensed
- ☐ Inflamed
- ☐ Infuriated
- ☐ Insulting
- ☐ Irritated
- ☐ Offensive
- ☐ Provoked
- ☐ Resentful
- ☐ Sore
- ☐ Unpleasant
- ☐ Upset
- ☐ Worked Up

😢 SAD
- ☐ Anguish
- ☐ Desolate
- ☐ Desperate
- ☐ Dismayed
- ☐ Grief
- ☐ Grieved
- ☐ Lonely
- ☐ Mournful
- ☐ Pained
- ☐ Pessimistic
- ☐ Sorrowful
- ☐ Tearful
- ☐ Unhappy

😐 INDIFFERENT
- ☐ Bored
- ☐ Cold
- ☐ Disinterested
- ☐ Dull
- ☐ Insensitive
- ☐ Lifeless
- ☐ Neutral
- ☐ Nonchalant
- ☐ Preoccupied
- ☐ Reserved
- ☐ Weary

😨 AFRAID
- ☐ Alarmed
- ☐ Anxious
- ☐ Cowardly
- ☐ Doubtful
- ☐ Fearful
- ☐ Frightened
- ☐ Menaced
- ☐ Nervous
- ☐ Panic
- ☐ Quaking
- ☐ Restless
- ☐ Scared
- ☐ Shaky
- ☐ Suspicious
- ☐ Terrified
- ☐ Threatened
- ☐ Timid
- ☐ Wary
- ☐ Worried

😣 HURT
- ☐ Aching
- ☐ Afflicted
- ☐ Agonized
- ☐ Alienated
- ☐ Appalled
- ☐ Crushed
- ☐ Dejected
- ☐ Deprived
- ☐ Heartbroken
- ☐ Humiliated
- ☐ Injured
- ☐ Offended
- ☐ Pained
- ☐ Rejected
- ☐ Tormented
- ☐ Tortured
- ☐ Victimized
- ☐ Wronged

Notes:
_____
_____
_____

8 Pitfalls to avoid

- ☐ Me-too-ism. Don't start telling your story, or comparing your story to theirs.
- ☐ Moralizing, preaching, being judgmental
- ☐ Asking a direct question to satisfy your own curiosity
- ☐ Being an interviewer rather then a listener
- ☐ Giving advice (try fixing it)
- ☐ Cheap consolation. *"Oh, that's not to bad"*
- ☐ Arguing or disagreeing with the speaker
- ☐ Analyzing or interpreting
- ☐ Ignoring obvious heavy emotions

Date: _____

PLEASANT FEELINGS

OPEN
- ☐ Accepting
- ☐ Amazed
- ☐ Confident
- ☐ Easy
- ☐ Free
- ☐ Interested
- ☐ Kind
- ☐ Receptive
- ☐ Reliable
- ☐ Satisfied
- ☐ Sympathetic
- ☐ Understanding

INTERESTED
- ☐ Absorbed
- ☐ Affected
- ☐ Concerned
- ☐ Curious
- ☐ Engrossed
- ☐ Fascinated
- ☐ Inquisitive
- ☐ Intrigued
- ☐ Nosy
- ☐ Snoopy

ALIVE
- ☐ Animated
- ☐ Courageous
- ☐ Energetic
- ☐ Free
- ☐ Frisky
- ☐ Impulsive
- ☐ Liberated
- ☐ Optimistic
- ☐ Playful
- ☐ Provocative
- ☐ Spirited
- ☐ Thrilled
- ☐ Wonderful

STRONG
- ☐ Certain
- ☐ Dynamic
- ☐ Free
- ☐ Hardy
- ☐ Impulsive
- ☐ Rebellious
- ☐ Secure
- ☐ Sure
- ☐ Tenacious
- ☐ Unique

LOVE
- ☐ Admiration
- ☐ Affectionate
- ☐ Attracted
- ☐ Close
- ☐ Comforted
- ☐ Considerate
- ☐ Devoted
- ☐ Drawn toward
- ☐ Loved
- ☐ Loving
- ☐ Passionate
- ☐ Sensitive
- ☐ Sympathy
- ☐ Tender
- ☐ Touched
- ☐ Warm

POSITIVE
- ☐ Anxious
- ☐ Bold
- ☐ Brave
- ☐ Challenged
- ☐ Confident
- ☐ Daring
- ☐ Determined
- ☐ Eager
- ☐ Earnest
- ☐ Enthusiastic
- ☐ Excited
- ☐ Hopeful
- ☐ Inspired
- ☐ Intent
- ☐ Keen
- ☐ Optimistic
- ☐ Re-enforced

GOOD
- ☐ At ease
- ☐ Blessed
- ☐ Bright
- ☐ Calm
- ☐ Certain
- ☐ Clever
- ☐ Comfortable
- ☐ Content
- ☐ Encouraged
- ☐ Free and easy
- ☐ Peaceful
- ☐ Pleased
- ☐ Quiet
- ☐ Reassured
- ☐ Relaxed
- ☐ Serene
- ☐ Surprised

HAPPY
- ☐ Cheerful
- ☐ Delighted
- ☐ Ecstatic
- ☐ Elated
- ☐ Festive
- ☐ Fortunate
- ☐ Glad
- ☐ Gleeful
- ☐ Great
- ☐ Important
- ☐ Joyous
- ☐ Jubilant
- ☐ Lucky
- ☐ Merry
- ☐ Overjoyed
- ☐ Satisfied
- ☐ Sunny
- ☐ Thankful

Read and check off ✓

Preparing to listen
- ☐ Remember to put your mind and feelings in neutral gear.
- ☐ Your body posture must say, *"I' am open, very interested, affirmative, attentive."*
- ☐ Maintain good eye contact.
- ☐ Give the speaker a verbal door opening, showing your readiness to listen.

While Listening
- ☐ Track what the speaker is saying in both content and feeling levels
- ☐ Stay with the content of communication
- ☐ Listen for and identify the basic general feeling; anger, fear, joy, resentment, etc.
- ☐ Suspend judgment; open yourself to the presence of their heart.

Responding
- ☐ Use oral responses, which are affirming, which say, *"I am with you"*, *"I understand."*
- ☐ Feed general feelings back to the speaker. *"You seem to feel this has been a good experience for you"*
- ☐ Stay an inch ahead of the speaker, not a mile.

UNPLEASANT FEELINGS

😞 HELPLESS
- ☐ Alone
- ☐ Despair
- ☐ Distressed
- ☐ Dominated
- ☐ Empty
- ☐ Fatigued
- ☐ Forced
- ☐ Frustrated
- ☐ Hesitant
- ☐ In A Stew
- ☐ Incapable
- ☐ Inferior
- ☐ Paralyzed
- ☐ Pathetic
- ☐ Tragic
- ☐ Useless
- ☐ Vulnerable
- ☐ Woeful

😕 CONFUSED
- ☐ Disillusioned
- ☐ Distrustful
- ☐ Doubtful
- ☐ Embarrassed
- ☐ Hesitant
- ☐ Indecisive
- ☐ Lost
- ☐ Misgiving
- ☐ Perplexed
- ☐ Pessimistic
- ☐ Shy
- ☐ Skeptical
- ☐ Stupefied
- ☐ Tense
- ☐ Unbelieving
- ☐ Uncertain
- ☐ Uneasy
- ☐ Unsure
- ☐ Upset

😔 DEPRESSED
- ☐ A Sense of Loss
- ☐ Abominable
- ☐ Ashamed
- ☐ Bad
- ☐ Despicable
- ☐ Detestable
- ☐ Diminished
- ☐ Disappointed
- ☐ Discouraged
- ☐ Disgusting
- ☐ Dissatisfied
- ☐ Guilty
- ☐ In Despair
- ☐ Lousy
- ☐ Miserable
- ☐ Powerless
- ☐ Repugnant
- ☐ Sulky
- ☐ Terrible

😠 ANGRY
- ☐ Aggressive
- ☐ Annoyed
- ☐ Bitter
- ☐ Boiling
- ☐ Cross
- ☐ Enraged
- ☐ Fuming
- ☐ Hateful
- ☐ Hostile
- ☐ Incensed
- ☐ Inflamed
- ☐ Infuriated
- ☐ Insulting
- ☐ Irritated
- ☐ Offensive
- ☐ Provoked
- ☐ Resentful
- ☐ Sore
- ☐ Unpleasant
- ☐ Upset
- ☐ Worked Up

😢 SAD
- ☐ Anguish
- ☐ Desolate
- ☐ Desperate
- ☐ Dismayed
- ☐ Grief
- ☐ Grieved
- ☐ Lonely
- ☐ Mournful
- ☐ Pained
- ☐ Pessimistic
- ☐ Sorrowful
- ☐ Tearful
- ☐ Unhappy

😐 INDIFFERENT
- ☐ Bored
- ☐ Cold
- ☐ Disinterested
- ☐ Dull
- ☐ Insensitive
- ☐ Lifeless
- ☐ Neutral
- ☐ Nonchalant
- ☐ Preoccupied
- ☐ Reserved
- ☐ Weary

😨 AFRAID
- ☐ Alarmed
- ☐ Anxious
- ☐ Cowardly
- ☐ Doubtful
- ☐ Fearful
- ☐ Frightened
- ☐ Menaced
- ☐ Nervous
- ☐ Panic
- ☐ Quaking
- ☐ Restless
- ☐ Scared
- ☐ Shaky
- ☐ Suspicious
- ☐ Terrified
- ☐ Threatened
- ☐ Timid
- ☐ Wary
- ☐ Worried

😟 HURT
- ☐ Aching
- ☐ Afflicted
- ☐ Agonized
- ☐ Alienated
- ☐ Appalled
- ☐ Crushed
- ☐ Dejected
- ☐ Deprived
- ☐ Heartbroken
- ☐ Humiliated
- ☐ Injured
- ☐ Offended
- ☐ Pained
- ☐ Rejected
- ☐ Tormented
- ☐ Tortured
- ☐ Victimized
- ☐ Wronged

Notes: _____
_____
_____
_____

8 Pitfalls to avoid

- ☐ Me-too-ism. Don't start telling your story, or comparing your story to theirs.
- ☐ Moralizing, preaching, being judgmental
- ☐ Asking a direct question to satisfy your own curiosity
- ☐ Being an interviewer rather then a listener
- ☐ Giving advice (try fixing it)
- ☐ Cheap consolation. *"Oh, that's not to bad"*
- ☐ Arguing or disagreeing with the speaker
- ☐ Analyzing or interpreting
- ☐ Ignoring obvious heavy emotions

Date: _____

PLEASANT FEELINGS

OPEN
- ☐ Accepting
- ☐ Amazed
- ☐ Confident
- ☐ Easy
- ☐ Free
- ☐ Interested
- ☐ Kind
- ☐ Receptive
- ☐ Reliable
- ☐ Satisfied
- ☐ Sympathetic
- ☐ Understanding

INTERESTED
- ☐ Absorbed
- ☐ Affected
- ☐ Concerned
- ☐ Curious
- ☐ Engrossed
- ☐ Fascinated
- ☐ Inquisitive
- ☐ Intrigued
- ☐ Nosy
- ☐ Snoopy

ALIVE
- ☐ Animated
- ☐ Courageous
- ☐ Energetic
- ☐ Free
- ☐ Frisky
- ☐ Impulsive
- ☐ Liberated
- ☐ Optimistic
- ☐ Playful
- ☐ Provocative
- ☐ Spirited
- ☐ Thrilled
- ☐ Wonderful

STRONG
- ☐ Certain
- ☐ Dynamic
- ☐ Free
- ☐ Hardy
- ☐ Impulsive
- ☐ Rebellious
- ☐ Secure
- ☐ Sure
- ☐ Tenacious
- ☐ Unique

LOVE
- ☐ Admiration
- ☐ Affectionate
- ☐ Attracted
- ☐ Close
- ☐ Comforted
- ☐ Considerate
- ☐ Devoted
- ☐ Drawn toward
- ☐ Loved
- ☐ Loving
- ☐ Passionate
- ☐ Sensitive
- ☐ Sympathy
- ☐ Tender
- ☐ Touched
- ☐ Warm

POSITIVE
- ☐ Anxious
- ☐ Bold
- ☐ Brave
- ☐ Challenged
- ☐ Confident
- ☐ Daring
- ☐ Determined
- ☐ Eager
- ☐ Earnest
- ☐ Enthusiastic
- ☐ Excited
- ☐ Hopeful
- ☐ Inspired
- ☐ Intent
- ☐ Keen
- ☐ Optimistic
- ☐ Re-enforced

GOOD
- ☐ At ease
- ☐ Blessed
- ☐ Bright
- ☐ Calm
- ☐ Certain
- ☐ Clever
- ☐ Comfortable
- ☐ Content
- ☐ Encouraged
- ☐ Free and easy
- ☐ Peaceful
- ☐ Pleased
- ☐ Quiet
- ☐ Reassured
- ☐ Relaxed
- ☐ Serene
- ☐ Surprised

HAPPY
- ☐ Cheerful
- ☐ Delighted
- ☐ Ecstatic
- ☐ Elated
- ☐ Festive
- ☐ Fortunate
- ☐ Glad
- ☐ Gleeful
- ☐ Great
- ☐ Important
- ☐ Joyous
- ☐ Jubilant
- ☐ Lucky
- ☐ Merry
- ☐ Overjoyed
- ☐ Satisfied
- ☐ Sunny
- ☐ Thankful

Read and check off
✓

Preparing to listen
- ☐ Remember to put your mind and feelings in neutral gear.
- ☐ Your body posture must say, *"I am open, very interested, affirmative, attentive."*
- ☐ Maintain good eye contact.
- ☐ Give the speaker a verbal door opening, showing your readiness to listen.

While Listening
- ☐ Track what the speaker is saying in both content and feeling levels
- ☐ Stay with the content of communication
- ☐ Listen for and identify the basic general feeling; anger, fear, joy, resentment, etc.
- ☐ Suspend judgment; open yourself to the presence of their heart.

Responding
- ☐ Use oral responses, which are affirming, which say, *"I am with you"*, *"I understand."*
- ☐ Feed general feelings back to the speaker. *"You seem to feel this has been a good experience for you"*
- ☐ Stay an inch ahead of the speaker, not a mile.

UNPLEASANT FEELINGS

😊 HELPLESS
- ☐ Alone
- ☐ Despair
- ☐ Distressed
- ☐ Dominated
- ☐ Empty
- ☐ Fatigued
- ☐ Forced
- ☐ Frustrated
- ☐ Hesitant
- ☐ In A Stew
- ☐ Incapable
- ☐ Inferior
- ☐ Paralyzed
- ☐ Pathetic
- ☐ Tragic
- ☐ Useless
- ☐ Vulnerable
- ☐ Woeful

😕 CONFUSED
- ☐ Disillusioned
- ☐ Distrustful
- ☐ Doubtful
- ☐ Embarrassed
- ☐ Hesitant
- ☐ Indecisive
- ☐ Lost
- ☐ Misgiving
- ☐ Perplexed
- ☐ Pessimistic
- ☐ Shy
- ☐ Skeptical
- ☐ Stupefied
- ☐ Tense
- ☐ Unbelieving
- ☐ Uncertain
- ☐ Uneasy
- ☐ Unsure
- ☐ Upset

😔 DEPRESSED
- ☐ A Sense of Loss
- ☐ Abominable
- ☐ Ashamed
- ☐ Bad
- ☐ Despicable
- ☐ Detestable
- ☐ Diminished
- ☐ Disappointed
- ☐ Discouraged
- ☐ Disgusting
- ☐ Dissatisfied
- ☐ Guilty
- ☐ In Despair
- ☐ Lousy
- ☐ Miserable
- ☐ Powerless
- ☐ Repugnant
- ☐ Sulky
- ☐ Terrible

😠 ANGRY
- ☐ Aggressive
- ☐ Annoyed
- ☐ Bitter
- ☐ Boiling
- ☐ Cross
- ☐ Enraged
- ☐ Fuming
- ☐ Hateful
- ☐ Hostile
- ☐ Incensed
- ☐ Inflamed
- ☐ Infuriated
- ☐ Insulting
- ☐ Irritated
- ☐ Offensive
- ☐ Provoked
- ☐ Resentful
- ☐ Sore
- ☐ Unpleasant
- ☐ Upset
- ☐ Worked Up

😢 SAD
- ☐ Anguish
- ☐ Desolate
- ☐ Desperate
- ☐ Dismayed
- ☐ Grief
- ☐ Grieved
- ☐ Lonely
- ☐ Mournful
- ☐ Pained
- ☐ Pessimistic
- ☐ Sorrowful
- ☐ Tearful
- ☐ Unhappy

😐 INDIFFERENT
- ☐ Bored
- ☐ Cold
- ☐ Disinterested
- ☐ Dull
- ☐ Insensitive
- ☐ Lifeless
- ☐ Neutral
- ☐ Nonchalant
- ☐ Preoccupied
- ☐ Reserved
- ☐ Weary

😨 AFRAID
- ☐ Alarmed
- ☐ Anxious
- ☐ Cowardly
- ☐ Doubtful
- ☐ Fearful
- ☐ Frightened
- ☐ Menaced
- ☐ Nervous
- ☐ Panic
- ☐ Quaking
- ☐ Restless
- ☐ Scared
- ☐ Shaky
- ☐ Suspicious
- ☐ Terrified
- ☐ Threatened
- ☐ Timid
- ☐ Wary
- ☐ Worried

😟 HURT
- ☐ Aching
- ☐ Afflicted
- ☐ Agonized
- ☐ Alienated
- ☐ Appalled
- ☐ Crushed
- ☐ Dejected
- ☐ Deprived
- ☐ Heartbroken
- ☐ Humiliated
- ☐ Injured
- ☐ Offended
- ☐ Pained
- ☐ Rejected
- ☐ Tormented
- ☐ Tortured
- ☐ Victimized
- ☐ Wronged

Notes: _____
_____
_____

8 Pitfalls to avoid
- ☐ Me-too-ism. Don't start telling your story, or comparing your story to theirs.
- ☐ Moralizing, preaching, being judgmental
- ☐ Asking a direct question to satisfy your own curiosity
- ☐ Being an interviewer rather then a listener
- ☐ Giving advice (try fixing it)
- ☐ Cheap consolation. *"Oh, that's not to bad"*
- ☐ Arguing or disagreeing with the speaker
- ☐ Analyzing or interpreting
- ☐ Ignoring obvious heavy emotions

Date: _____

PLEASANT FEELINGS

OPEN
- ☐ Accepting
- ☐ Amazed
- ☐ Confident
- ☐ Easy
- ☐ Free
- ☐ Interested
- ☐ Kind
- ☐ Receptive
- ☐ Reliable
- ☐ Satisfied
- ☐ Sympathetic
- ☐ Understanding

INTERESTED
- ☐ Absorbed
- ☐ Affected
- ☐ Concerned
- ☐ Curious
- ☐ Engrossed
- ☐ Fascinated
- ☐ Inquisitive
- ☐ Intrigued
- ☐ Nosy
- ☐ Snoopy

ALIVE
- ☐ Animated
- ☐ Courageous
- ☐ Energetic
- ☐ Free
- ☐ Frisky
- ☐ Impulsive
- ☐ Liberated
- ☐ Optimistic
- ☐ Playful
- ☐ Provocative
- ☐ Spirited
- ☐ Thrilled
- ☐ Wonderful

STRONG
- ☐ Certain
- ☐ Dynamic
- ☐ Free
- ☐ Hardy
- ☐ Impulsive
- ☐ Rebellious
- ☐ Secure
- ☐ Sure
- ☐ Tenacious
- ☐ Unique

LOVE
- ☐ Admiration
- ☐ Affectionate
- ☐ Attracted
- ☐ Close
- ☐ Comforted
- ☐ Considerate
- ☐ Devoted
- ☐ Drawn toward
- ☐ Loved
- ☐ Loving
- ☐ Passionate
- ☐ Sensitive
- ☐ Sympathy
- ☐ Tender
- ☐ Touched
- ☐ Warm

POSITIVE
- ☐ Anxious
- ☐ Bold
- ☐ Brave
- ☐ Challenged
- ☐ Confident
- ☐ Daring
- ☐ Determined
- ☐ Eager
- ☐ Earnest
- ☐ Enthusiastic
- ☐ Excited
- ☐ Hopeful
- ☐ Inspired
- ☐ Intent
- ☐ Keen
- ☐ Optimistic
- ☐ Re-enforced

GOOD
- ☐ At ease
- ☐ Blessed
- ☐ Bright
- ☐ Calm
- ☐ Certain
- ☐ Clever
- ☐ Comfortable
- ☐ Content
- ☐ Encouraged
- ☐ Free and easy
- ☐ Peaceful
- ☐ Pleased
- ☐ Quiet
- ☐ Reassured
- ☐ Relaxed
- ☐ Serene
- ☐ Surprised

HAPPY
- ☐ Cheerful
- ☐ Delighted
- ☐ Ecstatic
- ☐ Elated
- ☐ Festive
- ☐ Fortunate
- ☐ Glad
- ☐ Gleeful
- ☐ Great
- ☐ Important
- ☐ Joyous
- ☐ Jubilant
- ☐ Lucky
- ☐ Merry
- ☐ Overjoyed
- ☐ Satisfied
- ☐ Sunny
- ☐ Thankful

Read and check off
✓

Preparing to listen
- ☐ Remember to put your mind and feelings in neutral gear.
- ☐ Your body posture must say, *"I am open, very interested, affirmative, attentive."*
- ☐ Maintain good eye contact.
- ☐ Give the speaker a verbal door opening, showing your readiness to listen.

While Listening
- ☐ Track what the speaker is saying in both content and feeling levels
- ☐ Stay with the content of communication
- ☐ Listen for and identify the basic general feeling; anger, fear, joy, resentment, etc.
- ☐ Suspend judgment; open yourself to the presence of their heart.

Responding
- ☐ Use oral responses, which are affirming, which say, *"I am with you"*, *"I understand."*
- ☐ Feed general feelings back to the speaker. *"You seem to feel this has been a good experience for you"*
- ☐ Stay an inch ahead of the speaker, not a mile.

UNPLEASANT FEELINGS

HELPLESS
- [ ] Alone
- [ ] Despair
- [ ] Distressed
- [ ] Dominated
- [ ] Empty
- [ ] Fatigued
- [ ] Forced
- [ ] Frustrated
- [ ] Hesitant
- [ ] In A Stew
- [ ] Incapable
- [ ] Inferior
- [ ] Paralyzed
- [ ] Pathetic
- [ ] Tragic
- [ ] Useless
- [ ] Vulnerable
- [ ] Woeful

SAD
- [ ] Anguish
- [ ] Desolate
- [ ] Desperate
- [ ] Dismayed
- [ ] Grief
- [ ] Grieved
- [ ] Lonely
- [ ] Mournful
- [ ] Pained
- [ ] Pessimistic
- [ ] Sorrowful
- [ ] Tearful
- [ ] Unhappy

CONFUSED
- [ ] Disillusioned
- [ ] Distrustful
- [ ] Doubtful
- [ ] Embarrassed
- [ ] Hesitant
- [ ] Indecisive
- [ ] Lost
- [ ] Misgiving
- [ ] Perplexed
- [ ] Pessimistic
- [ ] Shy
- [ ] Skeptical
- [ ] Stupefied
- [ ] Tense
- [ ] Unbelieving
- [ ] Uncertain
- [ ] Uneasy
- [ ] Unsure
- [ ] Upset

INDIFFERENT
- [ ] Bored
- [ ] Cold
- [ ] Disinterested
- [ ] Dull
- [ ] Insensitive
- [ ] Lifeless
- [ ] Neutral
- [ ] Nonchalant
- [ ] Preoccupied
- [ ] Reserved
- [ ] Weary

DEPRESSED
- [ ] A Sense of Loss
- [ ] Abominable
- [ ] Ashamed
- [ ] Bad
- [ ] Despicable
- [ ] Detestable
- [ ] Diminished
- [ ] Disappointed
- [ ] Discouraged
- [ ] Disgusting
- [ ] Dissatisfied
- [ ] Guilty
- [ ] In Despair
- [ ] Lousy
- [ ] Miserable
- [ ] Powerless
- [ ] Repugnant
- [ ] Sulky
- [ ] Terrible

AFRAID
- [ ] Alarmed
- [ ] Anxious
- [ ] Cowardly
- [ ] Doubtful
- [ ] Fearful
- [ ] Frightened
- [ ] Menaced
- [ ] Nervous
- [ ] Panic
- [ ] Quaking
- [ ] Restless
- [ ] Scared
- [ ] Shaky
- [ ] Suspicious
- [ ] Terrified
- [ ] Threatened
- [ ] Timid
- [ ] Wary
- [ ] Worried

ANGRY
- [ ] Aggressive
- [ ] Annoyed
- [ ] Bitter
- [ ] Boiling
- [ ] Cross
- [ ] Enraged
- [ ] Fuming
- [ ] Hateful
- [ ] Hostile
- [ ] Incensed
- [ ] Inflamed
- [ ] Infuriated
- [ ] Insulting
- [ ] Irritated
- [ ] Offensive
- [ ] Provoked
- [ ] Resentful
- [ ] Sore
- [ ] Unpleasant
- [ ] Upset
- [ ] Worked Up

HURT
- [ ] Aching
- [ ] Afflicted
- [ ] Agonized
- [ ] Alienated
- [ ] Appalled
- [ ] Crushed
- [ ] Dejected
- [ ] Deprived
- [ ] Heartbroken
- [ ] Humiliated
- [ ] Injured
- [ ] Offended
- [ ] Pained
- [ ] Rejected
- [ ] Tormented
- [ ] Tortured
- [ ] Victimized
- [ ] Wronged

Notes: _____
_____
_____
_____

8 Pitfalls to avoid
- [ ] Me-too-ism. Don't start telling your story, or comparing your story to theirs.
- [ ] Moralizing, preaching, being judgmental
- [ ] Asking a direct question to satisfy your own curiosity
- [ ] Being an interviewer rather then a listener
- [ ] Giving advice (try fixing it)
- [ ] Cheap consolation. *"Oh, that's not to bad"*
- [ ] Arguing or disagreeing with the speaker
- [ ] Analyzing or interpreting
- [ ] Ignoring obvious heavy emotions

Date: _____

PLEASANT FEELINGS

OPEN
- ☐ Accepting
- ☐ Amazed
- ☐ Confident
- ☐ Easy
- ☐ Free
- ☐ Interested
- ☐ Kind
- ☐ Receptive
- ☐ Reliable
- ☐ Satisfied
- ☐ Sympathetic
- ☐ Understanding

INTERESTED
- ☐ Absorbed
- ☐ Affected
- ☐ Concerned
- ☐ Curious
- ☐ Engrossed
- ☐ Fascinated
- ☐ Inquisitive
- ☐ Intrigued
- ☐ Nosy
- ☐ Snoopy

ALIVE
- ☐ Animated
- ☐ Courageous
- ☐ Energetic
- ☐ Free
- ☐ Frisky
- ☐ Impulsive
- ☐ Liberated
- ☐ Optimistic
- ☐ Playful
- ☐ Provocative
- ☐ Spirited
- ☐ Thrilled
- ☐ Wonderful

STRONG
- ☐ Certain
- ☐ Dynamic
- ☐ Free
- ☐ Hardy
- ☐ Impulsive
- ☐ Rebellious
- ☐ Secure
- ☐ Sure
- ☐ Tenacious
- ☐ Unique

LOVE
- ☐ Admiration
- ☐ Affectionate
- ☐ Attracted
- ☐ Close
- ☐ Comforted
- ☐ Considerate
- ☐ Devoted
- ☐ Drawn toward
- ☐ Loved
- ☐ Loving
- ☐ Passionate
- ☐ Sensitive
- ☐ Sympathy
- ☐ Tender
- ☐ Touched
- ☐ Warm

POSITIVE
- ☐ Anxious
- ☐ Bold
- ☐ Brave
- ☐ Challenged
- ☐ Confident
- ☐ Daring
- ☐ Determined
- ☐ Eager
- ☐ Earnest
- ☐ Enthusiastic
- ☐ Excited
- ☐ Hopeful
- ☐ Inspired
- ☐ Intent
- ☐ Keen
- ☐ Optimistic
- ☐ Re-enforced

GOOD
- ☐ At ease
- ☐ Blessed
- ☐ Bright
- ☐ Calm
- ☐ Certain
- ☐ Clever
- ☐ Comfortable
- ☐ Content
- ☐ Encouraged
- ☐ Free and easy
- ☐ Peaceful
- ☐ Pleased
- ☐ Quiet
- ☐ Reassured
- ☐ Relaxed
- ☐ Serene
- ☐ Surprised

HAPPY
- ☐ Cheerful
- ☐ Delighted
- ☐ Ecstatic
- ☐ Elated
- ☐ Festive
- ☐ Fortunate
- ☐ Glad
- ☐ Gleeful
- ☐ Great
- ☐ Important
- ☐ Joyous
- ☐ Jubilant
- ☐ Lucky
- ☐ Merry
- ☐ Overjoyed
- ☐ Satisfied
- ☐ Sunny
- ☐ Thankful

Read and check off

✓

Preparing to listen
- ☐ Remember to put your mind and feelings in neutral gear.
- ☐ Your body posture must say, *"I' am open, very interested, affirmative, attentive."*
- ☐ Maintain good eye contact.
- ☐ Give the speaker a verbal door opening, showing your readiness to listen.

While Listening
- ☐ Track what the speaker is saying in both content and feeling levels
- ☐ Stay with the content of communication
- ☐ Listen for and identify the basic general feeling; anger, fear, joy, resentment, etc.
- ☐ Suspend judgment; open yourself to the presence of their heart.

Responding
- ☐ Use oral responses, which are affirming, which say, *"I am with you", "I understand."*
- ☐ Feed general feelings back to the speaker. *"You seem to feel this has been a good experience for you"*
- ☐ Stay an inch ahead of the speaker, not a mile.

UNPLEASANT FEELINGS

😞 HELPLESS
- ☐ Alone
- ☐ Despair
- ☐ Distressed
- ☐ Dominated
- ☐ Empty
- ☐ Fatigued
- ☐ Forced
- ☐ Frustrated
- ☐ Hesitant
- ☐ In A Stew
- ☐ Incapable
- ☐ Inferior
- ☐ Paralyzed
- ☐ Pathetic
- ☐ Tragic
- ☐ Useless
- ☐ Vulnerable
- ☐ Woeful

😕 SAD
- ☐ Anguish
- ☐ Desolate
- ☐ Desperate
- ☐ Dismayed
- ☐ Grief
- ☐ Grieved
- ☐ Lonely
- ☐ Mournful
- ☐ Pained
- ☐ Pessimistic
- ☐ Sorrowful
- ☐ Tearful
- ☐ Unhappy

😐 CONFUSED
- ☐ Disillusioned
- ☐ Distrustful
- ☐ Doubtful
- ☐ Embarrassed
- ☐ Hesitant
- ☐ Indecisive
- ☐ Lost
- ☐ Misgiving
- ☐ Perplexed
- ☐ Pessimistic
- ☐ Shy
- ☐ Skeptical
- ☐ Stupefied
- ☐ Tense
- ☐ Unbelieving
- ☐ Uncertain
- ☐ Uneasy
- ☐ Unsure
- ☐ Upset

😑 INDIFFERENT
- ☐ Bored
- ☐ Cold
- ☐ Disinterested
- ☐ Dull
- ☐ Insensitive
- ☐ Lifeless
- ☐ Neutral
- ☐ Nonchalant
- ☐ Preoccupied
- ☐ Reserved
- ☐ Weary

😞 DEPRESSED
- ☐ A Sense of Loss
- ☐ Abominable
- ☐ Ashamed
- ☐ Bad
- ☐ Despicable
- ☐ Detestable
- ☐ Diminished
- ☐ Disappointed
- ☐ Discouraged
- ☐ Disgusting
- ☐ Dissatisfied
- ☐ Guilty
- ☐ In Despair
- ☐ Lousy
- ☐ Miserable
- ☐ Powerless
- ☐ Repugnant
- ☐ Sulky
- ☐ Terrible

😨 AFRAID
- ☐ Alarmed
- ☐ Anxious
- ☐ Cowardly
- ☐ Doubtful
- ☐ Fearful
- ☐ Frightened
- ☐ Menaced
- ☐ Nervous
- ☐ Panic
- ☐ Quaking
- ☐ Restless
- ☐ Scared
- ☐ Shaky
- ☐ Suspicious
- ☐ Terrified
- ☐ Threatened
- ☐ Timid
- ☐ Wary
- ☐ Worried

😠 ANGRY
- ☐ Aggressive
- ☐ Annoyed
- ☐ Bitter
- ☐ Boiling
- ☐ Cross
- ☐ Enraged
- ☐ Fuming
- ☐ Hateful
- ☐ Hostile
- ☐ Incensed
- ☐ Inflamed
- ☐ Infuriated
- ☐ Insulting
- ☐ Irritated
- ☐ Offensive
- ☐ Provoked
- ☐ Resentful
- ☐ Sore
- ☐ Unpleasant
- ☐ Upset
- ☐ Worked Up

😢 HURT
- ☐ Aching
- ☐ Afflicted
- ☐ Agonized
- ☐ Alienated
- ☐ Appalled
- ☐ Crushed
- ☐ Dejected
- ☐ Deprived
- ☐ Heartbroken
- ☐ Humiliated
- ☐ Injured
- ☐ Offended
- ☐ Pained
- ☐ Rejected
- ☐ Tormented
- ☐ Tortured
- ☐ Victimized
- ☐ Wronged

Notes: _____
_____
_____
_____

8 Pitfalls to avoid
- ☐ Me-too-ism. Don't start telling your story, or comparing your story to theirs.
- ☐ Moralizing, preaching, being judgmental
- ☐ Asking a direct question to satisfy your own curiosity
- ☐ Being an interviewer rather then a listener
- ☐ Giving advice (try fixing it)
- ☐ Cheap consolation. *"Oh, that's not to bad"*
- ☐ Arguing or disagreeing with the speaker
- ☐ Analyzing or interpreting
- ☐ Ignoring obvious heavy emotions

Date: _____

PLEASANT FEELINGS

OPEN
- [ ] Accepting
- [ ] Amazed
- [ ] Confident
- [ ] Easy
- [ ] Free
- [ ] Interested
- [ ] Kind
- [ ] Receptive
- [ ] Reliable
- [ ] Satisfied
- [ ] Sympathetic
- [ ] Understanding

INTERESTED
- [ ] Absorbed
- [ ] Affected
- [ ] Concerned
- [ ] Curious
- [ ] Engrossed
- [ ] Fascinated
- [ ] Inquisitive
- [ ] Intrigued
- [ ] Nosy
- [ ] Snoopy

ALIVE
- [ ] Animated
- [ ] Courageous
- [ ] Energetic
- [ ] Free
- [ ] Frisky
- [ ] Impulsive
- [ ] Liberated
- [ ] Optimistic
- [ ] Playful
- [ ] Provocative
- [ ] Spirited
- [ ] Thrilled
- [ ] Wonderful

STRONG
- [ ] Certain
- [ ] Dynamic
- [ ] Free
- [ ] Hardy
- [ ] Impulsive
- [ ] Rebellious
- [ ] Secure
- [ ] Sure
- [ ] Tenacious
- [ ] Unique

LOVE
- [ ] Admiration
- [ ] Affectionate
- [ ] Attracted
- [ ] Close
- [ ] Comforted
- [ ] Considerate
- [ ] Devoted
- [ ] Drawn toward
- [ ] Loved
- [ ] Loving
- [ ] Passionate
- [ ] Sensitive
- [ ] Sympathy
- [ ] Tender
- [ ] Touched
- [ ] Warm

POSITIVE
- [ ] Anxious
- [ ] Bold
- [ ] Brave
- [ ] Challenged
- [ ] Confident
- [ ] Daring
- [ ] Determined
- [ ] Eager
- [ ] Earnest
- [ ] Enthusiastic
- [ ] Excited
- [ ] Hopeful
- [ ] Inspired
- [ ] Intent
- [ ] Keen
- [ ] Optimistic
- [ ] Re-enforced

GOOD
- [ ] At ease
- [ ] Blessed
- [ ] Bright
- [ ] Calm
- [ ] Certain
- [ ] Clever
- [ ] Comfortable
- [ ] Content
- [ ] Encouraged
- [ ] Free and easy
- [ ] Peaceful
- [ ] Pleased
- [ ] Quiet
- [ ] Reassured
- [ ] Relaxed
- [ ] Serene
- [ ] Surprised

HAPPY
- [ ] Cheerful
- [ ] Delighted
- [ ] Ecstatic
- [ ] Elated
- [ ] Festive
- [ ] Fortunate
- [ ] Glad
- [ ] Gleeful
- [ ] Great
- [ ] Important
- [ ] Joyous
- [ ] Jubilant
- [ ] Lucky
- [ ] Merry
- [ ] Overjoyed
- [ ] Satisfied
- [ ] Sunny
- [ ] Thankful

Read and check off
✓

Preparing to listen
- [ ] Remember to put your mind and feelings in neutral gear.
- [ ] Your body posture must say, *"I' am open, very interested, affirmative, attentive."*
- [ ] Maintain good eye contact.
- [ ] Give the speaker a verbal door opening, showing your readiness to listen.

While Listening
- [ ] Track what the speaker is saying in both content and feeling levels
- [ ] Stay with the content of communication
- [ ] Listen for and identify the basic general feeling; anger, fear, joy, resentment, etc.
- [ ] Suspend judgment; open yourself to the presence of their heart.

Responding
- [ ] Use oral responses, which are affirming, which say, *"I am with you"*, *"I understand."*
- [ ] Feed general feelings back to the speaker. *"You seem to feel this has been a good experience for you"*
- [ ] Stay an inch ahead of the speaker, not a mile.

UNPLEASANT FEELINGS

HELPLESS
- [ ] Alone
- [ ] Despair
- [ ] Distressed
- [ ] Dominated
- [ ] Empty
- [ ] Fatigued
- [ ] Forced
- [ ] Frustrated
- [ ] Hesitant
- [ ] In A Stew
- [ ] Incapable
- [ ] Inferior
- [ ] Paralyzed
- [ ] Pathetic
- [ ] Tragic
- [ ] Useless
- [ ] Vulnerable
- [ ] Woeful

CONFUSED
- [ ] Disillusioned
- [ ] Distrustful
- [ ] Doubtful
- [ ] Embarrassed
- [ ] Hesitant
- [ ] Indecisive
- [ ] Lost
- [ ] Misgiving
- [ ] Perplexed
- [ ] Pessimistic
- [ ] Shy
- [ ] Skeptical
- [ ] Stupefied
- [ ] Tense
- [ ] Unbelieving
- [ ] Uncertain
- [ ] Uneasy
- [ ] Unsure
- [ ] Upset

DEPRESSED
- [ ] A Sense of Loss
- [ ] Abominable
- [ ] Ashamed
- [ ] Bad
- [ ] Despicable
- [ ] Detestable
- [ ] Diminished
- [ ] Disappointed
- [ ] Discouraged
- [ ] Disgusting
- [ ] Dissatisfied
- [ ] Guilty
- [ ] In Despair
- [ ] Lousy
- [ ] Miserable
- [ ] Powerless
- [ ] Repugnant
- [ ] Sulky
- [ ] Terrible

ANGRY
- [ ] Aggressive
- [ ] Annoyed
- [ ] Bitter
- [ ] Boiling
- [ ] Cross
- [ ] Enraged
- [ ] Fuming
- [ ] Hateful
- [ ] Hostile
- [ ] Incensed
- [ ] Inflamed
- [ ] Infuriated
- [ ] Insulting
- [ ] Irritated
- [ ] Offensive
- [ ] Provoked
- [ ] Resentful
- [ ] Sore
- [ ] Unpleasant
- [ ] Upset
- [ ] Worked Up

SAD
- [ ] Anguish
- [ ] Desolate
- [ ] Desperate
- [ ] Dismayed
- [ ] Grief
- [ ] Grieved
- [ ] Lonely
- [ ] Mournful
- [ ] Pained
- [ ] Pessimistic
- [ ] Sorrowful
- [ ] Tearful
- [ ] Unhappy

INDIFFERENT
- [ ] Bored
- [ ] Cold
- [ ] Disinterested
- [ ] Dull
- [ ] Insensitive
- [ ] Lifeless
- [ ] Neutral
- [ ] Nonchalant
- [ ] Preoccupied
- [ ] Reserved
- [ ] Weary

AFRAID
- [ ] Alarmed
- [ ] Anxious
- [ ] Cowardly
- [ ] Doubtful
- [ ] Fearful
- [ ] Frightened
- [ ] Menaced
- [ ] Nervous
- [ ] Panic
- [ ] Quaking
- [ ] Restless
- [ ] Scared
- [ ] Shaky
- [ ] Suspicious
- [ ] Terrified
- [ ] Threatened
- [ ] Timid
- [ ] Wary
- [ ] Worried

HURT
- [ ] Aching
- [ ] Afflicted
- [ ] Agonized
- [ ] Alienated
- [ ] Appalled
- [ ] Crushed
- [ ] Dejected
- [ ] Deprived
- [ ] Heartbroken
- [ ] Humiliated
- [ ] Injured
- [ ] Offended
- [ ] Pained
- [ ] Rejected
- [ ] Tormented
- [ ] Tortured
- [ ] Victimized
- [ ] Wronged

Notes: _____
_____
_____

8 Pitfalls to avoid
- [ ] Me-too-ism. Don't start telling your story, or comparing your story to theirs.
- [ ] Moralizing, preaching, being judgmental
- [ ] Asking a direct question to satisfy your own curiosity
- [ ] Being an interviewer rather then a listener
- [ ] Giving advice (try fixing it)
- [ ] Cheap consolation. *"Oh, that's not to bad"*
- [ ] Arguing or disagreeing with the speaker
- [ ] Analyzing or interpreting
- [ ] Ignoring obvious heavy emotions

Date: _____

PLEASANT FEELINGS

OPEN
- ☐ Accepting
- ☐ Amazed
- ☐ Confident
- ☐ Easy
- ☐ Free
- ☐ Interested
- ☐ Kind
- ☐ Receptive
- ☐ Reliable
- ☐ Satisfied
- ☐ Sympathetic
- ☐ Understanding

INTERESTED
- ☐ Absorbed
- ☐ Affected
- ☐ Concerned
- ☐ Curious
- ☐ Engrossed
- ☐ Fascinated
- ☐ Inquisitive
- ☐ Intrigued
- ☐ Nosy
- ☐ Snoopy

ALIVE
- ☐ Animated
- ☐ Courageous
- ☐ Energetic
- ☐ Free
- ☐ Frisky
- ☐ Impulsive
- ☐ Liberated
- ☐ Optimistic
- ☐ Playful
- ☐ Provocative
- ☐ Spirited
- ☐ Thrilled
- ☐ Wonderful

STRONG
- ☐ Certain
- ☐ Dynamic
- ☐ Free
- ☐ Hardy
- ☐ Impulsive
- ☐ Rebellious
- ☐ Secure
- ☐ Sure
- ☐ Tenacious
- ☐ Unique

LOVE
- ☐ Admiration
- ☐ Affectionate
- ☐ Attracted
- ☐ Close
- ☐ Comforted
- ☐ Considerate
- ☐ Devoted
- ☐ Drawn toward
- ☐ Loved
- ☐ Loving
- ☐ Passionate
- ☐ Sensitive
- ☐ Sympathy
- ☐ Tender
- ☐ Touched
- ☐ Warm

POSITIVE
- ☐ Anxious
- ☐ Bold
- ☐ Brave
- ☐ Challenged
- ☐ Confident
- ☐ Daring
- ☐ Determined
- ☐ Eager
- ☐ Earnest
- ☐ Enthusiastic
- ☐ Excited
- ☐ Hopeful
- ☐ Inspired
- ☐ Intent
- ☐ Keen
- ☐ Optimistic
- ☐ Re-enforced

GOOD
- ☐ At ease
- ☐ Blessed
- ☐ Bright
- ☐ Calm
- ☐ Certain
- ☐ Clever
- ☐ Comfortable
- ☐ Content
- ☐ Encouraged
- ☐ Free and easy
- ☐ Peaceful
- ☐ Pleased
- ☐ Quiet
- ☐ Reassured
- ☐ Relaxed
- ☐ Serene
- ☐ Surprised

HAPPY
- ☐ Cheerful
- ☐ Delighted
- ☐ Ecstatic
- ☐ Elated
- ☐ Festive
- ☐ Fortunate
- ☐ Glad
- ☐ Gleeful
- ☐ Great
- ☐ Important
- ☐ Joyous
- ☐ Jubilant
- ☐ Lucky
- ☐ Merry
- ☐ Overjoyed
- ☐ Satisfied
- ☐ Sunny
- ☐ Thankful

Read and check off
✓

Preparing to listen
- ☐ Remember to put your mind and feelings in neutral gear.
- ☐ Your body posture must say, *"I' am open, very interested, affirmative, attentive."*
- ☐ Maintain good eye contact.
- ☐ Give the speaker a verbal door opening, showing your readiness to listen.

While Listening
- ☐ Track what the speaker is saying in both content and feeling levels
- ☐ Stay with the content of communication
- ☐ Listen for and identify the basic general feeling; anger, fear, joy, resentment, etc.
- ☐ Suspend judgment; open yourself to the presence of their heart.

Responding
- ☐ Use oral responses, which are affirming, which say, *"I am with you"*, *"I understand."*
- ☐ Feed general feelings back to the speaker. *"You seem to feel this has been a good experience for you"*
- ☐ Stay an inch ahead of the speaker, not a mile.

UNPLEASANT FEELINGS

😨 HELPLESS
- ☐ Alone
- ☐ Despair
- ☐ Distressed
- ☐ Dominated
- ☐ Empty
- ☐ Fatigued
- ☐ Forced
- ☐ Frustrated
- ☐ Hesitant
- ☐ In A Stew
- ☐ Incapable
- ☐ Inferior
- ☐ Paralyzed
- ☐ Pathetic
- ☐ Tragic
- ☐ Useless
- ☐ Vulnerable
- ☐ Woeful

😕 CONFUSED
- ☐ Disillusioned
- ☐ Distrustful
- ☐ Doubtful
- ☐ Embarrassed
- ☐ Hesitant
- ☐ Indecisive
- ☐ Lost
- ☐ Misgiving
- ☐ Perplexed
- ☐ Pessimistic
- ☐ Shy
- ☐ Skeptical
- ☐ Stupefied
- ☐ Tense
- ☐ Unbelieving
- ☐ Uncertain
- ☐ Uneasy
- ☐ Unsure
- ☐ Upset

😔 DEPRESSED
- ☐ A Sense of Loss
- ☐ Abominable
- ☐ Ashamed
- ☐ Bad
- ☐ Despicable
- ☐ Detestable
- ☐ Diminished
- ☐ Disappointed
- ☐ Discouraged
- ☐ Disgusting
- ☐ Dissatisfied
- ☐ Guilty
- ☐ In Despair
- ☐ Lousy
- ☐ Miserable
- ☐ Powerless
- ☐ Repugnant
- ☐ Sulky
- ☐ Terrible

😠 ANGRY
- ☐ Aggressive
- ☐ Annoyed
- ☐ Bitter
- ☐ Boiling
- ☐ Cross
- ☐ Enraged
- ☐ Fuming
- ☐ Hateful
- ☐ Hostile
- ☐ Incensed
- ☐ Inflamed
- ☐ Infuriated
- ☐ Insulting
- ☐ Irritated
- ☐ Offensive
- ☐ Provoked
- ☐ Resentful
- ☐ Sore
- ☐ Unpleasant
- ☐ Upset
- ☐ Worked Up

😢 SAD
- ☐ Anguish
- ☐ Desolate
- ☐ Desperate
- ☐ Dismayed
- ☐ Grief
- ☐ Grieved
- ☐ Lonely
- ☐ Mournful
- ☐ Pained
- ☐ Pessimistic
- ☐ Sorrowful
- ☐ Tearful
- ☐ Unhappy

😐 INDIFFERENT
- ☐ Bored
- ☐ Cold
- ☐ Disinterested
- ☐ Dull
- ☐ Insensitive
- ☐ Lifeless
- ☐ Neutral
- ☐ Nonchalant
- ☐ Preoccupied
- ☐ Reserved
- ☐ Weary

😨 AFRAID
- ☐ Alarmed
- ☐ Anxious
- ☐ Cowardly
- ☐ Doubtful
- ☐ Fearful
- ☐ Frightened
- ☐ Menaced
- ☐ Nervous
- ☐ Panic
- ☐ Quaking
- ☐ Restless
- ☐ Scared
- ☐ Shaky
- ☐ Suspicious
- ☐ Terrified
- ☐ Threatened
- ☐ Timid
- ☐ Wary
- ☐ Worried

😣 HURT
- ☐ Aching
- ☐ Afflicted
- ☐ Agonized
- ☐ Alienated
- ☐ Appalled
- ☐ Crushed
- ☐ Dejected
- ☐ Deprived
- ☐ Heartbroken
- ☐ Humiliated
- ☐ Injured
- ☐ Offended
- ☐ Pained
- ☐ Rejected
- ☐ Tormented
- ☐ Tortured
- ☐ Victimized
- ☐ Wronged

Notes: _____
_____
_____

8 Pitfalls to avoid
- ☐ Me-too-ism. Don't start telling your story, or comparing your story to theirs.
- ☐ Moralizing, preaching, being judgmental
- ☐ Asking a direct question to satisfy your own curiosity
- ☐ Being an interviewer rather then a listener
- ☐ Giving advice (try fixing it)
- ☐ Cheap consolation. *"Oh, that's not to bad"*
- ☐ Arguing or disagreeing with the speaker
- ☐ Analyzing or interpreting
- ☐ Ignoring obvious heavy emotions

Date: _____

PLEASANT FEELINGS

😁 OPEN
- ☐ Accepting
- ☐ Amazed
- ☐ Confident
- ☐ Easy
- ☐ Free
- ☐ Interested
- ☐ Kind
- ☐ Receptive
- ☐ Reliable
- ☐ Satisfied
- ☐ Sympathetic
- ☐ Understanding

🤔 INTERESTED
- ☐ Absorbed
- ☐ Affected
- ☐ Concerned
- ☐ Curious
- ☐ Engrossed
- ☐ Fascinated
- ☐ Inquisitive
- ☐ Intrigued
- ☐ Nosy
- ☐ Snoopy

😃 ALIVE
- ☐ Animated
- ☐ Courageous
- ☐ Energetic
- ☐ Free
- ☐ Frisky
- ☐ Impulsive
- ☐ Liberated
- ☐ Optimistic
- ☐ Playful
- ☐ Provocative
- ☐ Spirited
- ☐ Thrilled
- ☐ Wonderful

😤 STRONG
- ☐ Certain
- ☐ Dynamic
- ☐ Free
- ☐ Hardy
- ☐ Impulsive
- ☐ Rebellious
- ☐ Secure
- ☐ Sure
- ☐ Tenacious
- ☐ Unique

😍 LOVE
- ☐ Admiration
- ☐ Affectionate
- ☐ Attracted
- ☐ Close
- ☐ Comforted
- ☐ Considerate
- ☐ Devoted
- ☐ Drawn toward
- ☐ Loved
- ☐ Loving
- ☐ Passionate
- ☐ Sensitive
- ☐ Sympathy
- ☐ Tender
- ☐ Touched
- ☐ Warm

🙂 POSITIVE
- ☐ Anxious
- ☐ Bold
- ☐ Brave
- ☐ Challenged
- ☐ Confident
- ☐ Daring
- ☐ Determined
- ☐ Eager
- ☐ Earnest
- ☐ Enthusiastic
- ☐ Excited
- ☐ Hopeful
- ☐ Inspired
- ☐ Intent
- ☐ Keen
- ☐ Optimistic
- ☐ Re-enforced

🙂 GOOD
- ☐ At ease
- ☐ Blessed
- ☐ Bright
- ☐ Calm
- ☐ Certain
- ☐ Clever
- ☐ Comfortable
- ☐ Content
- ☐ Encouraged
- ☐ Free and easy
- ☐ Peaceful
- ☐ Pleased
- ☐ Quiet
- ☐ Reassured
- ☐ Relaxed
- ☐ Serene
- ☐ Surprised

😊 HAPPY
- ☐ Cheerful
- ☐ Delighted
- ☐ Ecstatic
- ☐ Elated
- ☐ Festive
- ☐ Fortunate
- ☐ Glad
- ☐ Gleeful
- ☐ Great
- ☐ Important
- ☐ Joyous
- ☐ Jubilant
- ☐ Lucky
- ☐ Merry
- ☐ Overjoyed
- ☐ Satisfied
- ☐ Sunny
- ☐ Thankful

Read and check off
✓

Preparing to listen
- ☐ Remember to put your mind and feelings in neutral gear.
- ☐ Your body posture must say, *"I' am open, very interested, affirmative, attentive."*
- ☐ Maintain good eye contact.
- ☐ Give the speaker a verbal door opening, showing your readiness to listen.

While Listening
- ☐ Track what the speaker is saying in both content and feeling levels
- ☐ Stay with the content of communication
- ☐ Listen for and identify the basic general feeling; anger, fear, joy, resentment, etc.
- ☐ Suspend judgment; open yourself to the presence of their heart.

Responding
- ☐ Use oral responses, which are affirming, which say, *"I am with you"*, *"I understand."*
- ☐ Feed general feelings back to the speaker. *"You seem to feel this has been a good experience for you"*
- ☐ Stay an inch ahead of the speaker, not a mile.

UNPLEASANT FEELINGS

☹ HELPLESS
- ☐ Alone
- ☐ Despair
- ☐ Distressed
- ☐ Dominated
- ☐ Empty
- ☐ Fatigued
- ☐ Forced
- ☐ Frustrated
- ☐ Hesitant
- ☐ In A Stew
- ☐ Incapable
- ☐ Inferior
- ☐ Paralyzed
- ☐ Pathetic
- ☐ Tragic
- ☐ Useless
- ☐ Vulnerable
- ☐ Woeful

☹ CONFUSED
- ☐ Disillusioned
- ☐ Distrustful
- ☐ Doubtful
- ☐ Embarrassed
- ☐ Hesitant
- ☐ Indecisive
- ☐ Lost
- ☐ Misgiving
- ☐ Perplexed
- ☐ Pessimistic
- ☐ Shy
- ☐ Skeptical
- ☐ Stupefied
- ☐ Tense
- ☐ Unbelieving
- ☐ Uncertain
- ☐ Uneasy
- ☐ Unsure
- ☐ Upset

☹ DEPRESSED
- ☐ A Sense of Loss
- ☐ Abominable
- ☐ Ashamed
- ☐ Bad
- ☐ Despicable
- ☐ Detestable
- ☐ Diminished
- ☐ Disappointed
- ☐ Discouraged
- ☐ Disgusting
- ☐ Dissatisfied
- ☐ Guilty
- ☐ In Despair
- ☐ Lousy
- ☐ Miserable
- ☐ Powerless
- ☐ Repugnant
- ☐ Sulky
- ☐ Terrible

☹ ANGRY
- ☐ Aggressive
- ☐ Annoyed
- ☐ Bitter
- ☐ Boiling
- ☐ Cross
- ☐ Enraged
- ☐ Fuming
- ☐ Hateful
- ☐ Hostile
- ☐ Incensed
- ☐ Inflamed
- ☐ Infuriated
- ☐ Insulting
- ☐ Irritated
- ☐ Offensive
- ☐ Provoked
- ☐ Resentful
- ☐ Sore
- ☐ Unpleasant
- ☐ Upset
- ☐ Worked Up

☹ SAD
- ☐ Anguish
- ☐ Desolate
- ☐ Desperate
- ☐ Dismayed
- ☐ Grief
- ☐ Grieved
- ☐ Lonely
- ☐ Mournful
- ☐ Pained
- ☐ Pessimistic
- ☐ Sorrowful
- ☐ Tearful
- ☐ Unhappy

☹ INDIFFERENT
- ☐ Bored
- ☐ Cold
- ☐ Disinterested
- ☐ Dull
- ☐ Insensitive
- ☐ Lifeless
- ☐ Neutral
- ☐ Nonchalant
- ☐ Preoccupied
- ☐ Reserved
- ☐ Weary

☹ AFRAID
- ☐ Alarmed
- ☐ Anxious
- ☐ Cowardly
- ☐ Doubtful
- ☐ Fearful
- ☐ Frightened
- ☐ Menaced
- ☐ Nervous
- ☐ Panic
- ☐ Quaking
- ☐ Restless
- ☐ Scared
- ☐ Shaky
- ☐ Suspicious
- ☐ Terrified
- ☐ Threatened
- ☐ Timid
- ☐ Wary
- ☐ Worried

☹ HURT
- ☐ Aching
- ☐ Afflicted
- ☐ Agonized
- ☐ Alienated
- ☐ Appalled
- ☐ Crushed
- ☐ Dejected
- ☐ Deprived
- ☐ Heartbroken
- ☐ Humiliated
- ☐ Injured
- ☐ Offended
- ☐ Pained
- ☐ Rejected
- ☐ Tormented
- ☐ Tortured
- ☐ Victimized
- ☐ Wronged

Notes: _____
_____
_____
_____

8 Pitfalls to avoid
- ☐ Me-too-ism. Don't start telling your story, or comparing your story to theirs.
- ☐ Moralizing, preaching, being judgmental
- ☐ Asking a direct question to satisfy your own curiosity
- ☐ Being an interviewer rather then a listener
- ☐ Giving advice (try fixing it)
- ☐ Cheap consolation. *"Oh, that's not to bad"*
- ☐ Arguing or disagreeing with the speaker
- ☐ Analyzing or interpreting
- ☐ Ignoring obvious heavy emotions

Date: _____

PLEASANT FEELINGS

OPEN
- ☐ Accepting
- ☐ Amazed
- ☐ Confident
- ☐ Easy
- ☐ Free
- ☐ Interested
- ☐ Kind
- ☐ Receptive
- ☐ Reliable
- ☐ Satisfied
- ☐ Sympathetic
- ☐ Understanding

INTERESTED
- ☐ Absorbed
- ☐ Affected
- ☐ Concerned
- ☐ Curious
- ☐ Engrossed
- ☐ Fascinated
- ☐ Inquisitive
- ☐ Intrigued
- ☐ Nosy
- ☐ Snoopy

ALIVE
- ☐ Animated
- ☐ Courageous
- ☐ Energetic
- ☐ Free
- ☐ Frisky
- ☐ Impulsive
- ☐ Liberated
- ☐ Optimistic
- ☐ Playful
- ☐ Provocative
- ☐ Spirited
- ☐ Thrilled
- ☐ Wonderful

STRONG
- ☐ Certain
- ☐ Dynamic
- ☐ Free
- ☐ Hardy
- ☐ Impulsive
- ☐ Rebellious
- ☐ Secure
- ☐ Sure
- ☐ Tenacious
- ☐ Unique

LOVE
- ☐ Admiration
- ☐ Affectionate
- ☐ Attracted
- ☐ Close
- ☐ Comforted
- ☐ Considerate
- ☐ Devoted
- ☐ Drawn toward
- ☐ Loved
- ☐ Loving
- ☐ Passionate
- ☐ Sensitive
- ☐ Sympathy
- ☐ Tender
- ☐ Touched
- ☐ Warm

POSITIVE
- ☐ Anxious
- ☐ Bold
- ☐ Brave
- ☐ Challenged
- ☐ Confident
- ☐ Daring
- ☐ Determined
- ☐ Eager
- ☐ Earnest
- ☐ Enthusiastic
- ☐ Excited
- ☐ Hopeful
- ☐ Inspired
- ☐ Intent
- ☐ Keen
- ☐ Optimistic
- ☐ Re-enforced

GOOD
- ☐ At ease
- ☐ Blessed
- ☐ Bright
- ☐ Calm
- ☐ Certain
- ☐ Clever
- ☐ Comfortable
- ☐ Content
- ☐ Encouraged
- ☐ Free and easy
- ☐ Peaceful
- ☐ Pleased
- ☐ Quiet
- ☐ Reassured
- ☐ Relaxed
- ☐ Serene
- ☐ Surprised

HAPPY
- ☐ Cheerful
- ☐ Delighted
- ☐ Ecstatic
- ☐ Elated
- ☐ Festive
- ☐ Fortunate
- ☐ Glad
- ☐ Gleeful
- ☐ Great
- ☐ Important
- ☐ Joyous
- ☐ Jubilant
- ☐ Lucky
- ☐ Merry
- ☐ Overjoyed
- ☐ Satisfied
- ☐ Sunny
- ☐ Thankful

Read and check off ✓

Preparing to listen
- ☐ Remember to put your mind and feelings in neutral gear.
- ☐ Your body posture must say, *"I' am open, very interested, affirmative, attentive."*
- ☐ Maintain good eye contact.
- ☐ Give the speaker a verbal door opening, showing your readiness to listen.

While Listening
- ☐ Track what the speaker is saying in both content and feeling levels
- ☐ Stay with the content of communication
- ☐ Listen for and identify the basic general feeling; anger, fear, joy, resentment, etc.
- ☐ Suspend judgment; open yourself to the presence of their heart.

Responding
- ☐ Use oral responses, which are affirming, which say, *"I am with you"*, *"I understand."*
- ☐ Feed general feelings back to the speaker. *"You seem to feel this has been a good experience for you"*
- ☐ Stay an inch ahead of the speaker, not a mile.

UNPLEASANT FEELINGS

☹ HELPLESS
- ☐ Alone
- ☐ Despair
- ☐ Distressed
- ☐ Dominated
- ☐ Empty
- ☐ Fatigued
- ☐ Forced
- ☐ Frustrated
- ☐ Hesitant
- ☐ In A Stew
- ☐ Incapable
- ☐ Inferior
- ☐ Paralyzed
- ☐ Pathetic
- ☐ Tragic
- ☐ Useless
- ☐ Vulnerable
- ☐ Woeful

☹ SAD
- ☐ Anguish
- ☐ Desolate
- ☐ Desperate
- ☐ Dismayed
- ☐ Grief
- ☐ Grieved
- ☐ Lonely
- ☐ Mournful
- ☐ Pained
- ☐ Pessimistic
- ☐ Sorrowful
- ☐ Tearful
- ☐ Unhappy

☹ CONFUSED
- ☐ Disillusioned
- ☐ Distrustful
- ☐ Doubtful
- ☐ Embarrassed
- ☐ Hesitant
- ☐ Indecisive
- ☐ Lost
- ☐ Misgiving
- ☐ Perplexed
- ☐ Pessimistic
- ☐ Shy
- ☐ Skeptical
- ☐ Stupefied
- ☐ Tense
- ☐ Unbelieving
- ☐ Uncertain
- ☐ Uneasy
- ☐ Unsure
- ☐ Upset

☹ INDIFFERENT
- ☐ Bored
- ☐ Cold
- ☐ Disinterested
- ☐ Dull
- ☐ Insensitive
- ☐ Lifeless
- ☐ Neutral
- ☐ Nonchalant
- ☐ Preoccupied
- ☐ Reserved
- ☐ Weary

☹ DEPRESSED
- ☐ A Sense of Loss
- ☐ Abominable
- ☐ Ashamed
- ☐ Bad
- ☐ Despicable
- ☐ Detestable
- ☐ Diminished
- ☐ Disappointed
- ☐ Discouraged
- ☐ Disgusting
- ☐ Dissatisfied
- ☐ Guilty
- ☐ In Despair
- ☐ Lousy
- ☐ Miserable
- ☐ Powerless
- ☐ Repugnant
- ☐ Sulky
- ☐ Terrible

☹ AFRAID
- ☐ Alarmed
- ☐ Anxious
- ☐ Cowardly
- ☐ Doubtful
- ☐ Fearful
- ☐ Frightened
- ☐ Menaced
- ☐ Nervous
- ☐ Panic
- ☐ Quaking
- ☐ Restless
- ☐ Scared
- ☐ Shaky
- ☐ Suspicious
- ☐ Terrified
- ☐ Threatened
- ☐ Timid
- ☐ Wary
- ☐ Worried

☹ ANGRY
- ☐ Aggressive
- ☐ Annoyed
- ☐ Bitter
- ☐ Boiling
- ☐ Cross
- ☐ Enraged
- ☐ Fuming
- ☐ Hateful
- ☐ Hostile
- ☐ Incensed
- ☐ Inflamed
- ☐ Infuriated
- ☐ Insulting
- ☐ Irritated
- ☐ Offensive
- ☐ Provoked
- ☐ Resentful
- ☐ Sore
- ☐ Unpleasant
- ☐ Upset
- ☐ Worked Up

☹ HURT
- ☐ Aching
- ☐ Afflicted
- ☐ Agonized
- ☐ Alienated
- ☐ Appalled
- ☐ Crushed
- ☐ Dejected
- ☐ Deprived
- ☐ Heartbroken
- ☐ Humiliated
- ☐ Injured
- ☐ Offended
- ☐ Pained
- ☐ Rejected
- ☐ Tormented
- ☐ Tortured
- ☐ Victimized
- ☐ Wronged

Notes: _____
_____
_____
_____

8 Pitfalls to avoid
- ☐ Me-too-ism. Don't start telling your story, or comparing your story to theirs.
- ☐ Moralizing, preaching, being judgmental
- ☐ Asking a direct question to satisfy your own curiosity
- ☐ Being an interviewer rather then a listener
- ☐ Giving advice (try fixing it)
- ☐ Cheap consolation. *"Oh, that's not to bad"*
- ☐ Arguing or disagreeing with the speaker
- ☐ Analyzing or interpreting
- ☐ Ignoring obvious heavy emotions

Date: _____

PLEASANT FEELINGS

OPEN
- ☐ Accepting
- ☐ Amazed
- ☐ Confident
- ☐ Easy
- ☐ Free
- ☐ Interested
- ☐ Kind
- ☐ Receptive
- ☐ Reliable
- ☐ Satisfied
- ☐ Sympathetic
- ☐ Understanding

INTERESTED
- ☐ Absorbed
- ☐ Affected
- ☐ Concerned
- ☐ Curious
- ☐ Engrossed
- ☐ Fascinated
- ☐ Inquisitive
- ☐ Intrigued
- ☐ Nosy
- ☐ Snoopy

ALIVE
- ☐ Animated
- ☐ Courageous
- ☐ Energetic
- ☐ Free
- ☐ Frisky
- ☐ Impulsive
- ☐ Liberated
- ☐ Optimistic
- ☐ Playful
- ☐ Provocative
- ☐ Spirited
- ☐ Thrilled
- ☐ Wonderful

STRONG
- ☐ Certain
- ☐ Dynamic
- ☐ Free
- ☐ Hardy
- ☐ Impulsive
- ☐ Rebellious
- ☐ Secure
- ☐ Sure
- ☐ Tenacious
- ☐ Unique

LOVE
- ☐ Admiration
- ☐ Affectionate
- ☐ Attracted
- ☐ Close
- ☐ Comforted
- ☐ Considerate
- ☐ Devoted
- ☐ Drawn toward
- ☐ Loved
- ☐ Loving
- ☐ Passionate
- ☐ Sensitive
- ☐ Sympathy
- ☐ Tender
- ☐ Touched
- ☐ Warm

POSITIVE
- ☐ Anxious
- ☐ Bold
- ☐ Brave
- ☐ Challenged
- ☐ Confident
- ☐ Daring
- ☐ Determined
- ☐ Eager
- ☐ Earnest
- ☐ Enthusiastic
- ☐ Excited
- ☐ Hopeful
- ☐ Inspired
- ☐ Intent
- ☐ Keen
- ☐ Optimistic
- ☐ Re-enforced

GOOD
- ☐ At ease
- ☐ Blessed
- ☐ Bright
- ☐ Calm
- ☐ Certain
- ☐ Clever
- ☐ Comfortable
- ☐ Content
- ☐ Encouraged
- ☐ Free and easy
- ☐ Peaceful
- ☐ Pleased
- ☐ Quiet
- ☐ Reassured
- ☐ Relaxed
- ☐ Serene
- ☐ Surprised

HAPPY
- ☐ Cheerful
- ☐ Delighted
- ☐ Ecstatic
- ☐ Elated
- ☐ Festive
- ☐ Fortunate
- ☐ Glad
- ☐ Gleeful
- ☐ Great
- ☐ Important
- ☐ Joyous
- ☐ Jubilant
- ☐ Lucky
- ☐ Merry
- ☐ Overjoyed
- ☐ Satisfied
- ☐ Sunny
- ☐ Thankful

Read and check off ✓

Preparing to listen
- ☐ Remember to put your mind and feelings in neutral gear.
- ☐ Your body posture must say, *"I am open, very interested, affirmative, attentive."*
- ☐ Maintain good eye contact.
- ☐ Give the speaker a verbal door opening, showing your readiness to listen.

While Listening
- ☐ Track what the speaker is saying in both content and feeling levels
- ☐ Stay with the content of communication
- ☐ Listen for and identify the basic general feeling; anger, fear, joy, resentment, etc.
- ☐ Suspend judgment; open yourself to the presence of their heart.

Responding
- ☐ Use oral responses, which are affirming, which say, *"I am with you"*, *"I understand."*
- ☐ Feed general feelings back to the speaker. *"You seem to feel this has been a good experience for you"*
- ☐ Stay an inch ahead of the speaker, not a mile.

UNPLEASANT FEELINGS

HELPLESS
- [ ] Alone
- [ ] Despair
- [ ] Distressed
- [ ] Dominated
- [ ] Empty
- [ ] Fatigued
- [ ] Forced
- [ ] Frustrated
- [ ] Hesitant
- [ ] In A Stew
- [ ] Incapable
- [ ] Inferior
- [ ] Paralyzed
- [ ] Pathetic
- [ ] Tragic
- [ ] Useless
- [ ] Vulnerable
- [ ] Woeful

CONFUSED
- [ ] Disillusioned
- [ ] Distrustful
- [ ] Doubtful
- [ ] Embarrassed
- [ ] Hesitant
- [ ] Indecisive
- [ ] Lost
- [ ] Misgiving
- [ ] Perplexed
- [ ] Pessimistic
- [ ] Shy
- [ ] Skeptical
- [ ] Stupefied
- [ ] Tense
- [ ] Unbelieving
- [ ] Uncertain
- [ ] Uneasy
- [ ] Unsure
- [ ] Upset

DEPRESSED
- [ ] A Sense of Loss
- [ ] Abominable
- [ ] Ashamed
- [ ] Bad
- [ ] Despicable
- [ ] Detestable
- [ ] Diminished
- [ ] Disappointed
- [ ] Discouraged
- [ ] Disgusting
- [ ] Dissatisfied
- [ ] Guilty
- [ ] In Despair
- [ ] Lousy
- [ ] Miserable
- [ ] Powerless
- [ ] Repugnant
- [ ] Sulky
- [ ] Terrible

ANGRY
- [ ] Aggressive
- [ ] Annoyed
- [ ] Bitter
- [ ] Boiling
- [ ] Cross
- [ ] Enraged
- [ ] Fuming
- [ ] Hateful
- [ ] Hostile
- [ ] Incensed
- [ ] Inflamed
- [ ] Infuriated
- [ ] Insulting
- [ ] Irritated
- [ ] Offensive
- [ ] Provoked
- [ ] Resentful
- [ ] Sore
- [ ] Unpleasant
- [ ] Upset
- [ ] Worked Up

SAD
- [ ] Anguish
- [ ] Desolate
- [ ] Desperate
- [ ] Dismayed
- [ ] Grief
- [ ] Grieved
- [ ] Lonely
- [ ] Mournful
- [ ] Pained
- [ ] Pessimistic
- [ ] Sorrowful
- [ ] Tearful
- [ ] Unhappy

INDIFFERENT
- [ ] Bored
- [ ] Cold
- [ ] Disinterested
- [ ] Dull
- [ ] Insensitive
- [ ] Lifeless
- [ ] Neutral
- [ ] Nonchalant
- [ ] Preoccupied
- [ ] Reserved
- [ ] Weary

AFRAID
- [ ] Alarmed
- [ ] Anxious
- [ ] Cowardly
- [ ] Doubtful
- [ ] Fearful
- [ ] Frightened
- [ ] Menaced
- [ ] Nervous
- [ ] Panic
- [ ] Quaking
- [ ] Restless
- [ ] Scared
- [ ] Shaky
- [ ] Suspicious
- [ ] Terrified
- [ ] Threatened
- [ ] Timid
- [ ] Wary
- [ ] Worried

HURT
- [ ] Aching
- [ ] Afflicted
- [ ] Agonized
- [ ] Alienated
- [ ] Appalled
- [ ] Crushed
- [ ] Dejected
- [ ] Deprived
- [ ] Heartbroken
- [ ] Humiliated
- [ ] Injured
- [ ] Offended
- [ ] Pained
- [ ] Rejected
- [ ] Tormented
- [ ] Tortured
- [ ] Victimized
- [ ] Wronged

Notes: _____
_____
_____
_____

8 Pitfalls to avoid
- [ ] Me-too-ism. Don't start telling your story, or comparing your story to theirs.
- [ ] Moralizing, preaching, being judgmental
- [ ] Asking a direct question to satisfy your own curiosity
- [ ] Being an interviewer rather then a listener
- [ ] Giving advice (try fixing it)
- [ ] Cheap consolation. *"Oh, that's not to bad"*
- [ ] Arguing or disagreeing with the speaker
- [ ] Analyzing or interpreting
- [ ] Ignoring obvious heavy emotions

Date: _____

PLEASANT FEELINGS

OPEN
- ☐ Accepting
- ☐ Amazed
- ☐ Confident
- ☐ Easy
- ☐ Free
- ☐ Interested
- ☐ Kind
- ☐ Receptive
- ☐ Reliable
- ☐ Satisfied
- ☐ Sympathetic
- ☐ Understanding

INTERESTED
- ☐ Absorbed
- ☐ Affected
- ☐ Concerned
- ☐ Curious
- ☐ Engrossed
- ☐ Fascinated
- ☐ Inquisitive
- ☐ Intrigued
- ☐ Nosy
- ☐ Snoopy

ALIVE
- ☐ Animated
- ☐ Courageous
- ☐ Energetic
- ☐ Free
- ☐ Frisky
- ☐ Impulsive
- ☐ Liberated
- ☐ Optimistic
- ☐ Playful
- ☐ Provocative
- ☐ Spirited
- ☐ Thrilled
- ☐ Wonderful

STRONG
- ☐ Certain
- ☐ Dynamic
- ☐ Free
- ☐ Hardy
- ☐ Impulsive
- ☐ Rebellious
- ☐ Secure
- ☐ Sure
- ☐ Tenacious
- ☐ Unique

LOVE
- ☐ Admiration
- ☐ Affectionate
- ☐ Attracted
- ☐ Close
- ☐ Comforted
- ☐ Considerate
- ☐ Devoted
- ☐ Drawn toward
- ☐ Loved
- ☐ Loving
- ☐ Passionate
- ☐ Sensitive
- ☐ Sympathy
- ☐ Tender
- ☐ Touched
- ☐ Warm

POSITIVE
- ☐ Anxious
- ☐ Bold
- ☐ Brave
- ☐ Challenged
- ☐ Confident
- ☐ Daring
- ☐ Determined
- ☐ Eager
- ☐ Earnest
- ☐ Enthusiastic
- ☐ Excited
- ☐ Hopeful
- ☐ Inspired
- ☐ Intent
- ☐ Keen
- ☐ Optimistic
- ☐ Re-enforced

GOOD
- ☐ At ease
- ☐ Blessed
- ☐ Bright
- ☐ Calm
- ☐ Certain
- ☐ Clever
- ☐ Comfortable
- ☐ Content
- ☐ Encouraged
- ☐ Free and easy
- ☐ Peaceful
- ☐ Pleased
- ☐ Quiet
- ☐ Reassured
- ☐ Relaxed
- ☐ Serene
- ☐ Surprised

HAPPY
- ☐ Cheerful
- ☐ Delighted
- ☐ Ecstatic
- ☐ Elated
- ☐ Festive
- ☐ Fortunate
- ☐ Glad
- ☐ Gleeful
- ☐ Great
- ☐ Important
- ☐ Joyous
- ☐ Jubilant
- ☐ Lucky
- ☐ Merry
- ☐ Overjoyed
- ☐ Satisfied
- ☐ Sunny
- ☐ Thankful

Read and check off
✓

Preparing to listen
- ☐ Remember to put your mind and feelings in neutral gear.
- ☐ Your body posture must say, *"I' am open, very interested, affirmative, attentive."*
- ☐ Maintain good eye contact.
- ☐ Give the speaker a verbal door opening, showing your readiness to listen.

While Listening
- ☐ Track what the speaker is saying in both content and feeling levels
- ☐ Stay with the content of communication
- ☐ Listen for and identify the basic general feeling; anger, fear, joy, resentment, etc.
- ☐ Suspend judgment; open yourself to the presence of their heart.

Responding
- ☐ Use oral responses, which are affirming, which say, *"I am with you", "I understand."*
- ☐ Feed general feelings back to the speaker. *"You seem to feel this has been a good experience for you"*
- ☐ Stay an inch ahead of the speaker, not a mile.

UNPLEASANT FEELINGS

😧 HELPLESS
- ☐ Alone
- ☐ Despair
- ☐ Distressed
- ☐ Dominated
- ☐ Empty
- ☐ Fatigued
- ☐ Forced
- ☐ Frustrated
- ☐ Hesitant
- ☐ In A Stew
- ☐ Incapable
- ☐ Inferior
- ☐ Paralyzed
- ☐ Pathetic
- ☐ Tragic
- ☐ Useless
- ☐ Vulnerable
- ☐ Woeful

😕 CONFUSED
- ☐ Disillusioned
- ☐ Distrustful
- ☐ Doubtful
- ☐ Embarrassed
- ☐ Hesitant
- ☐ Indecisive
- ☐ Lost
- ☐ Misgiving
- ☐ Perplexed
- ☐ Pessimistic
- ☐ Shy
- ☐ Skeptical
- ☐ Stupefied
- ☐ Tense
- ☐ Unbelieving
- ☐ Uncertain
- ☐ Uneasy
- ☐ Unsure
- ☐ Upset

😔 DEPRESSED
- ☐ A Sense of Loss
- ☐ Abominable
- ☐ Ashamed
- ☐ Bad
- ☐ Despicable
- ☐ Detestable
- ☐ Diminished
- ☐ Disappointed
- ☐ Discouraged
- ☐ Disgusting
- ☐ Dissatisfied
- ☐ Guilty
- ☐ In Despair
- ☐ Lousy
- ☐ Miserable
- ☐ Powerless
- ☐ Repugnant
- ☐ Sulky
- ☐ Terrible

😠 ANGRY
- ☐ Aggressive
- ☐ Annoyed
- ☐ Bitter
- ☐ Boiling
- ☐ Cross
- ☐ Enraged
- ☐ Fuming
- ☐ Hateful
- ☐ Hostile
- ☐ Incensed
- ☐ Inflamed
- ☐ Infuriated
- ☐ Insulting
- ☐ Irritated
- ☐ Offensive
- ☐ Provoked
- ☐ Resentful
- ☐ Sore
- ☐ Unpleasant
- ☐ Upset
- ☐ Worked Up

🙁 SAD
- ☐ Anguish
- ☐ Desolate
- ☐ Desperate
- ☐ Dismayed
- ☐ Grief
- ☐ Grieved
- ☐ Lonely
- ☐ Mournful
- ☐ Pained
- ☐ Pessimistic
- ☐ Sorrowful
- ☐ Tearful
- ☐ Unhappy

😑 INDIFFERENT
- ☐ Bored
- ☐ Cold
- ☐ Disinterested
- ☐ Dull
- ☐ Insensitive
- ☐ Lifeless
- ☐ Neutral
- ☐ Nonchalant
- ☐ Preoccupied
- ☐ Reserved
- ☐ Weary

😨 AFRAID
- ☐ Alarmed
- ☐ Anxious
- ☐ Cowardly
- ☐ Doubtful
- ☐ Fearful
- ☐ Frightened
- ☐ Menaced
- ☐ Nervous
- ☐ Panic
- ☐ Quaking
- ☐ Restless
- ☐ Scared
- ☐ Shaky
- ☐ Suspicious
- ☐ Terrified
- ☐ Threatened
- ☐ Timid
- ☐ Wary
- ☐ Worried

😞 HURT
- ☐ Aching
- ☐ Afflicted
- ☐ Agonized
- ☐ Alienated
- ☐ Appalled
- ☐ Crushed
- ☐ Dejected
- ☐ Deprived
- ☐ Heartbroken
- ☐ Humiliated
- ☐ Injured
- ☐ Offended
- ☐ Pained
- ☐ Rejected
- ☐ Tormented
- ☐ Tortured
- ☐ Victimized
- ☐ Wronged

Notes: _____
_____
_____
_____

8 Pitfalls to avoid
- ☐ Me-too-ism. Don't start telling your story, or comparing your story to theirs.
- ☐ Moralizing, preaching, being judgmental
- ☐ Asking a direct question to satisfy your own curiosity
- ☐ Being an interviewer rather then a listener
- ☐ Giving advice (try fixing it)
- ☐ Cheap consolation. *"Oh, that's not to bad"*
- ☐ Arguing or disagreeing with the speaker
- ☐ Analyzing or interpreting
- ☐ Ignoring obvious heavy emotions

Date: _____

PLEASANT FEELINGS

☺ OPEN
- ☐ Accepting
- ☐ Amazed
- ☐ Confident
- ☐ Easy
- ☐ Free
- ☐ Interested
- ☐ Kind
- ☐ Receptive
- ☐ Reliable
- ☐ Satisfied
- ☐ Sympathetic
- ☐ Understanding

☺ INTERESTED
- ☐ Absorbed
- ☐ Affected
- ☐ Concerned
- ☐ Curious
- ☐ Engrossed
- ☐ Fascinated
- ☐ Inquisitive
- ☐ Intrigued
- ☐ Nosy
- ☐ Snoopy

☺ ALIVE
- ☐ Animated
- ☐ Courageous
- ☐ Energetic
- ☐ Free
- ☐ Frisky
- ☐ Impulsive
- ☐ Liberated
- ☐ Optimistic
- ☐ Playful
- ☐ Provocative
- ☐ Spirited
- ☐ Thrilled
- ☐ Wonderful

☺ STRONG
- ☐ Certain
- ☐ Dynamic
- ☐ Free
- ☐ Hardy
- ☐ Impulsive
- ☐ Rebellious
- ☐ Secure
- ☐ Sure
- ☐ Tenacious
- ☐ Unique

☺ LOVE
- ☐ Admiration
- ☐ Affectionate
- ☐ Attracted
- ☐ Close
- ☐ Comforted
- ☐ Considerate
- ☐ Devoted
- ☐ Drawn toward
- ☐ Loved
- ☐ Loving
- ☐ Passionate
- ☐ Sensitive
- ☐ Sympathy
- ☐ Tender
- ☐ Touched
- ☐ Warm

☺ POSITIVE
- ☐ Anxious
- ☐ Bold
- ☐ Brave
- ☐ Challenged
- ☐ Confident
- ☐ Daring
- ☐ Determined
- ☐ Eager
- ☐ Earnest
- ☐ Enthusiastic
- ☐ Excited
- ☐ Hopeful
- ☐ Inspired
- ☐ Intent
- ☐ Keen
- ☐ Optimistic
- ☐ Re-enforced

☺ GOOD
- ☐ At ease
- ☐ Blessed
- ☐ Bright
- ☐ Calm
- ☐ Certain
- ☐ Clever
- ☐ Comfortable
- ☐ Content
- ☐ Encouraged
- ☐ Free and easy
- ☐ Peaceful
- ☐ Pleased
- ☐ Quiet
- ☐ Reassured
- ☐ Relaxed
- ☐ Serene
- ☐ Surprised

☺ HAPPY
- ☐ Cheerful
- ☐ Delighted
- ☐ Ecstatic
- ☐ Elated
- ☐ Festive
- ☐ Fortunate
- ☐ Glad
- ☐ Gleeful
- ☐ Great
- ☐ Important
- ☐ Joyous
- ☐ Jubilant
- ☐ Lucky
- ☐ Merry
- ☐ Overjoyed
- ☐ Satisfied
- ☐ Sunny
- ☐ Thankful

check off ✓

Preparing to listen
- ☐ Remember to put your mind and feelings in neutral gear.
- ☐ Your body posture must say, *"I am open, very interested, affirmative, attentive."*
- ☐ Maintain good eye contact.
- ☐ Give the speaker a verbal door opening, showing your readiness to listen.

While Listening
- ☐ Track what the speaker is saying in both content and feeling levels
- ☐ Stay with the content of communication
- ☐ Listen for and identify the basic general feeling; anger, fear, joy, resentment, etc.
- ☐ Suspend judgment; open yourself to the presence of their heart.

Responding
- ☐ Use oral responses, which are affirming, which say, *"I am with you", "I understand."*
- ☐ Feed general feelings back to the speaker. *"You seem to feel this has been a good experience for you"*
- ☐ Stay an inch ahead of the speaker, not a mile.

UNPLEASANT FEELINGS

😨 HELPLESS
- [ ] Alone
- [ ] Despair
- [ ] Distressed
- [ ] Dominated
- [ ] Empty
- [ ] Fatigued
- [ ] Forced
- [ ] Frustrated
- [ ] Hesitant
- [ ] In A Stew
- [ ] Incapable
- [ ] Inferior
- [ ] Paralyzed
- [ ] Pathetic
- [ ] Tragic
- [ ] Useless
- [ ] Vulnerable
- [ ] Woeful

😕 CONFUSED
- [ ] Disillusioned
- [ ] Distrustful
- [ ] Doubtful
- [ ] Embarrassed
- [ ] Hesitant
- [ ] Indecisive
- [ ] Lost
- [ ] Misgiving
- [ ] Perplexed
- [ ] Pessimistic
- [ ] Shy
- [ ] Skeptical
- [ ] Stupefied
- [ ] Tense
- [ ] Unbelieving
- [ ] Uncertain
- [ ] Uneasy
- [ ] Unsure
- [ ] Upset

😞 DEPRESSED
- [ ] A Sense of Loss
- [ ] Abominable
- [ ] Ashamed
- [ ] Bad
- [ ] Despicable
- [ ] Detestable
- [ ] Diminished
- [ ] Disappointed
- [ ] Discouraged
- [ ] Disgusting
- [ ] Dissatisfied
- [ ] Guilty
- [ ] In Despair
- [ ] Lousy
- [ ] Miserable
- [ ] Powerless
- [ ] Repugnant
- [ ] Sulky
- [ ] Terrible

😠 ANGRY
- [ ] Aggressive
- [ ] Annoyed
- [ ] Bitter
- [ ] Boiling
- [ ] Cross
- [ ] Enraged
- [ ] Fuming
- [ ] Hateful
- [ ] Hostile
- [ ] Incensed
- [ ] Inflamed
- [ ] Infuriated
- [ ] Insulting
- [ ] Irritated
- [ ] Offensive
- [ ] Provoked
- [ ] Resentful
- [ ] Sore
- [ ] Unpleasant
- [ ] Upset
- [ ] Worked Up

😢 SAD
- [ ] Anguish
- [ ] Desolate
- [ ] Desperate
- [ ] Dismayed
- [ ] Grief
- [ ] Grieved
- [ ] Lonely
- [ ] Mournful
- [ ] Pained
- [ ] Pessimistic
- [ ] Sorrowful
- [ ] Tearful
- [ ] Unhappy

😐 INDIFFERENT
- [ ] Bored
- [ ] Cold
- [ ] Disinterested
- [ ] Dull
- [ ] Insensitive
- [ ] Lifeless
- [ ] Neutral
- [ ] Nonchalant
- [ ] Preoccupied
- [ ] Reserved
- [ ] Weary

😨 AFRAID
- [ ] Alarmed
- [ ] Anxious
- [ ] Cowardly
- [ ] Doubtful
- [ ] Fearful
- [ ] Frightened
- [ ] Menaced
- [ ] Nervous
- [ ] Panic
- [ ] Quaking
- [ ] Restless
- [ ] Scared
- [ ] Shaky
- [ ] Suspicious
- [ ] Terrified
- [ ] Threatened
- [ ] Timid
- [ ] Wary
- [ ] Worried

😔 HURT
- [ ] Aching
- [ ] Afflicted
- [ ] Agonized
- [ ] Alienated
- [ ] Appalled
- [ ] Crushed
- [ ] Dejected
- [ ] Deprived
- [ ] Heartbroken
- [ ] Humiliated
- [ ] Injured
- [ ] Offended
- [ ] Pained
- [ ] Rejected
- [ ] Tormented
- [ ] Tortured
- [ ] Victimized
- [ ] Wronged

Notes:
_____
_____
_____
_____

8 Pitfalls to avoid
- [ ] Me-too-ism. Don't start telling your story, or comparing your story to theirs.
- [ ] Moralizing, preaching, being judgmental
- [ ] Asking a direct question to satisfy your own curiosity
- [ ] Being an interviewer rather then a listener
- [ ] Giving advice (try fixing it)
- [ ] Cheap consolation. *"Oh, that's not to bad"*
- [ ] Arguing or disagreeing with the speaker
- [ ] Analyzing or interpreting
- [ ] Ignoring obvious heavy emotions

Date: _____

98.

PLEASANT FEELINGS

OPEN
- ☐ Accepting
- ☐ Amazed
- ☐ Confident
- ☐ Easy
- ☐ Free
- ☐ Interested
- ☐ Kind
- ☐ Receptive
- ☐ Reliable
- ☐ Satisfied
- ☐ Sympathetic
- ☐ Understanding

INTERESTED
- ☐ Absorbed
- ☐ Affected
- ☐ Concerned
- ☐ Curious
- ☐ Engrossed
- ☐ Fascinated
- ☐ Inquisitive
- ☐ Intrigued
- ☐ Nosy
- ☐ Snoopy

ALIVE
- ☐ Animated
- ☐ Courageous
- ☐ Energetic
- ☐ Free
- ☐ Frisky
- ☐ Impulsive
- ☐ Liberated
- ☐ Optimistic
- ☐ Playful
- ☐ Provocative
- ☐ Spirited
- ☐ Thrilled
- ☐ Wonderful

STRONG
- ☐ Certain
- ☐ Dynamic
- ☐ Free
- ☐ Hardy
- ☐ Impulsive
- ☐ Rebellious
- ☐ Secure
- ☐ Sure
- ☐ Tenacious
- ☐ Unique

LOVE
- ☐ Admiration
- ☐ Affectionate
- ☐ Attracted
- ☐ Close
- ☐ Comforted
- ☐ Considerate
- ☐ Devoted
- ☐ Drawn toward
- ☐ Loved
- ☐ Loving
- ☐ Passionate
- ☐ Sensitive
- ☐ Sympathy
- ☐ Tender
- ☐ Touched
- ☐ Warm

POSITIVE
- ☐ Anxious
- ☐ Bold
- ☐ Brave
- ☐ Challenged
- ☐ Confident
- ☐ Daring
- ☐ Determined
- ☐ Eager
- ☐ Earnest
- ☐ Enthusiastic
- ☐ Excited
- ☐ Hopeful
- ☐ Inspired
- ☐ Intent
- ☐ Keen
- ☐ Optimistic
- ☐ Re-enforced

GOOD
- ☐ At ease
- ☐ Blessed
- ☐ Bright
- ☐ Calm
- ☐ Certain
- ☐ Clever
- ☐ Comfortable
- ☐ Content
- ☐ Encouraged
- ☐ Free and easy
- ☐ Peaceful
- ☐ Pleased
- ☐ Quiet
- ☐ Reassured
- ☐ Relaxed
- ☐ Serene
- ☐ Surprised

HAPPY
- ☐ Cheerful
- ☐ Delighted
- ☐ Ecstatic
- ☐ Elated
- ☐ Festive
- ☐ Fortunate
- ☐ Glad
- ☐ Gleeful
- ☐ Great
- ☐ Important
- ☐ Joyous
- ☐ Jubilant
- ☐ Lucky
- ☐ Merry
- ☐ Overjoyed
- ☐ Satisfied
- ☐ Sunny
- ☐ Thankful

Read and check off
✓

Preparing to listen
- ☐ Remember to put your mind and feelings in neutral gear.
- ☐ Your body posture must say, *"I am open, very interested, affirmative, attentive."*
- ☐ Maintain good eye contact.
- ☐ Give the speaker a verbal door opening, showing your readiness to listen.

While Listening
- ☐ Track what the speaker is saying in both content and feeling levels
- ☐ Stay with the content of communication
- ☐ Listen for and identify the basic general feeling; anger, fear, joy, resentment, etc.
- ☐ Suspend judgment; open yourself to the presence of their heart.

Responding
- ☐ Use oral responses, which are affirming, which say, *"I am with you", "I understand."*
- ☐ Feed general feelings back to the speaker. *"You seem to feel this has been a good experience for you"*
- ☐ Stay an inch ahead of the speaker, not a mile.

UNPLEASANT FEELINGS

😵 HELPLESS
- ☐ Alone
- ☐ Despair
- ☐ Distressed
- ☐ Dominated
- ☐ Empty
- ☐ Fatigued
- ☐ Forced
- ☐ Frustrated
- ☐ Hesitant
- ☐ In A Stew
- ☐ Incapable
- ☐ Inferior
- ☐ Paralyzed
- ☐ Pathetic
- ☐ Tragic
- ☐ Useless
- ☐ Vulnerable
- ☐ Woeful

😕 SAD
- ☐ Anguish
- ☐ Desolate
- ☐ Desperate
- ☐ Dismayed
- ☐ Grief
- ☐ Grieved
- ☐ Lonely
- ☐ Mournful
- ☐ Pained
- ☐ Pessimistic
- ☐ Sorrowful
- ☐ Tearful
- ☐ Unhappy

😐 CONFUSED
- ☐ Disillusioned
- ☐ Distrustful
- ☐ Doubtful
- ☐ Embarrassed
- ☐ Hesitant
- ☐ Indecisive
- ☐ Lost
- ☐ Misgiving
- ☐ Perplexed
- ☐ Pessimistic
- ☐ Shy
- ☐ Skeptical
- ☐ Stupefied
- ☐ Tense
- ☐ Unbelieving
- ☐ Uncertain
- ☐ Uneasy
- ☐ Unsure
- ☐ Upset

😐 INDIFFERENT
- ☐ Bored
- ☐ Cold
- ☐ Disinterested
- ☐ Dull
- ☐ Insensitive
- ☐ Lifeless
- ☐ Neutral
- ☐ Nonchalant
- ☐ Preoccupied
- ☐ Reserved
- ☐ Weary

😞 DEPRESSED
- ☐ A Sense of Loss
- ☐ Abominable
- ☐ Ashamed
- ☐ Bad
- ☐ Despicable
- ☐ Detestable
- ☐ Diminished
- ☐ Disappointed
- ☐ Discouraged
- ☐ Disgusting
- ☐ Dissatisfied
- ☐ Guilty
- ☐ In Despair
- ☐ Lousy
- ☐ Miserable
- ☐ Powerless
- ☐ Repugnant
- ☐ Sulky
- ☐ Terrible

😨 AFRAID
- ☐ Alarmed
- ☐ Anxious
- ☐ Cowardly
- ☐ Doubtful
- ☐ Fearful
- ☐ Frightened
- ☐ Menaced
- ☐ Nervous
- ☐ Panic
- ☐ Quaking
- ☐ Restless
- ☐ Scared
- ☐ Shaky
- ☐ Suspicious
- ☐ Terrified
- ☐ Threatened
- ☐ Timid
- ☐ Wary
- ☐ Worried

😠 ANGRY
- ☐ Aggressive
- ☐ Annoyed
- ☐ Bitter
- ☐ Boiling
- ☐ Cross
- ☐ Enraged
- ☐ Fuming
- ☐ Hateful
- ☐ Hostile
- ☐ Incensed
- ☐ Inflamed
- ☐ Infuriated
- ☐ Insulting
- ☐ Irritated
- ☐ Offensive
- ☐ Provoked
- ☐ Resentful
- ☐ Sore
- ☐ Unpleasant
- ☐ Upset
- ☐ Worked Up

😢 HURT
- ☐ Aching
- ☐ Afflicted
- ☐ Agonized
- ☐ Alienated
- ☐ Appalled
- ☐ Crushed
- ☐ Dejected
- ☐ Deprived
- ☐ Heartbroken
- ☐ Humiliated
- ☐ Injured
- ☐ Offended
- ☐ Pained
- ☐ Rejected
- ☐ Tormented
- ☐ Tortured
- ☐ Victimized
- ☐ Wronged

Notes: _____
_____
_____
_____

8 Pitfalls to avoid
- ☐ Me-too-ism. Don't start telling your story, or comparing your story to theirs.
- ☐ Moralizing, preaching, being judgmental
- ☐ Asking a direct question to satisfy your own curiosity
- ☐ Being an interviewer rather then a listener
- ☐ Giving advice (try fixing it)
- ☐ Cheap consolation. *"Oh, that's not to bad"*
- ☐ Arguing or disagreeing with the speaker
- ☐ Analyzing or interpreting
- ☐ Ignoring obvious heavy emotions

Date: _____

Definitions and Explanations

 ## Preparing to listen

☑ **Remember to put your mind and feelings in neutral gear.**

When preparing to listen to your partner, it is crucial to keep in mind the importance of putting your mind and feelings in neutral gear. By doing so, you create a space where you can truly listen and understand your partner's perspective without any preconceived notions or biases. This means setting aside any personal judgments or emotional reactions that may cloud your ability to empathize and connect with your loved one. By approaching the conversation with an open and neutral mindset, you pave the way for effective communication, mutual respect, and a deeper understanding of each other's thoughts and emotions. So, remember to embrace this mindset as you prepare to listen to your partner, allowing for a more meaningful and fulfilling exchange of ideas and feelings.

☑ **Your body posture must say, "I' am open, very interested, affirmative, attentive."**

When preparing to listen to your partner, it is crucial to ensure that your body posture exudes an air of openness, genuine interest, affirmation, and attentiveness. By adopting a relaxed yet engaged stance, you create an inviting atmosphere that encourages effective communication and understanding. Your body language should convey a sense of receptiveness, with your arms uncrossed and your posture leaning slightly forward, indicating your eagerness to hear what your partner has to say. Remember, the way you present yourself physically can greatly impact the quality of your communication, so strive to create a positive and receptive environment through your body posture.

Definitions and Explanations

 ## Preparing to listen

☑ **Maintain good eye contact.**

When preparing to listen to your partner, it is crucial to maintain good eye contact. By doing so, you demonstrate your attentiveness and show that you value what they have to say. Eye contact creates a sense of connection and trust, allowing for effective communication and understanding. It helps to establish a positive and respectful environment, where both parties feel heard and acknowledged. Moreover, maintaining eye contact enables you to pick up on nonverbal cues and emotions, enhancing your ability to empathize and respond appropriately. So, remember to keep your gaze focused on your partner, as it not only enhances the listening experience but also strengthens the bond between you.

☑ **Give the speaker a verbal door opening, showing your readiness to listen.**

Before you start listening to your partner, it's important to create a safe and welcoming environment for them to share their thoughts and feelings. One way to do this is by giving them a verbal door opening, which shows that you are ready and willing to listen. This can be as simple as saying "I'm here for you" or "I'm ready to listen whenever you're ready to talk." By providing this verbal cue, you are letting your partner know that you are fully present and engaged in the conversation, and that you value their perspective and feelings. This can help to build trust and strengthen your relationship, as well as facilitate more open and honest communication in the future. So when you're preparing to listen to your partner, remember to give them a verbal door opening and create a safe space for them to share.

NOTES

_____

_____

_____

Definitions and Explanations

While Listening

☑ **Track what the speaker is saying in both content and feeling levels.**

When you are listening to your partner, it is important to pay attention not only to the words they are saying but also to the emotions behind them. This means tracking both the content and feeling levels of their communication. By doing so, you can gain a deeper understanding of what they are trying to convey and respond in a more empathetic and effective way. It may also help you to identify any underlying issues or concerns that your partner may be struggling with. So, the next time you are having a conversation with your partner, make sure to listen with both your ears and your heart.

☑ **Stay with the content of communication.**

While engaging in a conversation with your partner, it is crucial to remain focused on the content being communicated. By actively listening and paying attention to what your partner is saying, you demonstrate respect and understanding. This not only allows you to fully comprehend their message but also helps to establish a strong connection and build trust within the relationship. By avoiding distractions and staying present in the moment, you can ensure that you are fully engaged in the conversation and able to respond appropriately. So, remember to prioritize the content of communication while listening to your partner, as it is the key to effective and meaningful conversations.

☑ **Listen for and identify the basic general feeling, anger, fear, joy, resentment, etc.**

While engaging in a conversation with your partner, it is crucial to actively listen and pay attention to their words, tone, and non-verbal cues. By doing so, you can effectively identify and understand their underlying emotions, such as anger, fear, joy, resentment, and more. This skill of empathetic listening not only strengthens your bond with your partner but also allows you to

Definitions and Explanations

 ## While Listening

respond in a more compassionate and supportive manner. So, remember to be fully present and attuned to their emotional state while listening, as it will greatly enhance your communication and foster a deeper connection with your loved one.

☑ **Suspend judgment; open yourself to the presence of their heart.**

While engaging in a heartfelt conversation with your partner, it is crucial to suspend judgment and truly open yourself to the presence of their heart. By doing so, you create a safe and nurturing space where both of you can freely express your thoughts, emotions, and vulnerabilities without fear of criticism or misunderstanding. This act of setting aside preconceived notions or biases allows for a deeper connection to form, fostering empathy, understanding, and compassion within your relationship. As you actively listen to your partner's words, pay attention not only to the surface level of what they are saying but also to the underlying emotions and intentions behind their words. By immersing yourself in their perspective and genuinely seeking to comprehend their experiences, you can cultivate a profound sense of intimacy and strengthen the bond you share. Remember, it is through the power of open-hearted listening that true connection and growth can flourish.

NOTES

_____

_____

_____

_____

_____

_____

Definitions and Explanations

 ## Responding

 Use oral responses which are affirming, which say "I'm with you", " I understand"

When engaging in conversations it is important to utilize verbal responses that convey affirmation and understanding. By expressing statements such as "I'm with you" and "I understand," you can effectively communicate your support and empathy towards the speaker. These affirming responses not only validate the speaker's thoughts and feelings but also create a sense of connection and rapport, fostering a more meaningful and productive conversation.

Feed general feelings back to the speaker. "You seem to feel this has been a good experience for you"

When responding to your partner, it is crucial to provide them with valuable feedback that acknowledges and validates their emotions. By feeding back general feelings to the speaker, you can effectively demonstrate your understanding and empathy towards their experience. For instance, you might express, "It is evident that you have found this to be a truly positive and enriching experience." This approach not only shows your attentiveness but also encourages open communication and fosters a supportive environment. By reframing the original statement in this manner, you can ensure that your response is both affirming and encouraging, strengthening the bond between you and your partner.

Stay an inch ahead of the speaker, not a mile.

When communicating with your partner, it's important to remember to stay on the same page. Instead of being miles apart in your understanding, try to stay just an inch ahead of them. This means actively listening to what they are saying and responding in a way that shows you understand their perspective. By doing this, you can avoid misunderstandings and work towards a stronger, more connected relationship. Remember, communication is key in any relationship, so take the time to really listen and understand your partner's point of view.

Definitions and Explanations

 9 Pitfalls to avoid

 Me-too-ism. Don't start telling your story or comparing your story to theirs.

When engaging in a conversation with your partner, it is crucial to be mindful of a potential pitfall known as Me-too-ism. This refers to the tendency of interjecting with your own story or comparing it to theirs, which can hinder effective communication. Instead, focus on actively listening to your partner's experiences and emotions, allowing them to express themselves fully without feeling overshadowed. By avoiding the urge to constantly relate back to your own experiences, you create a safe and supportive space for your partner to share their thoughts and feelings. Remember, genuine empathy and understanding are key in fostering a strong and healthy connection with your loved one.

☑ **Moralizing, preaching, being judgmental.**

When engaging in a conversation with your partner, it is important to avoid certain pitfalls that can hinder effective communication. One such pitfall is being moralizing, preaching, or judgmental. These behaviors can make your partner feel attacked or criticized, which can lead to defensiveness and a breakdown in communication. Instead, try to approach the conversation with an open mind and a willingness to listen to your partner's perspective. Focus on understanding their point of view rather than trying to convince them of your own. By avoiding moralizing, preaching, and judgmental behavior, you can create a safe and supportive environment for open and honest communication with your partner.

☑ **Asking a direct question to satisfy your own curiosity.**

When engaging in a conversation with your partner, it is crucial to be mindful of a potential pitfall that can hinder effective communication. One such pitfall is the tendency to ask direct questions solely to satisfy your own curiosity. By avoiding this pitfall, you can create a more open and supportive environment for your partner to express themselves freely. Instead of focusing on your own curiosity, strive to actively listen and empathize with your partner's

Definitions and Explanations

 ## 9 Pitfalls to avoid

thoughts and feelings. This will not only strengthen your bond but also foster a deeper understanding and connection between you both. Remember, effective communication is a two-way street, and by avoiding the pitfall of asking direct questions for your own curiosity, you can create a more enriching and fulfilling dialogue with your partner.

☑ **Being an interviewer rather than a listener**

When engaging in a conversation with your partner, it is crucial to be mindful of a potential pitfall: the tendency to adopt the role of an interviewer rather than a listener. By avoiding this pitfall, you can create a more meaningful and fulfilling exchange. Instead of approaching the conversation with a mindset of asking questions and seeking information, focus on actively listening to your partner's thoughts, feelings, and experiences. Show genuine interest and empathy, allowing them to express themselves freely. By doing so, you will foster a deeper connection, strengthen your bond, and create a safe space for open communication. Remember, being a listener rather than an interviewer is key to building a strong and healthy relationship.

☑ **Giving advice (try fixing it)**

When engaging in a conversation with your partner, it is crucial to be mindful of a potential pitfall that can hinder effective communication: refraining from giving advice or attempting to fix the situation. By avoiding the urge to provide immediate solutions, you create a safe and supportive environment where your partner feels heard and understood. Instead of jumping to conclusions or offering unsolicited advice, focus on actively listening to their concerns, validating their emotions, and empathizing with their experiences. This approach fosters a deeper connection and allows your partner to explore their thoughts and feelings more freely, ultimately leading to a more meaningful and productive conversation. Remember, sometimes all someone needs is a listening ear, and by avoiding the pitfall of giving advice, you can truly be there for your partner in a way that strengthens your bond and promotes effective communication.

Definitions and Explanations

 ## 9 Pitfalls to avoid

 Cheap consolation. "Oh, that's not too bad."

When listening to your partner, it is important to avoid the pitfall of offering cheap consolation. Saying things like "Oh, that's not too bad" may seem like a way to make your partner feel better, but it can actually be dismissive of their feelings and minimize the importance of what they are sharing with you. Instead, try to actively listen and validate their emotions. You can say things like "I can understand why you feel that way" or "That sounds really tough, I'm here for you." By acknowledging their feelings and showing empathy, you can create a stronger connection with your partner and build a foundation of trust and support in your relationship.

☑ **Arguing or disagreeing with the speaker**

When engaging in a conversation with your partner, it is crucial to be mindful of a potential pitfall that can hinder effective communication: refraining from arguing or disagreeing with them. By avoiding these counterproductive behaviors, you create a safe and open space for both parties to express their thoughts and feelings without fear of judgment or conflict. Instead, strive to actively listen and understand their perspective, fostering a sense of empathy and respect. Remember, the goal is not to suppress your own opinions or beliefs, but rather to prioritize the harmony and understanding within your relationship. By embracing this approach, you can cultivate a healthy and constructive dialogue that strengthens your connection and promotes mutual growth.

☑ **Analyzing or interpreting**

When engaging in a conversation with your partner, it is crucial to be mindful of a potential pitfall that can hinder effective communication: the tendency to analyze or interpret their words. By refraining from jumping to conclusions or making assumptions about their thoughts or intentions, you create a safe and open space for genuine understanding and connection. Instead, focus on actively listening to their words, acknowledging their emotions, and seeking

Definitions and Explanations
9 Pitfalls to avoid

clarification when needed. By avoiding the trap of analyzing or interpreting, you demonstrate respect, empathy, and a genuine desire to comprehend their perspective, fostering a stronger and more harmonious relationship.

☑ **Ignoring obvious heavy emotions**

When you are listening to your partner, it is crucial to be attentive to their emotions. One of the biggest mistakes you can make is to overlook the obvious heavy emotions that they may be experiencing. Ignoring these emotions can lead to misunderstandings and can even damage your relationship. It is important to acknowledge and validate your partner's feelings, even if you don't necessarily agree with them. By doing so, you are showing them that you care and that you are willing to support them through their emotional struggles. Remember, communication is a two-way street, and listening is just as important as speaking. So, the next time you are having a conversation with your partner, make sure to pay attention to their emotions and respond with empathy and understanding.

CONGRATULATIONS!

You are now armed with the four essential areas to focus on when it's your turn to be an exceptional listener. It may not be a walk in the park, but trust me, it's absolutely worth the effort. Research has shown that when individuals feel responsible for their partner's well-being, their listening skills tend to improve. And guess what? When your partner feels genuinely heard, their well-being flourishes. It's a win-win situation! Let's be there for each other and take on the responsibility of being attentive listeners for the sake of our loved ones health and a deep intimate relationship with them.

You are **Educated**, you are **Equipped** and now you have the opportunity to **Experience** an intimate connection with your partner. You now have a game plan, a blueprint, and a road map to become an engaged listener for your partner and your relationship. With the knowledge you now possess, you are well-prepared and ready to embark on a journey towards a deeper intimate connection. Imagine the possibilities!

This portion focuses on a couples workshop consisting of 7 actions, with a duration of 90 minutes, aimed at teaching and demonstrating the effectiveness of The Feeling First approach.

- Provide an explanation of the **Fill in Publishing presents** page, focusing on the functionality of journeys.
- Review the **Introduction page** to ensure a clear understanding of the journey ahead.
- Detail the process of completing pages 1 through 19 to demonstrate how it is done.
- Review every listening skill from page 101 to 109

The next 7 actions will prove this listening approach to be True, Effective and Successful.

Action #1

1) Everyone must divide in individual groups of 3 people per group. Do not have your partner in your group.

2) Each group must delegate a:

- Person A.
- Person B.
- Person C.

Action #2

1) **Person A will read the inverted question on the bottom of page 35 then proceed to ask Person B the question.**

   NOTE: Only person A. can read the question on page 35 to keep all other individuals unbiased, unprepared to keep this real.

2) **Person B. will answer the question asked by Person A.**

3) **Person C. will observe and score Person's A's listening skills.**

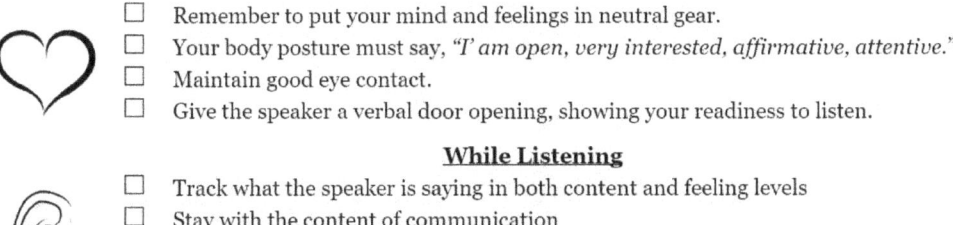

Person C evaluates and assess person A's listening abilities based on the four fundamental categories of listening listed below.

Terrible ←—to—→ Terrific
☐ ☐ ☐ ☐ ☐ ☐ ☐ ☐ ☐ ☐
1 2 3 4 5 6 7 8 9 10

Preparing to listen

☐ Remember to put your mind and feelings in neutral gear.
☐ Your body posture must say, *"I am open, very interested, affirmative, attentive."*
☐ Maintain good eye contact.
☐ Give the speaker a verbal door opening, showing your readiness to listen.

While Listening

☐ Track what the speaker is saying in both content and feeling levels
☐ Stay with the content of communication
☐ Listen for and identify the basic general feeling; anger, fear, joy, resentment, etc.
☐ Suspend judgment; open yourself to the presence of their heart.

Responding

☐ Use oral responses, which are affirming, which say, *"I am with you", "I understand."*
☐ Feed general feelings back to the speaker. *"You seem to feel this has been a good experience for you"*
☐ Stay an inch ahead of the speaker, not a mile.

8 Pitfalls to avoid

☐ Me-too-ism. Don't start telling your story, or comparing your story to theirs.
☐ Moralizing, preaching, being judgmental
☐ Asking a direct question to satisfy your own curiosity
☐ Being an interviewer rather then a listener
☐ Giving advice (try fixing it)
☐ Cheap consolation. *"Oh, that's not to bad"*
☐ Arguing or disagreeing with the speaker
☐ Analyzing or interpreting
☐ Ignoring obvious heavy emotions

Action #3

1) **Person B will read the inverted question on the bottom of page 42 then proceed to ask Person C the question.**

   NOTE: Only person B. can read the question on page 42 to keep all other individuals unbiased, unprepared to keep this real.

2) **Person C. will answer the question asked by Person B.**

3) **Person A. will observe and score Person's B's listening skills.**

A. Observes

Person A evaluates and assess person B's listening abilities based on the four fundamental categories of listening listed below.

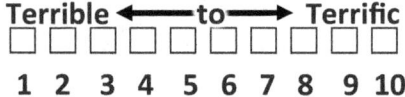

1 2 3 4 5 6 7 8 9 10

Preparing to listen
- ☐ Remember to put your mind and feelings in neutral gear.
- ☐ Your body posture must say, *"I' am open, very interested, affirmative, attentive."*
- ☐ Maintain good eye contact.
- ☐ Give the speaker a verbal door opening, showing your readiness to listen.

While Listening
- ☐ Track what the speaker is saying in both content and feeling levels
- ☐ Stay with the content of communication
- ☐ Listen for and identify the basic general feeling; anger, fear, joy, resentment, etc.
- ☐ Suspend judgment; open yourself to the presence of their heart.

Responding
- ☐ Use oral responses, which are affirming, which say, *"I am with you"*, *"I understand."*
- ☐ Feed general feelings back to the speaker. *"You seem to feel this has been a good experience for you"*
- ☐ Stay an inch ahead of the speaker, not a mile.

8 Pitfalls to avoid
- ☐ Me-too-ism. Don't start telling your story, or comparing your story to theirs.
- ☐ Moralizing, preaching, being judgmental
- ☐ Asking a direct question to satisfy your own curiosity
- ☐ Being an interviewer rather then a listener
- ☐ Giving advice (try fixing it)
- ☐ Cheap consolation. *"Oh, that's not to bad"*
- ☐ Arguing or disagreeing with the speaker
- ☐ Analyzing or interpreting
- ☐ Ignoring obvious heavy emotions

Action #4

1) Person C will read the inverted question on the bottom of page 64 then proceed to ask Person A the question.

   NOTE: Only person C. can read the question on page 64 to keep all other individuals unbiased, unprepared to keep this real.

1) Person A. will answer the question asked by Person C.
2) Person B will observe and score Person's C's listening skills.

B. Observes

Person B evaluates and assess person C's listening abilities based on the four fundamental categories of listening listed below.

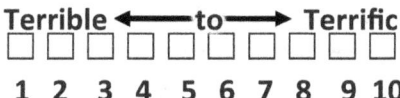

Preparing to listen
- ☐ Remember to put your mind and feelings in neutral gear.
- ☐ Your body posture must say, *"I' am open, very interested, affirmative, attentive."*
- ☐ Maintain good eye contact.
- ☐ Give the speaker a verbal door opening, showing your readiness to listen.

While Listening
- ☐ Track what the speaker is saying in both content and feeling levels
- ☐ Stay with the content of communication
- ☐ Listen for and identify the basic general feeling; anger, fear, joy, resentment, etc.
- ☐ Suspend judgment; open yourself to the presence of their heart.

Responding
- ☐ Use oral responses, which are affirming, which say, *"I am with you", "I understand."*
- ☐ Feed general feelings back to the speaker. *"You seem to feel this has been a good experience for you"*
- ☐ Stay an inch ahead of the speaker, not a mile.

8 Pitfalls to avoid
- ☐ Me-too-ism. Don't start telling your story, or comparing your story to theirs.
- ☐ Moralizing, preaching, being judgmental
- ☐ Asking a direct question to satisfy your own curiosity
- ☐ Being an interviewer rather then a listener
- ☐ Giving advice (try fixing it)
- ☐ Cheap consolation. *"Oh, that's not to bad"*
- ☐ Arguing or disagreeing with the speaker
- ☐ Analyzing or interpreting
- ☐ Ignoring obvious heavy emotions

Action #5

At this moment, it is appropriate to raise any questions that may arise. Additionally, we are encouraged to collectively examine pages 17 and 18, as they provide valuable information regarding the opportunities at hand and in the future.

Action #6

The partners reunite and locate a suitable space where they can dedicate some time to engage in this joint activity. They allocate 5 minutes to each partner, allowing them to individually practice the content found on pages 19 and 20.

The purpose of this exercise is for the partners to come together and utilize this designated time to improve their listening skills by practicing the material they just learned.

Action #7

This action paves the way for a brighter future, offering opportunities and rewards down the line.

- The partners come to a mutual agreement on the number of times they will meet each week, ensuring that both parties are satisfied with the frequency of their meetings. The frequency of the activity can vary from once a week to as often as seven times a week, or any number of times in between.

    ⇒ _____

- After determining the frequency, they proceed to select the specific days on which they will meet, taking into consideration their individual schedules and availability.

    ⇒ _____

- Once the days are decided, they move on to choosing the exact time at which they will meet, ensuring that it is convenient for both partners and allows for a productive and focused interaction.

    ⇒ _____

- Finally, they collaborate to select the ideal meeting place that suits their needs and preferences, taking into account factors such as accessibility, comfort, and the nature of their discussions.

    ⇒ _____